AUTHOR'S NOTE:

Fair warning, the topics covered in this collection of books are basic and more likely to help those just starting out on their publishing journey, rather than experienced authors.

Other titles by
Danielle Ackley-McPhail

THE ETERNAL CYCLE SERIES
Yesterday's Dreams
Tomorrow's Memories
Today's Promise

THE ETERNAL WANDERINGS SERIES
Eternal Wanderings

THE BAD-ASS FAERIE TALE SERIES
The Halfling's Court
The Redcap's Queen
The High King's Fool
(forthcoming)

THE SYSTEMA PARADOXA SERIES
The Play of Light

Baba Ali and the Clockwork Djinn
(with Day Al-Mohamed)

The Literary Handyman
Build-A-Book Workshop
More Tips From the Handyman

The Ginger KICK! Cookbook
Auntie D's Recipes (forthcoming)

SHORT FICTION
A Legacy of Stars
Transcendence
Consigned to the Sea
Flash in the Can
The Fox's Fire
The Kindly One
Dawns a New Day
Echoes of the Divine
The Die Is Cast
(with Mike McPhail)

The Literary Handyman Library

Volume One

Danielle Ackley-McPhail

PAPER
PHOENIX

PRESS

Pennsville, NJ

PUBLISHED BY
Paper Phoenix Press
A division of eSpec Books
PO Box 242
Pennsville, NJ 08070
www.especbooks.com

ISBN: 978-1-956463-05-7
ISBN (ebook): 978-1-956463-04-0

Interior Design: Danielle McPhail
Cover Design and Modification: Mike McPhail, McP Digital Graphics
Cover Art: Bryan Prindiville, http://www.bryanprindiville.com

Dedicated to Christopher Frost, who waited
unconscionably long for this project to be completed.

Contents

The Literary Handyman

Tips on Writing From Someone Who's Been There

"A Little Friendly Abuse" originally published as "Where Two, or Three, Or Twenty Are Gathered" in The Complete Fantasy Writer's Guide Volume Three: The Author's Grimoire, edited by Valerie Griswold-Ford and Lai Zhao, published by Dragon Moon Press, 2007.

"The Naming of Names", "The Tricky Art of Conversation", "Continuing the Conversation", and "Wrapping Up the Conversation" originally published under the ongoing column The Writer's Toolbox, in Allegory Magazine.

Dedication

To an awful lot of people who paid it both forward and back
along this journey of mine, including:
L. Jagi Lamplighter,
Jeffrey Lyman,
Lee C. Hillman,
David Goldstein
CJ Henderson,
Bernie Mojzes,
Ty Drago,
and all of my Yesterday's Dreamers

And especially for Mike, for giving up my time.

Contents

Craft

Business

It's Not Brain Surgery

There's a relatively famous anecdote about writing, one that has been ascribed to everyone from Stephen King to the late John D. MacDonald, author of the Travis McGee mysteries. It goes something like this:

> A writer and a brain surgeon are at a party and start talking about what each other does for a living. The brain surgeon says to the writer, "You know, I've always wanted to be a writer. I think I'll start tomorrow." The writer replies, "Really? I've always wanted to be a brain surgeon. I think I'll start tomorrow."

The point, of course, is that wanting to be a writer and *being* a writer are two very different things. I respectfully disagree and, in fact, tell the same story a bit differently:

> A writer is approached at a party by a woman who says wistfully, "Oh! You're a writer! I've always wanted to be a writer." And, to this, the writer replies, "Really? I've always wanted to be a brain surgeon."

My humble though adversarial point is that if you want to be a writer, you write. There's no other requirement, a fact that simply doesn't apply to most other avocations. For example, it isn't a very practical approach to brain surgery. Nevertheless, the very moment you put pen to paper (or words on a computer monitor) for no reason other than the desire to communicate with your fellow human beings, you are a writer.

Congratulations!

Now becoming a *good* writer; that's something else altogether.

Once you've committed yourself to authorship, where do you start? How do you find inspiration? How should your story be told? What sort of characters do you need to create in order to populate what sort of world? And once you have your finished tale, how should you market it? What happens when it's accepted or — more likely for new writers — when it's *not* ?

The Literary Handyman addresses these questions, and more.

Writing is a craft, like knitting or gardening. A person can, to some extent, be taught to write. All it takes is time, patience, and barrels full of practice. It also helps more than a little bit to have the advice of someone who's been there.

In November of 2009, Danielle first approached me with her idea of authoring a series of short essays on writing for my online fiction magazine *Allegory*. Her first such article, entitled "The Naming of Names" appeared in our Winter 2009 issue under the banner *The Writer's Toolbox*. That essay can be found in this volume, among her many others.

The reader response to her *Allegory* debut was so positive that I immediately reached out to Danielle for more, and she's since been our first ever non-staff columnist. Given the success of *The Writer's Toolbox*, when she later proposed compiling her work into *The Literary Handyman*, I was naturally excited at the prospect, and honored when she asked me to write the introduction.

Within these pages, Danielle's take on the craft of writing is intelligent, insightful, and often quite funny — as is the woman, herself. She tackles, with style and skill, everything from the mysteries of dialogue to the vagaries of the modern publishing world.

There's a good deal to be gleaned here. My advice is read it, enjoy it, and most importantly, use it. The path of a serious writer is lonely and often arduous. There's a lot to learn and a lot to do along the way.

And a literary handyman is — well — *handy*.

Ty Drago
Author, Editor, and Publisher

A Word Before We Get Started

First off... no... I'm not a guy, but *The Literary Handywoman* just didn't have the same charm.

Second off... this is and has always been a beginner's guide. If you are already established as an author this is all going to be basic knowledge for you.

Now... on to what I wanted to say!

Have you ever opened a toolbox? An honest-to-goodness working toolbox? No, I'm not talking about one owned by an obsessive-compulsive where everything is locked down and labeled. I mean just your everyday, jumbled collection of tools like most of us have somewhere in our homes. Yeah, that's the one... you open it up and have to paw through it to find precisely the right tool, but you know it's in there because this is a good handyman's toolbox.

Well, that's what I hope you'll find in this book. I'm less concerned with order and structure and everything in its place, this isn't a college course, after all. (Though to be honest, even if it was, I'd likely still do it my way.) Don't look for a step-by-step guide or an intensive refresher course on grammar and structure (those are out there in more than sufficient quantity already, and even if they weren't, I don't feel I'm the one to tackle explaining the English language).

No, I'm not teaching you how to be writers because frankly, everyone's process is different. Besides, if you have picked up this book it is likely you already *are* a writer. The rest comes with experience.

What I want to give you are the tools—the knowledge I have learned and the advice I have been given—for you to adapt in a manner that most benefits your growth as a writer. This is my effort to help you build that publishing career you are after (though I do recommend you consider it more of a serious hobby… there is less frustration that way) without imposing my own view of what that should be.

In *The Literary Handyman* you will discover a collection of mostly stand-alone articles. Some of them are brand new, others are recycled from either my column *If We'd Words Enough and Time* (from the defunct website www.fictionauts.com), or my column *The Writers' Toolbox* (previously featured in the online magazine *Allegory*, www.allegoryezine.com.) Since they were all written at different times and for different purposes I ask your patience as there will surely be some points that are repeated. That said, I like to think that much of what is here bears repeating, which is why they haven't been rewritten for the purpose of this handbook.

When all is said and done, these articles draw on my experience of over twenty years as a publishing professional, over fifteen of which I have also been a published author. Being a genre author, some of that will be evident in my examples, but for the most part the advice in these pages is not specific to genre writers. It is my hope that whatever you are inspired to write, you will benefit from what I have learned on my singular, ongoing journey.

Dream Big!

Danielle Ackley-McPhail

Craft

On Being Inspired

You know, there will be many people out there who will raise their voices in outrage at what I'm about to write.

So… are you ready for it?

Writers don't have to write every day to be writers.

No, really. This is not grounds for my turning in my union card. If you subscribe to the philosophy that you do need to write something every day, that is all well and good. I'm glad if it works for you and yes, one would hope by doing so you will hone your skills and produce both quality and quantity. For me, though, I just don't have the time. Now, that doesn't mean I am not a serious writer. To the contrary, I have six published novels to my name and countless short stories and articles that have seen print. (You can find a listing of these at the back of this book.) Of course, I've been doing this for a long time.

This does not mean that I don't *encourage* writers to write every day, just that I acknowledge that it isn't always practical, given the hectic schedules and volume of responsibilities that are common to each of us in today's society. That is why I am talking about this here and now, the very first thing, because I don't want anyone out there to feel they are somehow lacking because they can't dedicate some portion of time to their craft *every* day. I don't want any writers out there to be discouraged or feel they are anything less than what they are because they can't meet this dictate.

Now that I have made that clear, let's look at ways to get yourself writing when you do have time!

Being Practical

You've all had those times when you are not inspired or can't find the next thread in the story you are working on. I know you have. There isn't one of us that hasn't had a moment like that. There are ways around it, and sometimes they even work. Here are a few I've tried with some measure of success.

Polishing. If I can't make any progress writing new material, I force myself to start reading the piece from the beginning, correcting and tweaking as I go along. Occasionally, by the time I reach the end I am ready to pick up where I left off. This isn't precisely writing in that it doesn't always generate much in the way of new copy, but it does help me polish what I've already gotten down so I don't have to spend as much time cleaning up the story or novel later. Of course, if you feel you work better getting everything down first before you can edit, this may not be an option, in which case I have a few other suggestions.

Immersion. This can help with productivity, though not always. Remove distractions so that you don't have any option but to write. Put yourself in a secluded space, (or put a "do not disturb" sign on the door and flip the lock), put on some mood music (without words, I would recommend, unless that type of thing doesn't distract you), and make sure you have a snack and plenty to drink at hand. Now for this to work you need to make sure your computer is not a source of distraction on its own. For me, I had to remove all of the games that came pre-loaded and I have to stay disconnected from the internet, though that isn't always an option when I know I'll need to do research.

Multitasking. No, not quite in the traditional sense, but when I can't make headway on one project, I jump to another. This isn't always an option for everyone, but if you are like me and have three or four pieces going at once it can work. When I hit a stumbling block, it helps if I'm able to get somewhere on a different piece.

Assignments. If your goal is just to write, rather than to write on a dedicated project, get someone to give you an assignment or a challenge. Alternatives would be to set one for yourself, or to find a contest or submission opportunity on line and use the designated theme as your assignment. I find this helps when you aren't motivated because so many of us grew up used to English assignments. In some ways it is more comfortable and easier to mimic that experience because you have a focus and a deadline, rather than having to find the motivation from within yourself. This also has the added benefit of giving you a potential home for whatever you write. Joining a writer's group would be a similar incentive to be productive.

The Uncomfortable Truth

Nothing is going to work one hundred percent of the time. And if you force yourself, who is to say that the end product is going to be worth the effort? I am sure, as with myself, there are days where you are just totally unmotivated or incapable of writing. The trick is to let those happen. If you aren't geared up to write, forcing yourself isn't always going to have the effect you want, though sometimes it does work. If my literary neurons aren't firing, I crochet and watch movies, or if I really want to be totally unproductive and veg, I read a book from dawn until dusk... okay... midnight and beyond, but what is your point? Sometimes we need that decompression time... a reminder that life is more than work and a computer screen. This should be something you enjoy in life, not something that takes you away from it.

Put A Little Magic Into It

(Originally published in The Broad Sheet, the newsletter of
the international organization, Broad Universe.)

The world is full of wonder. Sometimes we forget that. Everything that happens contains a little bit of magic or miracle. As writers, particularly genre writers, we need to focus on that.

One of my favorite things is to take an event… just a normal event, and put a twist on it. Think what would make it different. An early example of this, in my eighth grade English class we had to write a story. My story was about the splendor of a moonrise, so overlooked and underappreciated in comparison to the sunrise. Now that is unusual in itself.

My narrator… a rubber band dropped in a garden.

What can I say; I've always been odd that way.

Writers are in a unique position where they get to reorder the readers' perception of the world. Give them rules and a framework for understanding and you can do anything you imagine. One way to do this is to create a social structure of knowledge for your characters. Think out the hows and whys and what-fors. Just remember, even with fantasy, logic has to be in there somewhere, or you better be prepared to explain why it isn't. Once you have that in place you can play in the new reality you've created exploring character dynamics and heroic challenges with your imagination as the guiding force. Nothing to hold you back but yourself. This can be a lot of work, but also a lot of fun for the author. Kind of like the first time you received a box of crayons…

at first you were a two-year-old Jackson Pollock, then as you gained control and understanding, a recognizable order began to take shape. First squiggles corresponded with the rough area on the page where they belonged, then a little while later you understood the concept of coloring within the lines, until ultimately you learned the joy of telling the lines to take a flying leap and made your own image.

In the speculative genres, we only have the lines we impose on ourselves.

One of the ways I like to explore this open field is to take the tropes everyone is familiar with and rearrange them. Currently I'm playing in the faerie realm. The twist: *my* faeries are bikers. Now, I know most people will say "What the heck?" But my bikers are modeled on the concept of faeries that kept generations of villagers leaving offerings on their hearths and hanging scissors over their babies' cradles. Old World faeries had teeth... and worse. They were tough and harsh and malevolent. They were warriors. I mingled a bit of the old-world with the new, channeled magic into wings of energy and introduced the peculiar nature of the biker culture, complete with legends of their own, to revitalize the Disney-fied fae.

There is so much of world myth that has been lost to common knowledge, but not lost to time. A little bit of exploration on the internet or at your local library and you can find so many forgotten treasures to revamp your speculative playground.

A good example of this are vampires. Yes, everyone has their own concept... from the Anita Blake novels to Sookie Stackhouse and beyond. But how much of what you read is modern invention of pop culture and how much is based on an actual existing myth? You would be surprised about how much of what everyone "knows" about vampires just from the Stoker novel is unsubstantiated by the actual legends found in nearly every culture. I have done research on vampires around the world for a current—unconventional—vampire novel I am working on and discovered only one legend that actually credits their version of vampires with not being able to go into the sun. If you want to explore an overdone subgenre do a little research, draw on uncommon knowledge about the common populous of our paranormal world... and if there is something so entrenched the readership will be in an uproar if you try and mess with it... rearrange what you cannot change.

One of my favorite things to do is find or devise an unanticipated reason for the assumptions everyone makes about a myth cycle. Just as an example, most elf or faerie fiction will claim that these creatures covet human young because they do not have many of their own. And why don't they have many of their own? It is popular belief that immortal (or near immortal) beings do not have the same need... compulsion... to reproduce as energetically. Since they live so long they don't need to worry about replacing themselves before it is too late... basically. For me, I wanted a different reason, one that had at least the illusion of being grounded in the existing mythology. My elves rarely have young because the Irish believe in reincarnation, but they believe that you come back as your descendants. With that in mind, in my novels, *Yesterday's Dreams* and *Tomorrow's Memories*, which are based on Irish mythology, the elves are incapable of having young unless one of them dies... because that frees up the soul to return. Finite amount of souls, death equals birth. That gives me some implication that there is a mythological basis.

I like to play that way. There is so much that you can do out of your own imagination or by exploring the underutilized aspects of existing mythology that can breathe new life into the speculative genres, setting your work apart from the cookie-cutter books that invariably begin to surface with the popularity of any particular trend in fiction.

Play, have fun, don't tie yourself down to what everyone *expects*. Above all, create.

Soul Food
Feeding Your Passion

(Originally published in the column If We'd Words Enough and Time)

Popcorn is nothing more than a butter vehicle. Let me say that again… popcorn is nothing more than a butter vehicle.

What the heck?! Right?

Now I'm sure your "What the heck?!" has completely different connotations from mine, so let's take a moment to explore them both: now my explanative was a shocked response, a spontaneous and completely understandable reaction to the blasphemy I myself have dared to utter. Popcorn, that light, airy manna, nothing more than a vehicle for something else? Those who know me can well understand my shock.

Here comes the surprise part: the blasphemy, for me, is true. Popcorn has absolutely no appeal for me dry. (Trust me, I am going somewhere with this.)

Shall we now examine your "What the heck?!"? That would be the "What the heck does this have to do with writing?!," right? Well I'm sorry, but it has everything to do with writing — once you stop to realize the written word is our popcorn.

Come on, don't walk away now… I know you're dying to find out where I'm going with this. You've come this far already…

In life, as in our writing, there are things that exist merely as a means to savor that which we love. Commercials exist so we can get our snacks; popcorn and crusty Italian bread exist so we can indulge in creamy butter; stale, near-tasteless tortilla chips are merely a means of getting flaming salsa to our tongues;

fights break out so that we can console ourselves with chocolate... you get the idea.

Well, when we write, our words exist so that we can write about what we love (such as buttered popcorn... I LOVE buttered popcorn) It is important to remember this—the part about the writing, not the popcorn—Words are our passion vehicle.

What is your passion? For me it is the richness of myth, an intricately woven tale full of hidden significance and vibrant descriptions. I love deep, evocative emotion and personal triumphs over adversity... not the kind that are handed to you on a platter, but the kind that required clawing and struggling and life-transforming decisions to obtain. I like poetry that is in your face and on your sleeve. And, if you couldn't tell, I like my nonfiction witty (I can only hope) and a little bit cheeky.

Now I know there is writing that pays the bills and writing that feeds your soul, and you might find yourself in a position where you must divide your time among both of them, but do not allow what you are required to do to crowd out what you are driven to do. Find the time to nurture your own creativity. If you are fortunate enough to have a choice in the bill-paying variety of writing, write what interests you, but even if you can't, be sure that you invest yourself in your words, let them carry your passion for all things, for only then will they be heard.

Remember, when we write, it reflects our beliefs, our interests, our souls. A piece of ourselves is left forever on the page, so make sure that what you leave behind is true to who you are, what you want the world to see. So, whatever you must write, for personal gratification or personal survival; find a way to make it yours. Turn everyone's expectations on their figurative ear and make your words a vehicle for whatever it is you need to say, what you believe in.

If you are not passionate about what you are writing, whether it be fiction, nonfiction, or poetry, then what is the point? Write first for yourself and only then can you speak to the masses.

Establishing Reality In Your Fantasy

I know… I know… seems like I'm contradicting myself, doesn't it? Not really. No matter what you are writing — science fiction, fantasy, romance, etc. — you need to establish some reality that your audience can identify with. Sometimes this draws on your own experience (after all, mostly we do write about what we know), but sometimes we want to explore something different. For my novel, *The Halfling's Court: A Bad-Ass Faerie Tale*, I wanted the backdrop of a biker bar with my primary character the leader of a biker gang. I am not a biker. I don't interact with bikers. I've only been on a motorcycle once.

Yeah… what was I thinking! Actually, I was thinking this is going to be really cool! It was also a lot of work, though. See, bikers aren't just tough men and women (or faeries, in the case of my novel) wearing leather and riding motor bikes. There is an entire culture there, right down to a unique language that to the uninitiated definitely needs translation. Fortunately for me, there are a lot of biker sites out there that have glossaries of terms that define the phrases for you and even put them into context. This was invaluable to me when I went to incorporate flavor into my story. Some of it was obvious and I could just substitute the terms for other words I would generally use, for example:

"What'll you have?" asked the hot, young mattress cover masquerading as a waitress.

But often I had to work a bit of explanation into the text. Case in point:

"You keep tellin' yourself that," she murmured, her gaze brutal in its wisdom. "These riders are here to make the run with you... with the Wind Walker."

He hissed through clenched teeth. "Anyone can be a wind walker; all it takes is treating people right, looking out for them on the road."

It was a challenge to insert just enough "color" without alienating the reader. I sprinkled in some motorcycle and biker facts, used the language where it felt appropriate and not forced and then let the story progress. It took research, but with the internet there is more than enough material out there on virtually anything you could want to use as a theme. And for what is not readily accessible, consider interviewing someone living in that culture or take a field trip (if that is an option) to observe people similar to the characters you wish to write. For me it was simple. My main character, Lance, is physically based on my uncle, and the secondary character Bubba is based on my brother. I have first-hand experience with their personalities and mindset as it applies to the culture I wanted to portray.

Once I had the biker elements incorporated I could work in the fantasy thread I needed for the story, in fact, in a way this was simpler than if I had chosen a different social group because believe it or not there are already fantasy elements in the biker world. Primary for my purposes was the legend of the road gremlin. See, the original biker gangs were made up of retired Air Force personnel. In the Air Force if something went wrong with a plane it was gremlins. When they transitioned into bikers that bit of legend came with them, morphed into road gremlins. To protect themselves from this hazard bikers hang little bells off their motorcycles. The ringing either scares the gremlins away from the bike before they get on, or it traps them in the bowl of the bell if they are already in residence. This was an ideal element for me to incorporate to link "reality" with "fantasy."

To further strengthen the link between my bikers and the magical realm of faeries my biker gang is called the Wild Hunt, mirroring the legendary Hunt found in myth and folklore, only substituting motorcycles for the horses the faeries would ride. Also to mirror the magical realm the hierarchy of a biker club mimics a Court (as in royal or faerie) structure, thus setting up the primary conflict in my tale.

When I applied magic to my characters it was something appropriate to their lifestyle… helmets spelled for protection, magic tattoos that link one character with another… things you would expect in real life, only with a magic twist.

After all, that is the challenge. Give a reader just enough that is familiar to them and then give it an unexpected twist. Now this context is urban fantasy, but a similar foundation can be applied to high fantasy equally as well. Just take the culture or social group you want to emulate and do your research, then find ways to adapt their identifying features to a fantasy setting.

Have fun, play with it, but definitely do your homework because if you don't capture the proper feel it doesn't matter how well written the other aspects of your story are, if one thing doesn't ring true it throws off the whole story.

The Naming of Names

(Originally published in Allegory Magazine, www.allegoryezine.com)

Have you realized how much a name can say about someone? Well, maybe not so much today, where the blending of culture and celebrity and downright boredom has led to some combinations that simply ignore things like tradition, religious/ethnic background, and even gender. But at one time you had a good chance of telling where a person was from, their sex, their occupation, and sometimes even roughly when they were born just by learning their name. Some places in the world you still can.

Our challenge as writers is to match that rich process. Parents on average name one, two, or at most a bare handful of children in their lifetime. Authors populate worlds. Now, not every character needs a name with layers of meaning. Many won't even need a name at all, but when the name does count, how do you go about finding or creating one?

Good question! Let's talk…

The Don'ts

First off, let's get some basics out of the way. There are a few things that you want to avoid when naming your characters. After all, you want them to complement your story, not detract from it.

Don't Get Cute. Unless there is a specific reason for it, such as you are writing a children's story or pulp fiction, try to avoid names that sound like they are the butt of a bad joke, like Hope

Bright or Candy Kane. Do it too often, or without a relevant reason, and you'll just make it harder for the reader to take your character—and your story—seriously.

Don't Be Difficult. Names have a structure we are familiar with. Even if it's in another language, we can generally recognize the pattern of a name. A well-constructed one is comfortable to say, as well as to hear (unless, of course, the voice is your mother's and she's using all three of yours at once).

Now this is mostly for those writing fantasy or science fiction, but if you are creating a name for an alien or non-human race, have mercy on your reader and try and mirror the above-mentioned pattern. For example, in the movie *The Fifth Element*, the perfect being had a name about thirty syllables long… for effect. It was quickly shortened to the more manageable and name-like Lelu.

Don't Echo. What do I mean by that? When you have a number of characters involved in a storyline, it is important that the reader be able to easily distinguish which character you are talking about at any given time. This need increases exponentially the more characters that are involved. So, even though in life it is quite common for people to at least partially share the same name or similar sounding names, you absolutely do not want your characters to do so—unless, of course, there is a very good reason for it that is integral to the plot. Mike and Ike makes for a catchy name for a candy, but have such a duo in a story and you could easily leave your reader confused when things really get going. Less common, but also something you should watch out for is having a character and a race, city, or other story element with similar sounding names. Like using Vargas from Vegas, this could be a rather unfortunate combination.

Don't Mirror Life. Unless you are writing historic fiction or your story has a specific need to include or allude to a figure from recorded history or current events, be careful of using name combinations for characters that mirror those of notable people that actually exist or did exist at one time when you aren't actually writing about that individual. Also be careful of mirroring the names of other distinct fictional characters. In extreme cases of either example, it could lead to accusations of libel or copyright violation, and possible legal action against you. (For the same reason, some in the industry often caution against using the name or representation of someone you know even with their permission, because it has been known to occasionally be poorly received. This, of course, is a personal choice you must make.)

The Do's

Once you are ready to actually get down to naming your characters there are a lot of things to consider, questions to ask yourself as you establish their persona, and steps you can take to ensure you have the right one. For our current purposes, let's assume you have already chosen your character's name.

Do Confirm. As I mentioned, sometimes a character's name will have some particular relevance—as with Harry Copperfield Blackstone Dresden, from Jim Butcher's *Dresden Files,* a wizard named after three of the world's greatest magicians—and sometimes it will just be something to identify who is who, but in either case run a web search on it once you have chosen. I recommend you look for several things: Are there any negative associations with real-life individuals? Does the (first) name have a meaning that is unfortunate, inapplicable, or perhaps apropos? Has a similar or identical name been used for a character in someone else's book? (With everyday kind of names, this isn't really an issue, but if the book is of a similar type to what you are writing, or if there are parallels in the plot or character development, they could be used to substantiate an accusation of plagiarism, such as in the case with Disney's Simba and the story of Kimba the White Lion. The best you could hope for in such situations is to be accused of a lack of originality. At the worst you will be looking for a lawyer.)

Do Be Consistent. Make sure your character's name is both spelled and used consistently throughout. Settle on the different variations you might use for formal and informal encounters, any titles, ranks, or honorifics, and do not vary from what you have established. An exception to this would be if your character has a particular nemesis or bully that uses an incorrect or ill-preferred variant of the name to annoy said character, or a friend or family member that can't or won't use the more common variant, but without malice.

Do Be Appropriate. Make sure you select a name in keeping with the time, setting, and social position of the character, where applicable. Also, make sure supporting characters have names that complement one another and work together to establish your environment. After all, having a character from a primitive tribe deep in the Brazilian rainforest named Charles isn't really going to be plausible (Unless, of course, you build some justification into the story).

The How-To's

Some people are good at picking names. Some agonize over it. I find if you have a method, it goes a lot simpler, and the joy: you aren't limited to just one! On those occasions where the name doesn't just come to me I have plenty of tricks for picking one out. Here are a few of them.

Morality Play Method. It was standard in these medieval works to name a character after the predominant trait they represented, such as Charity, Hope, Avarice, etc. That lacks a certain subtlety for modern works, except for the rare virtues that are accepted as names today. However, I still like the idea of this method, but with a twist. I write a lot of fantasy, usually mythology based; for those characters that I wish to use the MP method of naming I go to the language associated with whatever myth cycle I am using. For example, my first novel, *Yesterday's Dreams*, is based on Irish mythology. I wanted to name my antagonist Evil so I looked up the word in my Irish-English dictionary. Several different words were listed so I chose to go with "Olcas" because it seemed the most like an actual name. By an ironic twist, when I was later doing research into the mythology I ran across a rather nasty fellow from the actual legends named Olcas and I was able to adapt my plot to that myth rather nicely.

Defining Characteristics. A variant of the above, only the name represents a notable physical trait, rather than just the more usual virtues. An example would be my character Kerwin. When he first appeared in the short story "At the Crossroads" he was introduced as the Dubh Fae, Irish for the black fae. This had a dual purpose because he was dark in coloring and nature. When that story was expanded into my novel, *The Halfling's Court*, he needed a true name. It also turned out that he was an outcast among his own kind, shunned because of his dark, crude features. To that end he gained the name Kerwin, which means the little black one, in this case an insult to a grown fae.

Historic/Cultural Relevance. Depending on what type of story you are writing it might be applicable (as in the aforementioned *Dresden* reference) to add layers of meaning to your work by borrowing all or part of a name from the history books or newspapers. This is a little different than what I describe above in the "Don'ts" section. Do so with care. I tend to use this more for naming vessels or installations than people in my science fiction, and when I use it in my fantasy I'm more likely to borrow the name of an applicable mythological personage, than I am someone that actually lived. For example, I have a character that insisted on the nickname Scotch no matter how I tried to change it. I didn't discover the reason for the nickname until I'd written three more stories using the character... he was apparently Corporal Jack(son) Daniels, (thus the nickname Scotch) and it just hadn't come up on the page yet.

Made-up Names. For those that write fantasy or science fiction, at some point you are going to find yourself with a story where what we recognize as names just won't be applicable. You could just pick something obscure from another language, or you can make up something yourself either whole-cloth or echoing an actual name. If you do be sure to read it aloud to feel what it sounds like. Keep it simple and follow a recognizable pattern. If you start out with a complex name, be sure to establish a shorter version that will be easier on the reader when the action gets going (or yourself, should you be in a position to read your work aloud in front of an audience.) When you must make up a number of names for a common group, try to establish a unifying syntax so the reader can believe the individuals come from the same culture. Or, conversely, distinctly different syntax if the characters are from separate environments. Try to avoid apostrophes or Latin-construct endings, these have become somewhat cliché.

For Your Toolbox

To get you started on populating your worlds, here are some questions to consider in relation to the character and setting.

What time frame/setting are you writing in? Very important as in some cases this will determine if you use recognizable names or those that are made up or altered. Also, name usage changes over time, with old names falling out of favor and new ones being established. Lingual shift can even cause the spelling of established names to change, which you can use in your favor if writing a future piece.

Are there established naming protocols for this time frame? Some cultures, classes, and religions are very specific on how a child is to be named. Research some of these traditions to give a more realistic feel to your work.

What is the character's gender? Some names are clearly gender specific, while others are gender neutral. Over time, some have even switched their orientation. In some cultures names are unisex, with a change in suffix identifying gender, such as Angelo versus Angela, or Ivanov versus Ivanova. Whatever pattern you establish, remain consistent.

What is the character's social standing? While in most modern cultures names are not restricted by social class, they can be an indicator, such as the stereotypical Buffy, Muffy, and Biff of the well-to-do set, as characterized in fiction and media, or Billy-Joe-Jim-Bob and Katie Sue, for more rural individuals. Now I don't usually recommend such stereotypes, but they can be useful to quickly and cleanly establish a type of character... or turn one on its ear.

What is the character's ethnic background? Some names are specific to those of an ethnic group, or such groups have a variant of a common name, such as the Polish version of Agnes, which is Agnieszka. Be careful of using a clearly identifiable cultural name when not writing in that particular cultural setting or of choosing names from different cultures for members of the same group and assuming the reader won't notice. All they need to do is recognize one of the names to make assumptions about the characters that could be completely wrong. Not really an issue if you are writing in modern-day America, but if you are writing in a fantasy world a recognizable name could prevent the reader from immersing themselves in the created reality.

Is there a cultural/religious tradition in the naming of children? In centuries past, as in different societies today, children are named for relatives, saints, and other culturally determined conventions. This goes for surnames as well, where some children were identified by their personal name followed by their parent's name (Erikson) or occupation (Cooper).

The Summing Up

Basically, names should sound like names and they should fit your character and your story. With the advent of the internet it is relatively easy to find names from different cultures, variants on common names, and the meanings of names, not to mention historical documents such as census reports that can tell you particular names popular in a given era or region. If you are unsure, look to what exists in the world for inspiration; there are countless examples all around you!

So, with no further ado, let us commence with the naming of names!

Populating Worlds
The Imprecise Science Of Characterization

You know, as much as I have gone on about characters and those things that go into building them, I am astounded to realize that I have not, until now, written a dedicated article on creating characters. There is something wrong there. Something very wrong.

(… cue melodramatic music…)

I'm sure you want to know why, right?

Well… because I haven't had a reason to before! (I would have thought that one was simple.) Now as for why it is important to discuss character creation… that is much more complex.

Have you ever been at a party, or a function, or heck, just sitting quietly on the bus minding your own business and someone starts talking to you? Not a friend or a companion, just a stranger? Imagine they start telling you stories about themselves or people you don't know and frankly don't care about. They go on and on until your eyes want to cross and you contemplate getting off at the next stop, even though it isn't yours, just to get away from them.

Okay, maybe a little extreme, but the same thing goes for fiction. If the reader doesn't get a sense that they know the characters, they don't have a reason to care what happens to them. If they don't care, why read? If you don't catch their interest, a reader is going to just close the book and never open it up again. If you are lucky, they stop there; if not, look out for the scathing reviews.

Now… you don't want that, do you?

Didn't think so. As authors it is our job to make our characters real. And what is more, we have to make the reader care about them, even those they aren't supposed to like.

Let's take a look at how.

Putting a Face to the Name

We've already talked extensively about naming a character, so I won't go into that here, other than to say yes, they should have one. And once you have one, you should share it as soon as possible with the reader (unless, of course, there is a compelling reason to keep it to yourself for the time being.) But where do you go from there? I do a lot of gaming conventions, and not having created a game myself or been involved with a published one in any official capacity, at those conventions the only thing I can talk about as a guest panelist is — you guessed it — writing. You would be amazed at how many gamers want to be writers.

Okay… maybe not.

Anyway, the nice thing is that gamers already have plenty in common with writers. They tell stories and they create characters. They have help that writers generally don't, though. Gaming is a collaborative effort. While the players determine what their individual characters do, it is the Game Master (or GM) who is responsible for the plot and setting of the game, which is mutable depending on the choices made by the players. And when characters are generated (or rolled up) their capabilities and even some of their physical traits are dictated by the players' choices in relation to the process outlined in the game manual and the luck of the dice. (Each game is bloody different so I won't go into all of this, but trust me, I am going somewhere with it.) The game manual only takes them so far, though.

Now, as for why gamers have to roll up characters… It's a cheat sheet. By rolling up a set character before a game begins the player — and the GM — knows what that character is capable of, what they know, what they look like, and often even something of their history, depending on how in-depth the generation process is. This is important because everyone playing needs an idea of who they are dealing with.

The truth is, with gaming characters or fiction characters, the more the creator invests of themselves into the creation, the more interesting things are going to be. Even if the details don't come out right away — or even at all! — just the fact that they have been set helps make the character more real for the writer and the reader. The more you put into it at the beginning, the more everyone will get out of the experience in the end. That is one of the reasons I like to use gaming for an example because there are key points that must be filled in before the game can even be played:

Physical characteristics. This covers all of the basics: hair and eye color, age, build, height, weight, gender, and race. Sometimes there is more, sometimes less, but these are pretty standard. In gaming, most of this is just to get the player into the swing of things and so the GM can describe the characters to the other players when called for during the course of the game. It makes things more real. Don't forget things like scars, physical condition, and manner of dress. In fiction these details are vital for establishing the visual of the character in the reader's mind, as well as their personality. In addition to appearance, some traits determine what a character is physically capable of doing.

Learned skills. In gaming, when you roll up a character their abilities are dictated by the choices the player makes and the physical characteristics they either chose or which are determined by the roll of the dice. For example, if a gaming character has a "strength" rating of forty out of a possible one hundred — just saying — then they aren't going to be a broad-sword-wielding barbarian. And a female warrior with a charisma rating of three isn't going to be a beauty queen in her spare time.

Writers don't have those same restrictions. They get to choose what suits the purpose of the story and then it is their job to make it work. For them, characters can be or do anything, as long as the writer sets things up appropriately to make the claims plausible in the reader's mind. (Yes, that having been said, not all writers bother with the whole making it plausible bit... but frankly, do you want to be that kind of writer?) As writers you should have some basic idea of the specialized skills your character may need based on what that character is and what they are going to face. You can't anticipate everything, don't even try... and don't worry about it when something comes up that you didn't plan for; that is what revisions are for. It is important, though, not to give your character skills on the fly. Either establish that they learned certain things earlier, or actually have them go through the process of learning the new skill needed during the course of the story. You also don't want to claim abilities for them which your earlier description of them implies would be contrary to their nature. (Kind of like the examples in the first paragraph of this section only you are restricted by your own choices and not the luck of the dice.)

Personality traits. Some things will either naturally develop, or even change as you progress through your story, but some things are basic. Is your character a bore? Do they have an insecurity complex? Are they overly proud? Are they extremely nurturing or sneaky? You want to get an idea of this before you even start because the character's verbal and physical responses need to ring true. Actions and reactions are dependent upon personality and morality. If you don't set the guidelines the character will do so on their own and not always in a beneficial way. I know when I was writing my first novel my main character had a bad habit of being whiny in her dialogue throughout the first draft. Besides making her unsympathic and annoying, it was contrary to what I had established for her in the narrative. It also set her up as a weak character, which was okay in the beginning of the book, but needed to change radically by the end. Needless to say I had to go back and revise. By learning who the character is before you sit down to write you can head off such problems because it makes you more aware of how actions and dialogue relates to "who" that character is.

Flaws. Yes, I said flaws. Imperfections. Weaknesses. Interpersonal kryptonite. Physical handicaps. Everyone has them so don't make your characters perfect. Readers can't identify with perfect because *no one* has ever seen it in our lifetime. Flaws make characters more real, but in addition to that, flaws give them something to overcome (or for another character to exploit.) Such things are vital for advancing a plot and for bringing life to a story. To go back to my original gaming example, this is one of the reasons players roll for various attributes. The dice cannot be predicted and by using them the players introduce challenges to their characters that they then must work around or with to achieve their goals. (So in a way, writing is role-playing for one.)

Personal/family history. As individuals we interact with the world not only based on who and what we are, but also based on what has happened to us or those around us. It's called experience. Everyone has it. Your characters should as well. History is what drives our reactions; it is those layers of detail that give life depth. Know why your characters say and do the things they do. Understanding where a character comes from is as important to a reader, often, as seeing where they are going. Think of such details as threads in a tapestry. The thread is pretty in and of itself, but when you weave them together they form a rich image that is much more than the sum of its parts.

Environmental influences. We are all products of our environment. Culture, society, home life, politics, all of this affects our views and responses to different situations. Characters should be the same way. Think of the different racial, religious, and cultural stereotypes you are familiar with; sad to say, but they are stereotypes for a reason. When you place a character in a particular setting it will impact the way they talk, think, and act. These are learned behaviors. If your character has learned something different than his peers, you as the writer need to account for why. Whether your character adheres to the typecasts or is contrary to it, be mindful of the reader's expectations based on the information you have given them.

The Voices in Your Head

Listen. Your characters are there. Get to know them before you attempt to tell their tale. Know what to expect from them the way you would with a good partner, one you know well enough to anticipate their responses. This isn't to say that characters won't do things that surprise you. Things that are... forgive me... out of character, but as with all of us, there are reasons, you just have to figure out what they are.

Questions to Ask Yourself

Here are just a few things for you to think about while developing your characters. Not all of them will apply in every instance, but by applying some of the below you can add depth and richness to those populating your stories.

What is my character's name? Sometimes this will just be something that sounds right to you, sometimes there will be a deeper significance either to you personally, or to the plot in general, but in almost all cases, characters should have some form of name. (See the article on naming characters for a more in depth discussion about this.)

What does my character look like? Go all out on this. You might not use all the details but even if it only serves to set the character in your own mind so they are more real to you as you are writing, it strengthens your story and ultimately translates to the character being more real to the reader in the end. Also, there will be times when you need to distinguish between characters when their name doesn't come into play.

What is my character's personal background? I'm not just talking about what they do now, but where they came from, and who they hang out with, as well. Give at the very least your primary characters a history and some depth to their immediate lives. This includes family history, education, and even those deep, dark secrets we all have that we would rather no one else knew about. I'm not saying to weigh down your story with all of this stuff, but you don't know what will be relevant to the story until you are done. Do some preparation, have the information to hand, and that way as you are writing you can seed the story with whatever details flow in naturally. Even if something doesn't make it to the page it will still help you set in your own mind the appropriate reactions and personality traits of your character. By knowing where they've been you have a better understanding of who they are now.

What flaw does my character need to overcome? We all have them. There are always ways we can or outright need to improve. Don't neglect this aspect of your characters otherwise they will not only be flat and uninteresting, but also implausible. No one is perfect. Not even the make-believe. More than that, though, in fiction the flaws exist also to build tension, making them a vital tool.

Summing Up

Personality is important, as are physical traits. Not only do they give a sense of identity, but they also dictate what we — and our characters — are capable of. It is important for the author to have a firm grasp of that, particularly with longer works because if the details aren't locked down it is much easier for them to get jumbled as you go.

So You Think You Know...

(*Originally published as Kelly Green, Corned Beef and Cabbage, and Other Stereotypes That Have Little or Nothing to Do With the Irish in the column If We'd Words Enough and Time*)

Local color is very important in a story, it lends authenticity and helps draw the reader into whatever realm you want to immerse them.

It is so easy when writing to fall back on stereotypes that we have come to confuse with fact. In my early novels, *Yesterday's Dreams* and *Tomorrow's Memories*, I wrote about the Irish. Yeah, there is a wealth of stereotype there; some of it rooted in truth, and some of it made up either completely out of whole-cloth or based on outdated concepts more aptly termed — at least by me — Irish-Americanisms. Let's look at some of the misconceptions:

All Irish drink alcohol
If you are Irish you wear Kelly green
All Irish are religious
Corned beef and cabbage is an Irish dish

I am sure there are many more that we could come up with, but these are the most common, as well as the ones I discovered were not necessarily true when I actually went to Ireland. (Now, I focus on Ireland here only because it pertains to what I have written, but this applies to any culture or time period that you might have cause to write about.)

I know that stereotypes are a convenient and effective way to distinguish the locale or certain characters in a story, and if they are a minor part of the whole you may decide that for your purposes that is sufficient, however, when the element is a more significant part of your plot you want to depend on more than stereotype or your work will suffer.

If the place you want to capture in words is nearby then you are lucky. Just schedule a vacation or weekend get-away in your target area and talk to some people, see some sights, and sample the local flavor first hand. Now, if you are working with a culture that lies across an ocean you might not be able to indulge in a trip there to see for yourself the true local color that you want to capture in your writing. I didn't make it to Ireland until after my books were written, but a good Irish Pub helps fill in some of the details, (an authentic one, not just one capitalizing on the stereo-types, anyway.) This isn't always an option, though. There are several ways around not being able to visit the culture you want to write about:

- Internet sites dedicated to the region/culture you want to utilize

- Interviews with people originally from that area

- Visiting the cultural/ethnic neighborhoods found in many larger cities

- Research through books and local newspapers

- Phone calls to the Tourist Board for that area

- Slang dictionaries (regional and found on the internet)

Another facet of this dilemma is trying to write about a par-ticular locale, but in a different time. Granted, unless there are people still living that may remember the time you are aiming at, then you are out of luck as far as interviews go—anyone have an extra time machine laying around anywhere?—but that doesn't mean that there isn't a wealth of information out there just waiting for you to dig in.

Here are just a few sources you could plunder, and I am sure you can come up with a few on your own:

- Recreationalist groups (they exist for nearly every period in recorded history and for many cultures. The Society for Creative Anachronisms, or SCA, alone covers much more than just medieval England, for example.)

- Literary and journalistic archives (many libraries and universities have these going way back, and what you don't have in your local library you can often get through interlibrary loan. Microfilm is a bit trickier, but even that is migrating to the internet in many cases.)

- Old journals and letters (check with historic societies in the area you are focusing on)

- Museums and Historical Societies

These are by no means the only sources, just the first that come to mind. As writers there are many resources out there geared toward helping us get past the stumbling block of being born in a different era than that which we may want our stories to take place. For instance, the Writer's Digest Book Club alone has countless period reference books, such as *Everyday Life in the 1800's* and so on, not to mention guide books on making characters in different professions well... professional.

However you go about getting your information, remember this, your writing is only as good as the effort you put into it. If you want your work to be taken seriously, take a little time to do the research, make sure that your portrayals are more than just hasty stereotypes and flat depictions. The reader wants to see a world that comes alive through your words, not a two-dimensional view that merely mimics the world's preconceived notions.

Stereotypes might have their place, but it is not center stage and in the spotlight. Take the time to discover who your characters are and the worlds they really live in. Do justice to your work and to your readers. With so much research potential out there, particularly given the profusion of internet and TV documentaries geared toward just this sort of thing, building an accurate picture of something you have no exposure to at all on a regular basis is no longer the time-consuming excavation it once was.

Take a little effort... invest some time, you will be amazed at the difference it can make in your work.

The Tricky Art of Conversation

(Originally published in Allegory Magazine, www.allegoryezine.com)

There is no path so fraught with potential misstep than conversation. Bad enough talking to yourself—a whole other realm of fraught there—but bring another person into it and you get three things: What you said, what you thought you said, and what the other person heard.

Knowing what to say and when to say it... not so easy. *Am I getting my point across? Am I saying too much? Is this going to be taken wrong?* At some point we have all asked ourselves these questions; and that is just with verbal communication. Written dialogue... much more complex. And yet in fiction, as in life, conversations are what take you out of yourself—or the character's head—and integrate you into a living, breathing world.

Having trouble with that? Well, let's see if we can't extract your proverbial foot from your literary mouth...

What to Say

In writing, dialogue is one of the trickiest simple things to do. I know, contradiction, right? Not really. We talk every day. We hear people talk every day. It should be beyond easy to write two or more people holding a conversation.

Again, not really.

There are nuances of verbal communication that defy written expression, or at least are difficult to do full justice to. Expression, inflection, body language. Yes, you can include some or even all of that, but at what point does it begin to intrude, becoming cumbersome to read? Your task as a writer is to put in just enough cues to get your point across without slowing down the pace and flow inherent in natural conversation.

There are two ways you can learn this (besides through nifty how-to articles like this, which can only take you so far). First, go out and listen. Find a park or shopping mall or someplace where there are loads of people and sit yourself down. People watch, but more important, listen. Conversations are organic, each one unique. Some people are good at it and others aren't. By listening and observing you can get an objective feel for how different conversations proceed and what nonverbal vocabulary is involved.

Your second resource, read!

No, not a how-to book—I know, how ironic. One of the best ways to get the hang of written dialogue, or any other aspect of fiction writing, is to study what others have done… and sold! You want published examples for comparison because they have, in theory, been through the editing process. Now this doesn't guarantee they are examples of literary perfection but the works in print are representative of what is being accepted and published in today's market. You want to read more than a few books to get a proper feel for the dialogue. Pay attention not only to what is said and how, but to your own reaction to the author's attempt at replicating natural conversation. You don't necessarily need to read the full book—at least for the purpose of this exercise—skimming the dialogue should be enough to give you perspective (this might be a good time to dust off your library card). To save yourself some time, you might also ask your friends if they can recommend any books that had particularly good or bad dialogue.

Once you have a few examples of each, find a quiet place and try reading some of the selections out loud. This will help you identify the strengths and weaknesses in the written conversation. If something is awkward to speak aloud, it is usually awkward to read on the page as well, though that isn't always as consciously evident if you haven't first recited it. You might think if it isn't obvious, then it can't really be a problem, right? I wish, but the truth is that readers often pick up on these things on a subconscious level even if they can't readily identify why a particular passage is less effective or enjoyable than another.

Things you want to look for are comfortable pacing, dynamic exchange (meaning the back and forth between characters, not the snappy comebacks), conversational language suited to the character speaking, and nonverbal cues and clues. Everyone is going to have their own style, but dialogue should read like people actually speak, with appropriate tone for whatever setting it is occurring in.

The Art of It

Once you can recognize the mechanics of good dialogue it is time to move on to the conventions of conversation, more to the point, some of what to avoid.

Pace and Interaction. Think of dialogue as a tennis game. It's an exchange between two characters, sometimes recreational, sometimes competitive, occasionally adversarial, but always back and forth, like the ball going over the net. Think back on some of the conversations you've had in your life. I am sure there are those that ate away the hours without you realizing it because you were enjoying the exchange so thoroughly. By the same token, there were those you thought would never end. As an author, your objective is to find the right balance for the scene you are writing and the dynamics between the characters participating. Don't have one character dominate—unless, of course, that is the point—get a volley going. If one character goes on and on for some reason, make sure to interject with nonverbal reactions and exposition from the other character.

Information overload. Have you ever been trained in a job where the person training you just goes on and on, feeding you details without allowing you the chance to ask questions? If not, man, are you lucky! I can tell you that eventually, no matter how much you attempt to pay attention, your mind begins to shut off. There is only so much you can take in when you have no opportunity to process it. The same can happen in dialogue. If you have a character feeding detail after detail with very little interaction from the other character/s in the scene, the reader is going to miss some of what you wanted to get across. To avoid this, share the informational responsibility among your characters. Dialogue should be reactive: one character says one thing and the other has some kind of response, either through dialogue, nonverbal cues, or inner monologue. Dialogue should also be interspersed with action, otherwise the mind wanders. Come on, you know I'm right… just think about those family gatherings when you were young, expected to just sit there quietly as the adults talked around you. It is amazing the places the mind will take you faced with such tedium. Now, you don't want that for your readers, right?

Stating the obvious. There is no getting around the fact that everything you write on the page is meant to convey information to the reader. All of it. That's the entire point! One of the things you have to avoid, though, is being obvious about it. You want the reader to lose themselves in your universe, to be fully immersed in the story. The quickest way to yank them out of that immersion is to stage your dialogue in such a way that it is obviously there for the sole purpose of educating the reader. What do I mean by that? In a conversation with someone of a similar upbringing or whom you have an existing relationship with certain knowledge is common knowledge… to everyone but the newly introduced reader. One of the ways authors betray themselves is by have characters sharing information among themselves that they logically would have already been familiar with. It's kind of like when you want to tell someone something, but you don't feel you can directly, and instead you stage a conversation with someone else in front of that person so they overhear what you want them to know. Such conversations are rarely natural; same goes for dialogue.

Talking out of Character. If you have done your job properly each of your characters is going to some degree or other have a distinct personality. They will also have an established social position. This translates into a character's Voice (I'll be going into this in more depth in the next article: *Continuing the Conversation*). When writing dialogue, or even narrative, it is very important that your word choices for a character are in keeping with that Voice, otherwise you shatter the illusion you have built and the reader no longer believes in them.

Summing Up

Needless to say there is much more to dialogue than the little bit I've covered here. For now, follow the good examples, not the bad; remember to keep the right Voice in your head when writing from a particular character's point of view, and don't be a bore! Or rather, don't let your character's be, unless, of course that is their purpose in the tale.

Continuing the Conversation

(Originally published in Allegory Magazine, www.allegoryezine.com)

Do your characters talk to you? Come on, you can admit it.

No, really, it's a good thing!

Mine do — well, actually, they're more likely to argue with me, but that's beside the point…

If you can hear your characters in your head, clear and distinct and individual, that means they have their own Voice. Yes, Voice with a capital V. This is a very important part of the character's personality. With a capital V-Voice they have their own identity that sets them off from the other characters populating the story. Not just because you've said so, or because you've described them in very particular terms, or because of the things they say, but because the way they say them is unique only to them. Primarily, this pertains to dialogue, though not always. It depends on how much you use the narrative and point of view to establish your characters. For the purpose of this article we will focus on dialogue.

Getting the Conversation Started

So much of conversation is in how you say things. Your grasp of grammar — whether written or spoken — will determine how well you are understood. In person, you have the opportunity to clarify. On paper, you only get one chance. Because of this, even when you are trying to establish a character type you have to be sure to get your point across properly through word choice, sentence structure, and through the response of other characters, otherwise you are going to frustrate your reader. In my previous article, *The Tricky Art of Conversation*, I recommend reading selections of published dialogue to get a feel for what works and what doesn't. I again recommend that. My skill at writing effective dialogue without a doubt came out of my being a voracious reader since I was a young child. By the time I had to learn this stuff in school it was already coming naturally to me.

One of the most important things to remember is to break up your dialogue. Lectures, not conversations, are one person going on and on. Give your characters the opportunity to respond to one another, and if that isn't appropriate to the scene, inject a bit of narrative so we can see the silent participant's reactions to what is being said. In either case, always remember that more than one character is involved and don't let your reader forget either.

Personal Identity

Have you noticed in life how much you can tell about some people just from hearing them talk? I'm not talking friends, or family, or anyone you know intimately enough to pick up on the unspoken cues. I'm talking strangers, people you have just met. Now, as with most things in life, this doesn't go for everyone but there are several bits of personal information you can garner from a person's Voice — real life here, not fiction — those things are their general age, their gender, their education level, and their general geographic origins. This is because there are cues we all project without even realizing it. The words we choose, our diction, regional slang, or even just accent. These details are a part of our personal identity.

As writers it is our task to mimic those auditory cues to shape our characters. Now we are hindered a bit in this being a print medium — duh! — but by an intricate dance of narrative, dialogue, and character interaction you can accomplish the same goals. Let's look at the tools for the job:

Slang. This develops on several levels, for several reasons. Sometimes it comes out of technical language used among a given set of people, sometimes it is specific-use language developed by a ethnic or social group, or sometimes it stems from popular culture or results from poor education. Whatever the origin you need to take several things into account: the meaning of the slang, the context, and the appropriateness of its use by a particular character in a given situation. From my own works my novel, *The Halfling's Court*, is a perfect example. This book is set in my biker faerie universe — yes… I said *biker* faeries — and to write realistically in this context I had to do a lot of research into biker slang. I discovered they virtually have their own language, for instance, a mechanic is called a "Wrench," cars and their drivers are called "cages" and "cagers," respectively, and those thick, slick squiggles of tar used to repair cracks in the road are called "tar snakes," just to give you a sampling of what I mean.

Now, if we were to use this language in our everyday lives we would likely get more than a few eyebrows quirked at us, but in a biker bar, spoken with confidence and understanding, no one would bat an eye. I did not take myself down to the local biker bar, but I was very fortunate that there are a lot of websites on the internet that give a glossary of biker terms. Not only do they give you the language and the meaning, but they often put it in context as well. This made my job very simple and lent credibility to my biker characters. All it took was a little research. Of course, if you are lacking a convenient and detailed website, you can always interview someone of the appropriate demographic that uses the type of slang suited to the character you are trying to develop, or you can go to where such people are likely to be found and observe. Ironically enough, I've encountered this with the next installment of my biker faeries; that one includes roller derby girls and while I couldn't find a glossary on line, I was fortunate enough to contact the South Jersey Derby Girls and gained an invitation to one of their practices. We'll see how that one turns out. In the end, though, do the research, rather than relying on stereotypes and assumptions that may not be as authentic as you think they are.

Another caution, do not overdo this as it can become difficult for the reader if a story is too overloaded with such references, particularly if they are not intuitive to someone not a part of that culture. I always put a glossary in the back of my novels when I use a lot of slang or mythological references, but you also don't want to put your reader in the position of having to continually flip to the back just to understand what they are reading. Make your references clear and where necessary explain briefly and in a non-disruptive way in the context of the story.

Vocabulary/Grammar. This is related to slang, but not exactly the same. More often than not this is dictated by education level and career, though not always. Someone that is more well-read or educated might chose more complex words, or someone with a very technical occupation will reflect that in their speech. Of course, a character that wants to be perceived as well-read or educated might well adopt this manner of speech to mislead others.

Dialect. For our purposes, this is the written representation of regional accents. By itself it is only part of the picture but combined with the above two treatments it makes for a more three-dimensional character. Put into practice in literature it is generally the phonetic representation of some words or sounds representative of the verbal identity of an ethnic or regional group.

There are two schools of thought on this device. Some people absolutely loath written dialect. Others feel it has a transformative effect on the writing. In the end it all comes down to how you incorporate it. Done incorrectly — or correctly to excess — it can be tedious, even painful to read, especially if the character it is applied to is a primary focus character that appears and speaks often. With a lighter touch, it can be just enough to add flavor to a piece. But how do you decide how much is too much?

This is a dilemma I have run into personally. In my first novel, *Yesterday's Dreams*, three of my primary characters are Irish, complete with accent, as well as a number of secondary characters. It wasn't too bad, though I did catch some flack from reviewers. My approach to it was to take three conventions stereotypical of a brogue and apply them to those characters: the dropped consonant, primarily the "f" in of and the "g" in anything ending in –ing, substituting "ye" for "you," and " 'tis" and " 'twas" contractions. By selecting just these three alternations it was enough to get the point across without rendering the dialogue nearly indecipherable, as well as being easier to maintain consistency.

Pausing for a Breath

Now like I've said before, nothing is fool-proof or absolute. Take the above and consider it, then see how best to apply it to each character you write and specific interactions between those characters. If you are trying to set a particular feel, perhaps you want to go with a bit of dialect. If you need to establish a passing character quickly because they won't be around long, you might want to go with slang or specific vocabulary to get their Voice across. Whatever you chose, be consistent and don't let the device you use take undue attention away from the story you are telling. These are tools that should augment and complement your tale, not dominate them.

Wrapping Up the Conversation

(Originally published in Allegory Magazine, www.allegoryezine.com)

Dialogue is one of the writer's primary tools in mimicking real life. It can also be one of their greatest weaknesses. Good dialogue will do more to establish the personality of a character than any amount of description or narrative because, done correctly, it echoes things we have all experienced. Far-fetched as it might sound, you want the reader to forget they are reading… you want them to forget this is fiction. When your characters speak naturally through your words that state of immersion is possible. To accomplish this there are several things you need to understand about dialogue.

Identifying the Speaker

When you're having a conversation with someone, for the most part you know who is talking even when you can't see them. We have voice cues and context that help us distinguish the participants. In fiction, clearly, that aspect is missing. Instead the author must make plain which character is talking at any given time. There are several different schools of thought on this.

Stick with "said". When identifying the speaker some feel that substituting other words for "said" should be kept to a minimum. These individuals believe that "said" is one of those invisible words we are so used to that our eyes just gloss over it, acknowledging without catching on it or being disturbed by its repetition.

To substitute alternative words is to draw attention to the substitution and distract from the dialogue. For example:

> "I don't know what you mean," Corey said. "I have never been to that part of town."
> "But I was there, I saw you," Ralf said.

For the most part in literature, this is observed, particularly in traditional markets.

Vary your speech tags. Other people feel that the repetitiveness of "he said-she said" fosters an uncomfortable and obvious rhythm, particularly in dialogue-heavy passages. These individuals endorse using alternative words to "said" such as "commented," "answered," etc. Such substitution cuts down on the repetition, but can be more overt than simply saying said. For example:

> "When do you think you saw me there?" Corey asked.
> "Tuesday," Ralf responded.

(Personally, I prefer a happy medium between options one and two. If said suits, I use it, but if something else feels right, I substitute.)

Leave off the tag. No, not all together, all the time. But in a situation where the characters are established and it is clear who is talking, then yes, to improve the pace and flow of the dialogue, it is completely acceptable to have some of your dialogue go without a tag. For example:

> "Impossible!"
> "Well then you have a twin..." Ralf said, glaring at Corey. "And he's wearing the shirt I gave you for Christmas last year!"

Or

> "Impossible!"
> "That's interesting, Corey," Ralf said, "because you

were wearing the sweater you borrowed from me... the one my mom made for me!"

Alternate means of identifying the speaker. In some instances it is quite natural to use narrative or action to identify the speaker in place of the tag. For example:

> Corey whirled around. "I don't know what you mean. I have never been to that part of town."
> "But I was there, I saw you," Ralf said.

As you can see, there are many different options. The important thing is to pick the one that is comfortable for you, but also to be aware that when you are sending your work to a paying market, they might have their own preferences. See if the publication or publisher has a style guide on their website or if they mention a particular style guide they use, such as Chicago Manual of Style.

On a related note to the above, whether or not you use "said" or "commented" or some other alternative, keep in mind that word order is important, if it sounds awkward to read out loud then you shouldn't be using it in writing either. Word order is important and there is a current trend of writers transposing the subject and the verb in speech tags. For example:

> "But I was there, I saw you," said Ralf.

Now it might not seem like a big thing and when paired with a name it hardly seems wrong at all, but substitute a pronoun and the error glares:

> "But I was there, I saw you," said he.

Or substitute a different verb for just for the sake of example:

> "Ran he." versus "He ran."

Transposing a phrase might sound more poetic, or intimate, but many editors feel it is an indication of poor writing. So remember... noun first, then verb!

What to Talk About

Writers are faced with a particular challenge: how to convey necessary information to the reader without 1) resorting to info dumps, or 2) clearly leading the reader. The first is a conversation for another time. The second, though, applies to dialogue.

It is tempting to get your characters to do your dirty work for you, and don't get me wrong, that isn't a bad thing, you just have to be smart how you go about it. Unless you are writing for children give your reader credit for being observant. What do I mean by this? Don't spoon feed them, or write down to them. Written conversations between characters should be natural and purposeful. If you wouldn't have such a conversation in real life (personal circumstances aside) then your characters shouldn't be having it either. I'm not talking about the topics of conversation precisely, but the manner in which you conduct the conversation. Primarily, don't have your character regurgitate facts both of them clearly already know, when you do this you make it obvious that the conversation is being held for the purpose of the reader, rather than to advance the plot. If you want to reveal information by means of dialogue between characters be sure to weave in narrative to fill in those gaps in the reader's knowledge. For example:

"I saw your sister, Tammy, the other day," Carl said, pausing as if not sure he should go on. "She looked good. Barely even limped."

Ralf flinched. He hadn't seen her in months. Went out of his way to ensure he didn't. He was glad she was recovering from the accident but he didn't think he could face her yet. "Good. Good, I'm glad to hear it."

Now, you could argue that perhaps Ralf has more than one sister, in which case it would be natural for Carl to specify which one. On the other hand, I could argue that the name would be sufficient because after all, Ralf will know who Tammy is by context if nothing else, but as an example, let's assume there is both one sister and one Tammy. Here's how I would fix this:

"I saw your sister the other day," Carl said, pausing as if not sure he should go on. "She looked good. Barely even limped."

Ralf flinched. Tammy. He hadn't seen her in months. Went out of his way to ensure he didn't. He was glad she was recovering from the accident but he didn't think he could face her yet. "Good. Good, I'm glad to hear it."

Or

"I saw Tammy the other day," Carl said, pausing as if not sure he should go on. "She looked good. Barely even limped."

Ralf flinched. He hadn't seen his sister in months. Went out of his way to ensure he didn't. He was glad she was recovering from the accident but he didn't think he could face her yet. "Good. Good, I'm glad to hear it."

Establishing Personality

You have surely noticed that what a person says isn't always as important as the way they say it, right? This is applicable for personality, as well as intent.

"I don't know what you mean," Corey said, with a sly glint in his eye. "I have never been to that part of town."

Or

"I don't know what you mean," Corey said, his expression baffled. "I have never been to that part of town."

Or

"Dude, I don't know what you're talking about," Corey said, his expression sullen and his posture slouched.

Both word choice and physical description in the speech tags can in a few short words define a character, either overall or in reaction to a given situation.

The Final Word

So, when you sit down to write — dialogue or narrative — remember what your purpose is: to establish your characters and universe in a non-obtrusive manner, allowing the reader to immerse themselves in the reality you have built as completely as they are able, without the presence of the author intruding overtly on the experience. To accomplish this through dialogue, ask yourself the following questions:

- Is this a natural conversation?

- Does it convey knowledge already common to the character?

- Would this be better expressed in narrative?

- Does the dialogue fit the personality I have established for the character in question?

- What does the dialogue do to advance the plot or inform the reader of the back story?

Be natural, be age-appropriate (to your readers and your characters!), think of the words as actually coming out of a person's mouth. Better yet, get someone to read through it with you, each of you taking an appropriate character's lines of dialogue. See if your dialogue holds up as a conversation. Artificial dialogue can be the kiss of death to a good story. I know I myself see it almost as a personal affront when characters come across as patently fake independent of anything required by the plot. Look closely at your characters, be true to them and let *them* talk.

Spend Your Words Wisely

(Originally published in the column If We'd Words Enough and Time)

How many words does it take to tell a story?

Can't really answer that, can we? Or at least, not easily... There are too many variables, too many considerations. Is it a short story? A long one? A novel? A complex, or a simple one? What do you want to tell? What do you want to simply imply?

Who can say, really? A haiku can convey a story in seventeen syllables; Tolstoy required thousands of pages. Most of us are fortunate, we can answer the original question as simply as this: It takes as many words as it takes.

But then, who wants to be simple, anyway? In this world of done and redone and overdone, we want a challenge, don't we? At the time this article was originally written such websites as New Times – San Luis Obispo and AOL's Amazing Instant Novelist — and who knows how many others over the years — offered up that challenge every day: write a complete and compelling story in however many words strikes the sponsor site's fancy and no more. Usually they are generous, allowing a few hundred, at least. A challenge, but a relatively simple one.

Not so with New Times – San Luis Obispo. Are you ready for this? Maybe you better sit down... fifty-five words a story, nothing more!

Can't be done, you say? Well, there's the challenge, and the guidelines are very specific as to what constitutes a story: one or more characters, a setting, a conflict, and a resolution. It ain't easy (ooh! I can hear my grade school English teacher screeching from her grave, now!), but it can be done, as I will show you below. With the permission of my illustrious... anonymous partner in crime — let's just call him IrateIndigoSimian, why don't we? — I'd like to give you an example of the same story from a couple of different approaches:

> He had always loved her, ever since the first time he had laid eyes on her he had known she was the only one. He kissed her sleeping forehead gently and considered her betrayal.
>
> The recoil from the gun surprised him, the finality of it all didn't. He turned the gun toward himself next.

Simple... straightforward... uncomplicated. Nothing wrong with that. By the contest guidelines, this definitely works, but does it work well? Think about it, the author made use of all of his fifty-five words, "had" was used three times, "her" was used four times, and "he" was used five times; those three words make up more than twenty percent of the author's allotment. Ouch! Yeah, it works, but the impact the subject matter could have is diminished by the frivolous use of throw-away words. (Don't feel I'm being too harsh with IrateIndigoSimian, this was a first draft. We already hashed all of this out and he agrees.) Now, let's look at a later version of the story:

> Their love had been the thing keeping him alive for years now. Her betrayal severed their bond, his soul, his mind. His final kiss left a soft, warm ghost touch on her sleeping forehead.
>
> The recoil from the gun surprised him, the finality of it all didn't. He turned the gun toward himself next.

Not bad, this version has a decidedly different feel, putting everything out in the reader's face from the very beginning. You are immediately confronted with the character's betrayal and anger, and the ending is a logical progression, without surprise. This accomplishes something very different from the first draft, and as for economy, not one word, other than articles, appears more than three times. This is an honest, straightforward rendition of this piece, but for my own tastes, a little too much in your face, not subtle enough.

Now for a bit more subtlety: The next one is more ambiguous. Other than the main character's love, we aren't sure how this is going until the fourth line. With the emotions drawn on, the fondness that is admitted, the second paragraph is a shocker:

> He found he couldn't remember a time he hadn't loved her. Even now, his soul was entwined with hers. Her sleep was deceptively peaceful. He gently kissed her cool forehead and contemplated her betrayal.
>
> The recoil from the gun surprised him, the finality of it all didn't. He turned the gun toward himself next.

And the last is on a similar vein, with the betrayal hinted at in the third line, but not revealed until the fourth. This draws the reader in, hooks them, has them guessing. The words chosen have an emotional impact all their own; you feel his love, then his betrayal... and finally, your own shock:

> There was never a time he hadn't loved her. Even now, his soul was entwined with hers. She slept so sweetly... innocently... deceptively so. He gently kissed her cool forehead and contemplated her betrayal.
>
> The recoil from the gun surprised him, the finality of it all didn't. He turned the gun toward himself next.

With all fiction, and most decidedly in microfiction — or drabbles, as they are now called — you have to choose carefully. Think of the emotional investment of the words you put to the page... for example, in the last line of the first paragraph, the first version has the main character "considered" the woman's betrayal, in subsequent versions it was changed to "contemplated"... Considered is an everyday word, an ordinary word. Contemplated is more involved, more impact.

It is cliché, but no matter what the length of your prospective work you need to go for quality, not quantity, but most especially with something like this, where you only have so many words to use... each one has to score.

Words should have purpose, a goal, all of them used to good effect. Unless it is for a reason, never use more words than you have to; your work can drown in a profusion of "highfalutin' " words, as my Daddy liked to tell me. Use a fancy word because it lends something, because it enriches the beauty of your poetry or prose; by the same token, do not be afraid to use a simple "workaday" word, if it suits your purposes. Simply put, use a word because it does what you need it to do, not because it is delightfully pretentious.

And finally, because it bears repeating over and over — ironically enough — when you are writing and rewriting your work, no matter the length, always keep close watch, guarding against our natural impulses to repeatedly use the same familiar words, even if we have used them three times already on the same page. Many word processors (if not *all*) have a Thesaurus option, my greatest advice to you: use it.

Literary Detailing

You know, sometimes we just don't know when to stop. No. It's true, even I'm guilty (I know. *Shocker*.) We get so caught up in the language and discovery of these worlds in our head that we just pile on the detail. We get so caught up in the creativity that we have to build the universe right down to the thumbtacks on the wall, or we're worried about not being clear, or missing something important, until we end up with a literal checklist of all the steps that took our characters from A to B... for each scene.

Okay, so perhaps I exaggerate, but not completely. There are times in fiction that call for expansive detail and others where too much clutter kills the action. It is important to know how and when to hold back. There are two kinds of detail: relevant information, and window dressing. The relevant details might be regarding the character, the setting, or the plot; the stuff you must tell the reader for the story to work. The window dressing is what helps your story really come alive. It is what the characters experience through their five senses, the type of detail you would casually take note of in your day-to-day life.

Now, if you do your job properly, every part of your story will combine the above types of details with only the degree of each varying, but each scene will have a central focus: Some scenes are so you can get to know the characters and their conflicts and drives, some reveal details you'll need to know to understand what is going on, and others propel the story forward. What type of scene you are writing will determine how much detail is called for, and what type.

Plot-oriented scenes. These scenes are what we call the build-up. Something happens, or someone says something, or the protagonist finds — sometimes knowingly, but often not — the key to resolving everything. The reader learns where things are, how they work, and what's important. There is going to be detail there. Some of it is the whole point of the scene and sprinkled around that detail is backdrop, either to mask that this is an important detail or just to flesh out the scene so that it is not static.

Character-oriented scenes. For these scenes everything should be in terms of how it relates to the character: their motivations, their past, their goals. And let's not forget, their features and personality. Readers need to get to know your characters so depending on their level of importance, some characters get a little detail, some a lot. Inner monologues and self-examination are not frowned upon here, unless they go on for too long, but they shouldn't dominate the storyline. Of course, that also depends on the type of characters in the scene. Protagonists we should know like our own blood because we need to care what happens to them. Secondary characters, we should know their importance to the protagonist and some small amount of detail that impacts the story or their actions. Background characters, something to identify them, a name or a feature, but nothing else that doesn't directly relate to the scene they appear in or the part they play in the plot.

Action-oriented scenes. In most action scenes you either already know all or most of the players, or they are only relevant for what they are doing at the moment. This is about what is happening, what blows are struck and what plans are put into action... reactions and movement. The setting is only important in relation to its impact on the characters and its impact on what is taking place. You want short, sharp sentences where things are happening, not exposition or distraction.

Things to Consider

Once you have a handle on what scenes you are writing, here are some questions to help you keep focused as you tackle each one:

Is the scene a destination or a transition? If it is the former you have more leeway to go into detail because that is the point. If a scene is a transition you want to focus more on relevant details, rather than background stuff. Now, there is a caveat: if the point is to show an extended passage of time, expounding a bit more is to be expected.

Is it taking too long to get where you're going? If you personally start to feel like things are dragging, then that is a sure sign that they are. Pacing is important and too much detail can slow things down. Go back over the story and pare things back. Shorten sentences, take out detail you don't really need, even cut out whole sections and give us a fade-away before cutting to another character or just a later point in the story.

Is the detail relevant later? Sometimes we just put in detail because it is cool, and sometimes we mention something that seems totally irrelevant, but the entire story hinges on it. Be careful of focusing on something that isn't a key point too heavily because readers have come to assume that anything the author spends an extended time on will be important. It leaves them frustrated at the end if some such point turns out to be merely fluff.

Summing Up

Details are what will define your story: they are the building blocks of your universe, the soul of your characters. Be a little coy, be a little bold, and always proceed at the proper pace for the scene you are writing. Don't be afraid of detail or ignore it, but don't let it run away with you either.

Coming to Your Senses

No! Not like that. I know what it is like to have the writing bug. When you really have it, there's no getting rid of it. I'm talking the five senses, not common sense.

One thing I've learned over the years is that we pick up a lot of information in our day-to-day lives, most of it without even realizing. There is a constant influx of sights, sounds, smells, tastes, and touches. This influx helps us to define our world. Remove any one or more of these senses and the rest have to work that much harder.

Writers would do well to remember that. And I don't mean in relation to the characters.

I can see the look on your face now. *Huh?*

Let me explain. As writers one of our jobs is to create a world that the readers will be drawn into. For that to happen it has to be presented so that they can relate. We process our world through our senses. If you neglect that in your writing or depend only on the more common senses of sight, sound, and perhaps smell, those senses will have to work very hard to connect the reader with your created world, which will lack some of the dimension we've come to expect in life.

Now, I'm not saying to bombard the reader to the extent that a snail would move faster than your plot, but there are natural openings for sensory data in most fiction and those openings often go underutilized. You don't want paragraphs of nothing but description, but you can do a lot to integrate both your character and the reader into a setting by weaving in sensory data as the action progresses.

First, let's see what we have to work with:

Sight. Most authors have this one down pretty good. After all, we know you have to describe what's going on, and what is seen, right? In shorter works you mostly want to keep this down to relevant details, basic description of the setting or things that the characters are seeing as they move about. More focus is placed on something that is a key point in the story with the rest just setting the scene. In longer fiction, however, there is room to play.

Sound. The obvious things here are sudden sounds meant to indicate something is about to happen, or dialogue, but our world is so full of background sounds. That is where you will find depth in your literary universe. Children laughing. The sounds of cars. Birds singing. The argument down the street. These are common, every-day things. They are the pulse of life itself. Have your character note such sounds… or even the absence of such sounds, which can communicate a lot to the reader.

Smell. Again, often used in fiction to indicate something out of the ordinary; an alert that we should pay attention, but smells seem to be the sense most linked to memories. I know personally that the scent of the air just around mid-October, or early November has a distinct difference and I respond to that each time I smell it. Just mention that crisp, slightly mulchy aroma and all kinds of associations come to my mind: from raking multicolored leaves to the nip in the air on a Halloween night to the heavy weight of my cold-weather coat.

Taste. This doesn't just come into play when you eat or drink. Sometimes a scent on the air or clinging dust or any one of a myriad of things we encounter each day that touches or passes our lips. By choice or otherwise! Those things can tell you much about a setting or situation. Do not overlook this aspect of our environment. Sometimes we as writers even associate tastes with emotional responses, a good way to incorporate them when the actual taste buds are not possibly engaged.

Touch. There is no point in life when we are not touched by something: a breeze, a falling leaf, someone brushing by. When all of our other senses fail us, this is for the most part the one to remain faithful. In very few instances can we move about and not come in contact with our environment in some way. Our characters should likewise interact with their world.

A Matter of Depth

You knew all the above… pretty much, yes? It's a given. We don't think about it much, but there are certain things we just know. These are the simple basics of reality. Incontrovertible facts. When you are building a world, though, it is very important to go beyond the basics. Don't assume that the reader will get the depth of detail you are looking if you aren't giving them any cues. For example:

Tammy's coat brushed against Kyle's hand.

That tells us what happened, but not really anything else. What you want are the tactile clues that will resonate with the reader. Yes, with the above they will likely have a memory or some idea of what the sensation is like just from their own experience, but what if their experience isn't what you are going for? For example, what if you had something like this in mind:

Tammy brushed past Kyle, the heavy wool of her coat slapping hard against his hand.

Or

Kyle shivered at the slap of wet wool against his hand as Tammy brushed past him.

Both sentences basically say the same thing as far as the action goes, but the choice of adjectives gives very different sensory input. Don't leave all the work up to the reader; for your story to work you need to give the audience the proper cues. Okay. Let's take it a little further with the next example:

> The lights were off when Ricki arrived home. She unlocked the door and stepped inside. Moving carefully through the room she turned on the lights. Mac was sprawled on the floor.

You know the progression, but you don't know how Ricki feels and you don't get any sense of her interacting with her world. There is plenty of action/reaction, but as a reader you don't know how to react yourself to the words on the page. Now try this:

> The autumn breeze took on a deeper chill as Ricki pulled up in front of the house. The windows were dark and there were deep shadows around the door. The porch light was out, as was every light in the house. Ricki drew a sharp breath and scrambled out of the car as soon as it was in park. The door knob was icy beneath her hand as she unlocked the front door. Even before she stepped inside a metallic tang pinched her nose. A soft groan sounded from the darkness. With shaking hands she flipped on the light. Mac blinked up at her from where he sprawled on the floor, his expression dazed by more than just the sudden light.

This paragraph not only paints a picture for the reader, but gives cues on how the reader is supposed to feel. Yes it took longer, but this isn't a trip to the store we are talking about, it is an adventure in a brand new world.

Summing Up

It is a common adage in writing: Show, don't tell. The best way to do that is letting your character experience their reality through sensory input that will resonate with the reader. Think about what you want to convey not just about what your character is experiencing, but their surroundings and the emotional responses you want to inspire in any given scene. Every encounter will not call for all five senses, but engage them, when you can, more than singly or in pairs. After all, it is up to us as writers to create a comprehensive experience for the reader as they wander the pages of our universes.

The Short and the Long
of a Novel Idea

I was recently approached by an aspiring novelist. This writer was stymied because he wanted to write a novel, but his stories kept wrapping up in about fifty pages or less (assuming standard margin and double spacing, probably about 20 to 30,000 words) which makes them technically novellas. This is a common dilemma for writers, wanting to write a novel, but not knowing how to get started.

Let's start by looking at the difference between a short story and a novel. (besides word count, smart aleck!)

Well, part of what makes a short story different from a novel is back story; most short fiction has just the relevant information to the story being told. Novels, on the other hand, explore characters and events a bit more, including information that is not necessary to the story, but does develop the character or give the reader insight to why things are the way they are. You can also explore the setting in a bit more detail and that kind of thing. All of this makes for a richer, more layered universe where the reader gets the feeling that there are other, unseen things going on in the world around the characters.

The second thing that is the major difference between short stories and novels is multiple threads. Usually there is one overall plot to a short story and that is it. Novels have a primary plot, but a number of subplots that are related in some way but still differ from the main goal of the story. Sometimes the subplot will deal with the main character and sometimes it will be a separate story line where another character is the focus and your main character is secondary. So basically think of a novel as telling several stories at once, but interwoven.

To use a metaphor… novels are woven tapestries, whereas short stories are knitted afghans. Many individual threads versus one continuous yarn (for simplicity's sake, though there are always exceptions).

Start out with your characters and figure out three things about each one:

- What is their goal?
- What do they have to do to achieve that goal?
- What is preventing them from achieving that goal?

Sometimes there will be multiple answers to each of the above, but don't make it too complicated… Also, don't be afraid to alter things as you go. I start out with an idea and write a bit, then do some research related to what I've written and often that sparks other ideas relevant to what I am doing but different from what I'd planned. My work has much more life in it if I let it develop organically rather than sticking rigidly to my plan. Other writers put together an outline that lays out the key points of the entire novel. Some write the way I write, no method is more correct than another, so find the way that works for you.

Another method I have used is to write a number of short stories in the same universe, with the same characters. This has the same basic effect as a novel, particularly if you have an overall theme that continues from story to story, with a secondary theme that resolves itself by the end of the individual story. Each story should stand alone so that if anyone reads just that one, they won't feel lost or that they are missing part of the picture. Once you are done you can go back and link them into one big storyline, revising to take out repetitive detail, or just leave the stories as is and publish it as a collection instead of a novel, but with the same effect.

I'll give you an example from my own experience:

My novel, *The Halfling's Court: A Bad-Ass Faerie Tale*; when I first introduced my biker faeries of the Wild Hunt M.C. in the anthology *Bad-Ass Faeries* it was meant to be a stand-alone story. Entitled "At the Crossroads," the story dealt with a faerie challenge, but set in the modern day. Since it was a short story I put more effort into setting the feel of the universe than going in-depth into the characters motivations. Those I kept simple. Faerie biker wants faerie woman, faerie woman goes missing, faerie biker must ride to the rescue. As I said, I never meant it to be anything more... however... the story was so well received that when we went back to do the second volume in the series, *Just Plain Bad*, I decided to write in the same universe, this time with a story called "Within the Guardian Bell," borrowing on both faerie lore and biker lore pertaining to road gremlins. Again, the story was well-received.

I should not have been surprised when shortly thereafter a publisher showed interest in a Wild Hunt novel.

This posed quite a challenge for me because as I mentioned, the stories were meant to just be stories, and now I had to incorporate them into a novel. The character development was not as detailed as I would have done for a novel, but by the same token the writing was tightly woven, making it difficult to interject new copy building on the characters more. I managed, but not to everyone's satisfaction. From this I have learned that when I am writing a short story I will take the extra space and flesh out the characters a little more than necessary.

In addition to adding character detail and integrating new characters, I had the challenge of pruning away redundant details. After all, the stories originally were linked, but printed separately so enough detail had to be recapped from one to the other so that no matter which story was read, the person reading it didn't feel lost. This had the added benefit of tightening the writing and smoothing out the pace. When gathering related stories into a collection this is not so much of a concern as it is when you are fully integrating them into a novel, but still be aware of details too often repeated and perhaps edit them out in a few instances.

Now, when I was writing *The Halfling's Court* I was aware a third *Bad-Ass Faeries* anthology was coming up, so rather than have three stories all integrated into the same novel, I instead left a gap in the manuscript where some of the secondary action takes place off-page. I later came back and wrote that scene as a stand-alone story, "Seeing Red," which is also the linking story between *The Halfling's Court* and the upcoming sequel, *The Redcaps' Queen*.

So, as you can see, if you goal is a novel but it seems too daunting a task, try establishing a 'universe' through a series of short stories and you never know what might develop!

Writing Exercises

This section is meant to complement the articles you just completed reading. They are exercises I have used in writing seminars over the years and have found useful. I hope you do as well. There is one exercise to a page so that you may photocopy them if you wish to complete the exercise on the page with the instructions for reference. Feel free to do so for the purpose of honing your craft.

As mentioned in my opening note, there is no particular order here. Have fun!

Writing Exercise – Character Development: Take fifteen minutes and write a scene that starts off with the following elements (you can elect to add other elements and characters): A woman in one shoe, a broken branch, and a public place. Remember to show who your character is through action, thought, and expression. (Aim for 200 to 300 words).

Writing Exercise – Writing to the Senses: For each of the following listings write down three descriptions for each of the five senses (not all the senses will apply).

Example: A Fishing Wharf
Sight:
1. a long expanse of weathered pier,
2. sun sparkling off the water,
3. a lone pole propped against the rail

Smell:
1. the tang of brine on the wind,
2. the tarry aroma of the sun-heated planks,
3. the scent of roasting peanuts from a nearby vendor

Sound:
1. the strident cry of the gulls,
2. the gentle slap of water against the pilings,
3. the hissing zip of a cast fishing line

Taste:
1. a hint of salt as the surf sends a mist into my face,
2. the beefy taste of hot dog I bought on the boardwalk,
3. the flavor of fish

Touch:
1. the wet slap of a caught fish,
2. rough wood beneath my fingers,
3. the breeze tugging on my hair

A City Street Corner
Sight:
1.
2.
3.
Smell:
1.
2.
3.
Sound:
1.
2.
3.
Taste:
1.
2.
3.
Touch
1.
2.
3.

A Room in an Abandoned Building
Sight:
1.
2.
3.
Smell:
1.
2.
3.
Sound:
1.
2.
3.
Taste:
1.
2.
3.
Touch
1.
2.
3.

A Battlefield
Sight:
1.
2.
3.
Smell:
1.
2.
3.
Sound:
1.
2.
3.
Taste:
1.
2.
3.
Touch
1.
2.
3.

An Art Studio
Sight:
1.
2.
3.
Smell:
1.
2.
3.
Sound:
1.
2.
3.
Taste:
1.
2.
3.
Touch
1.
2.
3.

Writing Exercise – Writing to the Senses, Part Two: Write a brief scene based on one of the settings in the previous exercise, incorporating the details you have listed (you do not have to use all of them, just what fits the scene).

Writing Exercise – Description: Take four canvas bags or something you cannot see through. Have someone place a different item in each bag where you cannot see what they have put inside. These should be things that have very distinct textural feels. Reach in to each one, do not look, and then describe the contents in the space below. The object is not to guess or tell what the items are, but to express the tactile nature of the item.

1)

2)

3)

4)

Writing Exercise – The Five Senses: Do this as a group exercise, if possible. Gather a notebook, pen, blindfold, earplugs, and something to plug your nose, then take a field trip to somewhere with a lot of sensory input (if you are self-conscious, you can do this without the last three items); try a mall, the beach, a park or something similar. Once you are there attempt to isolate your senses one at a time, or at the least, focus on them individually. (Taste will be the most difficult. Try breathing through your mouth to capture elements on the air, or having the group provide you with edible things from where you happen to be.) Take some time with this and try and pinpoint the various sensory data you gather, as many things as possible for each sense (not all will apply), then write them down in your notebook. As a group, compare the different information you gathered. Save the notes for future use in your fiction.

Writing Exercise – Character Development: Take fifteen minutes and write a brief description of the following characters. Give them a name, a history, and physical and personality traits, and one character strength and one character weakness. Describe only, this is not a story.

A young woman in her twenties.

A little boy, no younger than three, no older than twelve.

Writing Exercise – Dialogue: Write three lines of dialogue to suit the description given. Keep in mind the character should be identified first, then the attribution (She said; Kyle replied, not said she or replied Kyle). Or experiment with using action and reaction to identify the speaker, rather than "she said."

1) argumentative:
"Don't bother to lie to me!" she said, her teeth gritting. "I found the receipt from the motel in your pocket."

2) romantic:
Tammy looked up at him through lowered lashes, a half smile tugging at her lips. "I don't have anywhere I need to be... unless you have somewhere to suggest?"

3) frightened:
"I... it was right there, I swear it was," Kyle stammered, the whites fully visible around his irises.

4) hurt:
"You know," she said, her voice low and trembling, "I expected that kind of thing from her... but... but you?"

5) excited:
"We won! Oh my God! We won!" She grabbed her partner by the shoulders and danced around with glee.

Writing Exercise – Dialogue: Time for another field trip. Go to a populated location and observe a nearby conversation. You don't need to be close enough to hear. Take notes on the nonverbal cues in the conversation, expression, body movement, vocal tone (if you can hear it). Write your own dialogue to match the observed cues, incorporating them into the narrative.

Writing Exercise – Characterization: Complete this exercise with a fellow writer or in a group. Take a primary character you have already created and write down everything you know about them. Be as thorough as possible, including physical and personality traits as well as personal history. Give that character sheet to your partner (you should receive one in return) and then each of you write a scene or short story utilizing the description you were given. Do not add character details beyond those provided. When complete, exchange and read what the other person has done with your character, noting the differences from your own interpretation and looking for gaps in the profile that leave your character less defined than you may have realized.

Writing Exercise – Local Color: Take a social or ethnic group you are familiar with and write a scene depicting the distinctive elements of that group. Do not depend on cliché, but rather things you have observed or experienced first hand. This can also be done as a field trip, though you should use caution in selecting the environment you enter for this purpose.

Writing Exercise – Naming/Characterization: This is a good exercise to do in a group. Make three separate lists of names, (first, last, and nicknames.) Have fun with it. For best results, make sure the names reflect diversity. You should have an equal number of each, but they should be separate lists. Take scissors and cut those lists into little strips containing one name each, keeping the piles separate. Put the first, last, and nicknames in separate bowls. Pick one slip of paper from each bowl and write down the resulting name. Take a few moments and write a brief description of that character to match the name. Be sure to include ethnic background and an explanation of how the character acquired the nickname.

Business

Always Another Day Away

(Originally published in the column If We'd Words Enough and Time)

So… you wonder why you don't get any writing done… right? Let me guess… Work gets in the way? You have Writer's Block? You're tired? You're not good enough? *Enh…* Wrong answer.

Procrastination… The Lazy-Eyed Monster

First off, let's see what Merriam-Webster's Colligate Dictionary has to say on this subject:

Main Entry: **pro·cras·ti·nate**
Function: *verb*
Inflected Form(s): **-nat·ed; -nat·ing**
Etymology: Latin *procrastinatus*, past participle of *procrastinare*, from *pro-* forward + *crastinus* of tomorrow, from *cras* tomorrow
Date: 1588
transitive senses : to put off intentionally and habitually
intransitive senses : to put off intentionally the doing of something that should be done
synonym see DELAY
- **pro·cras·ti·na·tion**
- **pro·cras·ti·na·tor**

So, you might say: No way! I would never *intentionally* put off writing, so this doesn't apply to me. *Enh…* wrong again… All of us do it, from time to time, me most of all. When I originally wrote this it was 7:16pm on Saturday night... guess when this column was due? Yup, Saturday. We may not realize we are doing it, but we are constantly making decisions that stand in the way of our writing progress.

It Will Just Take a Few Minutes...

What is it for you? Do you have to clean up the mess before you can concentrate? Do you need to catch that season finale, or you just won't be able to think straight? How many times have you gone for a snack? Or decided to check your email first? There are so many little things that get in the way of what we "really" want to do: write. To be truthful, I am sure that you don't even realize you are doing it; I know I don't most the time. The truth is the few minutes those tasks take can really add up.

How do you get around this? Writing time is writing time, baring emergencies — or impending spousal wrath — nothing is to interrupt it. Don't have a TV nearby, make sure your family stays clear (with the noted exception of the above instances), make sure your hunger and thirst contingencies are in place, and close your mind to the world outside your writing space. (This is not recommended for long stretches of time, unless you want those close to you to forget what you look like).

To Muse or Be-Muse?

Acceptance is the first step. Now repeat after me: I am a procrastinator. Very good... Now, do you know why? Everyone has their own reasons — admittedly, sometimes even valid.

A lack of inspiration. It can be rough not knowing what to write. I have definitely been there myself, from time to time. The ways I get around this, editing and assignments. If I find myself with a lack of inspiration — the dreaded Writer's Block — I do not let it stand in my way. You may not make headway in your storyline, but if you at the very least use your writing session to review what you have already written it serves several purposes: one, it allows you to catch mistakes like spelling and grammar; two, it gives you an opportunity to flesh out any sections that need it; and three, it re-familiarizes you with the work you have already done. All three of these can help summarily banish your lack of inspiration.

Another way around this is to use an outline, or keep a list of "things I need to write." I don't work well with an outline because I'm always radically diverging from it, but I do create lists in relation to my novels. I jot down any ideas or elements I want to be sure to incorporate in the finished product. When I find myself stumped and I have already polished what I've written before to a fare-thee-well, I read through my notes and ideas. It doesn't always work, but nothing will, every time. If nothing else, it does remind me of my goals.

If you don't have an ongoing project to help you along, have someone provide you with assignments, topics or situations for you to base your work on as an exercise. Think about it… most of us fell in love with writing thanks to some English teacher somewhere. Assignments and reports fostered our interest and cultivated our enthusiasm (presuming you did well at them, but then, if you hadn't you likely wouldn't be reading this, would you?)

For most of us, that is the seed that got this obsession started. But seeds need to be tended or they shrivel and die. How many of you realized that after the impetus of school was removed from your daily routine, your writing efforts became drastically reduced? I know mine did. It wasn't the enjoyment that fled, just the motivation. There was no sense of direction anymore. So recreate it. I had a friend give me assignments and I also found an on-line writing site with weekly writing contests. Without that, I never would have been published when I was. Whatever means you use to get past this stumbling block, be sure to write. Some in the industry insist that you must write every day, or you aren't a writer. I'm more practical than that. Life does get in the way, after all. To me as long as you make the effort to write *something* on a relatively regular basis, then you're still in the game. It is vital to write, though; to let your creativity out to play. It is the only way for your talent to grow.

Why Do Today What You Can Put Off 'Til Tomorrow?

Too much effort. I don't know about you, but I am lazy to the extreme when it comes to certain aspects of my writing. Part of this stems from too many steps, part comes from too much waiting, and yet another part comes from too much doubt. See, in my own experience, to use a cliché we can all relate to, I am used to being a big fish in a little pond and a little fish in the big pond.

I don't find writing to be too much of a problem, most of the time. In fact, I have more problems stopping when I *should* be doing other things. My biggest problem, and the source of my private procrastination habits, is in submitting my finished work for consideration in the various venues that exist for authors. It isn't a lack of desire to gain recognition. It isn't a lack of confidence in my talent. It is an overwhelming aversion to waiting and wondering. This will explain to you how, though I have written prolifically since the age of thirteen, it wasn't until I was thirty-one that my work was recognized in any way.

This is the roadblock that I must work my way past. So far, even now, I have made little effort to submit my work to any venue unless it was the simplest of procedures, or I felt I had something to set me off from being just another faceless by-line. I like places that accept electronic submissions (they tend to respond quicker) and if I have an introduction to those reviewing submissions, or even better, a previous connection to them, that is when I submit. I still look for those places I can submit electronically because it cuts out the transit-time portion of the waiting, but I have worked my way from submitting only when my work is solicited, or submitting when my work is recommended. The next step I have taken is to aggressively seek out sources that don't know me from Eve. It is tough for me, learning to wait patiently to see if any will find a home, but it is the next step in my professional growth. I know my work is appreciated by those that are familiar with it… but those professionals that are seeing it for the first time… daunting.

Why? Because despite what I have accomplished in the last nine years, my reason for procrastinating is a fear of rejection... a fear that this isn't good enough...

I resolve that I will work my way past that fear.

Now, my friend, you need to look at your own personal brand of procrastination and see what is required of you to overcome it. Only by freeing our dreams can they be realized.

In Godhood Is Perfection Found

(Originally published in the column If We'd Words Enough and Time)

... And nowhere else. Remember that. It's important.

You've written the next Great American Novel... you bask in the glow of the accomplishment and look down on all non-achievers with faint (and certainly justifiable) condescension. Neatly typed in complete observance of the submission guidelines of all the major publishers, you are ready for your deserved acclaim.

Yeah... it was kind of hard for me to not let it go to my head too... until my first less-than-glowing review came through citing the fact that my precious masterpiece was riddled with flaws even a mediocre editor should have caught. I learned an important lesson that day, and once I started rewriting *Yesterday's Dreams*, I had to admit the reviewer in question, as well as the three or four others that shared his opinion, were completely right. My story was delightful; my grasp of certain aspects of grammar was not.

Now, no publisher expects a manuscript to be flawless... if they did, copyeditors across the country would have no jobs. The lesson I have learned from this experience... well... the three lessons I learned from this experience, in fact, are as follows:

- Always remember the adage "To Err is Human..."

- Never assume my work is pristine

- And, never assume the editor will catch all my mistakes

I know! I know! That is what editors are there for, right? Well, you know, that is logical in theory, but all too often books are launched onto the shelves with absolutely no consideration given to the errors within, either because the publisher wants to save the cost of paying a copy editor or because they are in a rush to get the book on the shelves and assume the corrections can be done later. Besides, even if the copyeditor *does* practice great diligence and pours over every word, remember "To Err is Human..."

Yes... I expect you to tattoo that phrase right across the back of your hand so that you never forget. (Oh, *okay*, in indelible marker, then...) No one is perfect and there will always be mistakes. Even if you were to have a flawless grasp of the English language, there will always be such things as typos. More importantly, after a certain point, we become so familiar with our work that our mind tricks our eye into reading what we expect to see on the page rather than what is really there. In all the years I've been writing seriously I have never picked up one of my stories without finding something that needs correction or adjustment. Even Piers Anthony has the philosophy that typos and spelling errors sprout on the page after the editing process.

Ensuring the most correct version of your work is presented to the public falls to you. There are many potential errors in a manuscript that is tens of thousands or even hundreds of thousands of words long: spelling, grammatical, continuity, factual... You will never catch all of those errors alone, though it will start with yourself. The most important step in polishing your writing is your own attitude: Your mantra needs to be "No work is a finished piece." In fact, even once I have submitted a piece of what I hope is polished writing for publication consideration, I always include in my cover letter the disclaimer that any suggestions for the story's improvement are welcome, regardless of how many times I have already gone over it.

The next step in polishing your work is read-through, after read-through, after read-through, but remember, each time you personally review your work your effectiveness diminishes. There are several ways around this:

- Have your friends — both writers and non-writers — do a read-through for you, noting any errors they notice or questions they might have. (This is to see if the common reader has any issues, as well as those more familiar with the craft.)

- Join a Writer's Group at your local library, bookstore, or on-line, where your work will be critiqued, in theory, by those more knowledgeable of grammar and structure.

- Hire an editor before you submit the work anywhere. (Not always financially feasible, but if you do be sure to research their credentials first.)

The publisher should have the work edited again on their end before publication, but sometimes things don't go as we expect. If that happens in your case, it is to be hoped you will have already caught the majority of serious errors with the above efforts. This isn't about questioning the abilities of the staff and freelancers employed by publishers these days, but it is about taking responsibility for your own work and recognizing everything can use improvement. There are a lot of aspiring writers out there and not nearly as many publishing opportunities, but with so much competition, extraordinary steps will help in getting your work noticed and minimizing the possibility of embarrassing mistakes for which the audience, be they publishers, reviewers, or the reading public, will look to attribute to you, not some faceless editor who "should have caught it in the first place."

Remember… To Err Is Human… and there is no such thing as a finished piece.

Flexibility Is A Virtue

(Originally published in the column If We'd Words Enough and Time)

A wise old author once imparted on me a gem of advice: No matter what, be flexible. Note, I said "wise old author," not "dirty old author." The flexibility is in our writing and our mindset, and there are several different dimensions to this advice.

Flexibility in Novels

Okay, so you have written the next great novel of our century and you have been fortunate enough — with hope — to find someone willing to take a look at it. Good for you, excellent, in fact. This is nearly as hard to do as writing the book to begin with, particularly in this day and age of "no unsolicited manuscripts" (for those of you new to the business, this means your manuscript doesn't have a pimp... sorry... agent!).

Now, when you send your manuscript off — unfailingly following the submission guidelines to the letter — you will include a cover letter. This is where your flexibility begins. Your first impulse will be to tell the extremely fortunate editor what a treasure they have before them. Resist... believe me... resist. What you need to do is thank them for taking the time to consider your work and let them know you would be open to any suggestions they might make that would improve the quality of the manuscript.

Some of you might be prepared to stalk off in a huff right now and say "No way! This is my masterpiece, it is whole and complete and immaculate." And that is all well and good, but you know what the editor is going to say, "Well, this isn't quite what I was looking for, and this passage here is a little rough, and my god! The typos, the grammar… Maybe we can work with it… but…" It's true, and that is if you are lucky. Always be humble when you are asking someone to have faith in your work. That is the hardest, yet most important aspect of the flexibility you will need to be a writer.

Think you can manage that? Good, because that is only the beginning. If you are fortunate enough to make it through nego-tiations and sign a deal (after being asked to rewrite half the book already) then your manuscript goes to the copyeditor and the nightmare begins for it is their job to take your efforts and pick them apart down to nearly the cellular level and rebuild. If you are fortunate, you will recognize a glimmer of your original work in there somewhere… eventually.

Okay, so I exaggerate, but only a bit. I have a friend who is an established author with multiple books under his belt with a major publisher. He had to add fifty pages to his manuscript before the editor would even consider an agreement—because there wasn't enough war in it. The publisher already had the first two books in this tetraology and they would have turned down the third book because they were bloodthirsty. My friend was flexible, in went fifty pages of war. My author friend's reasoning? He will add the fifty pages because it is a matter of paying his dues and securing his place, because if he does not compromise now, he will not be in a position to set terms later in his career. And this is an already established author. Imagine what is asked of the aspiring author.

Do not… I repeat… do NOT make a big stink about changes the publisher wants to make in your work. Very few of us have the bargaining power of Stephen King or Danielle Steel, and if we alienate the editors, we never will. If there is a problem with the revisions (as in it makes the story make absolutely NO sense whatsoever) then talk the matter over with them, but always in a cooperative manner.

Flexibility in Short Fiction and Other Venues

Another way for a writer to establish themselves is through the publication of short fiction, articles, and poetry in magazines and anthologies. Once again, your query letter will be your key to holding the editor's attention long enough for them to consider your work. The way to do this is not to be flashy (the last thing you want is for your cover letter to take attention away from your actual work), but to be respectful. One or two short paragraphs indicating what you are sending and expressing an interest in suggestions that will improve the work. They don't want to work with prima donnas, they have enough of them with the big names.

Since many anthologies and magazine issues are theme driven, it can be in your favor to query the editor, asking if there was anything in particular they were looking for that they did not receive. I know an author that did this for an anthology that was to be about the old west, he asked the editor and it turned out that of all the things that were received, not one of them dealt with the building of the railroad. My friend whipped something out and it made it in to the anthology.

This won't work every time, but by being flexible and willing to give the editors what they want, rather than what you want to give them, you build your prospects for being invited to other projects in the future.

Now That You're as Twisted as a Pretzel...

No matter what venue or genre you write in, being humble and accommodating — within reason — will improve your chances of getting a foothold in the writing world. Eventually, if you are fortunate, you will be in a position to set terms, but the easier you are to work with and the less arrogant you become, the smoother your path to literary immortality will be.

Rejection and the Tender-Hearted Youth

(Originally published in the column If We'd Words Enough and Time)

Last One Picked for the Team

Do you have faith in yourself? Do you see the merit of your work? Well… then everyone else will too, won't they? Unfortunately, this is not an if-then situation. One of the greatest hurdles in the literary world is the constant, guaranteed threat of rejection. How you deal with this rejection will plot the course of your literary career for all time.

So, I guess the first question is: How bad do you want to be an author? You noticed I said author and not writer, right? Of course, you did. This is an important distinction. The moment you put pen to paper — or fingers to keys, or stylus to touch screen, or… you get the picture — you *are* a writer. The transition takes place with publication. When your name is on the professionally printed page the transformation begins and "writer" becomes "author." A heady sensation, though not as glamorous as you might think… but that is a topic for another time.

Make no doubt, the distinction between writer and author is an important one, for there are those who — though some of us cannot fathom it — have no desire to become the latter, whose entire goal in life is to content themselves with the wonder of being the former, all for their own sublime enjoyment. For the sake of perpetuating this article, let's assume "author" is your ultimate goal.

Maintaining a healthy perspective is the key... and cultivating at least a kernel of thick-skinned hubris. Without it you will scatter like dust on the wind after your first dozen or so rejections.

Dear John...

Rejection... even the word is abhorrent to us. It cuts us to the quick and lays bare our insecure hearts. Fear is not the little death... rejection is. It cultivates doubt and discouragement until we question our own value, the merit of our work. With each rejection a tiny part of our confidence dies... if we let it.

I have forced myself to view each rejection or negative review with a ruthless clarity. First, how readily — and honestly — can I refute what they say? If I cannot, then I would do well to listen with an open mind and learn from their observations. Do they complain of things that can be easily fixed? Is this the first time I have heard this particular criticism, or is it a recurring theme that uncovers something I must learn to work on in my writing? If I am going to court comments, I must extract every bit of value from them. Nothing is a finished work. The world, in every aspect, is in a constant state of change. Our work is a microcosm of the world.

Ultimately, the most common cause of rejection or other negative response — those reactions having nothing to do with the technical aspects of grammar, continuity, and construction — is personal preference. Not everything we write will appeal to all. It is not possible. Not only do we all look for different things in our reading, but we also bring to the experience different understandings. Some will be blind to our vision and death to the poetry of our words. That does not speak to our merit, only the observer's perception.

Always a Bridesmaid

"This is not quite the exceptional work I am able to add to my crowded plate right now."

"This story belongs to the world... in one or two more drafts... but I cannot see it for what it is: a published work."

Quite a blow to one's "golden child"… With each strike, a bit of the gold leaf flakes off, revealing the foundation as less-than-priceless. These are two of the most devastating responses I have ever received on my own work. Without a doubt, a humbling experience. And yet, if I allow myself to be blinded by the rejection, I have defeated myself.

A knee-jerk reaction is to accept the judgment without analyzing it. What is the standpoint these people are responding from? Is it personal preference? Is it with an eye to profit or marketability? Is there a flaw I can work around? Our ability to change, to adapt, is one of our greatest strengths. This is as true in our writing as any other part of our existence.

Woo the world, entice them… use confidence and skill to convince them, but be true to yourself. Your opinion should not be lost to the challenge of changing theirs.

Red Pill or Blue Pill?

Which would you chose? In the realm of literary success, will you chose self-delusion? A fantasy realm where only your own opinion matters? Or will you chose a proactive role; seeing every response, positive or negative, as a gauge, a tool to hone your skill? Do you hold tight to your conviction that your work puts the classics to shame? Or will you give serious thought to the humble acknowledgement that yes, even your masterpiece needs a bit of polish — or complete revitalization — before the world can see its merit? My advice to you: grow that thick skin. Don't let them tear you down with their brutal words. Recognize that every rejection is but one opinion. Take what you can of value from it, but refuse the debasement of your worth. One man's opinion… ten men's opinion… even a hundred's, is still just that: an opinion. Listen to what they say, and how they say it, not to validate, but to cull the indifference and gather to you any observation that might nurture and hone your talent.

A Little Friendly Abuse

*(Originally published as "Where Two or Three – Or Twenty – Are Gathered"
in The Complete Guide To Writing Fantasy: The Author's Grimoire,
by Dragon Moon Press)*

Writing, they say, is a solitary endeavor.

I say it is a journey you make with your friends: those you write for, those you write about, and those who make it all come together by helping you figure out where you went wrong.

True, for the most part you sit yourself before your computer... or typewriter... or clay tablet... and pretend the world outside your head is not there, but for those writing with the hope of publication this is only one third of the process (refining the resulting manuscript and promoting the finished product being the other two legs of this triumvirate). With that in mind, it is my task to tell you about one of the writer's most valuable tools: the Writer's Group.

What Exactly Are We Talking About?

On the off chance that it might actually be there, I looked up *Writer's Group* in The Oxford English Dictionary and alas, though countless triviality, including that which follows somewhere after Muffle, has made it into those exalted pages, *Writer's Group* has not. The same went for Miriam-Webster's, and the Cambridge Dictionary. Surprising considering you can't turn around without encountering someone that wants to be a writer. Well, that just leaves me to define the term for myself.

I say Writer's Groups are meetings of passions, minds, and on occasion bodies. The one key and unifying factor of such groups is that they be attended by, of course, writers — aspiring, established, and every stage in between. While such meetings can have varying objectives (which I will soon discuss), the key element is a desire to write (that is the passion I reference above, so you can stop looking for the X-rating at the top of this chapter).

To Put a Fine Edge on It

While I am sure there are countless variations on Writer's Groups in the world, I am going to focus on three basic types (and please keep in mind, these labels are my own): The Social Club, the Crucible, and the Community. Every group I have ever been a part of or encountered has been some combination of these three elements.

The Social Club. When you are shopping around for a group of your own, it is important to be sure of both what you are looking for, and what you are getting into. Not every Writer's Group focuses on polishing the craft.

I know. What is the sense in that? Well, some people like to socialize. This process — especially for someone who sits alone in front of a monitor, pretending the outside world doesn't exist — is made easier when there is common ground. What that means for you is that though the majority of people on or in the group are writers, the craft of writing may not be the primary topic of discussion. Participation and structure in the Social Club are characteristically relaxed.

That is not to say that such groups serve no purpose. Not only are they a place to commiserate and unwind among those who can relate, but they are also a means of networking with those in different tiers of the industry, or a pool to be tapped into if you yourself are looking for someone with certain writing-related skills. Think of it as the grapevine for writers, or a community bulletin board.

The Crucible. Do you have a general idea what this one is going to be like? Yeah, you're right, as painful as it sounds… well, for your ego, anyway. This is the intense, no-nonsense Writer's Group. Think of it as diametrically opposed to the Social Club previously discussed. There is generally a great deal of regulation, a firm obligation to *give* as much, if not more feedback than you receive, and the bitter blow to your ego is not softened when they tear down your work and help you build it back up again, better, stronger than it was before.

The main factor of the Crucible is structure. The process is very formal and regimented, with certain plateaus to be reached and maintained before you can fully benefit from all the group has to offer. One such point being that those participating must meet an obligation to review and critique a set number of submissions before they are entitled to submit their own work into the process. Once they have reached this point they must maintain a quota of so many reviews in a given period if they wish to retain their submission privileges. Many times, though not always, emphasis is given to highlighting the flaws of a work that they may be eradicated and repaired, rather than on giving note to the positive attributes of a piece.

This might seem cruel and counterproductive to some, but it is not. The point is not to be brutal and unfair, but to be frank and exacting. For some writers constructive criticism is the best way to refine their work. They do not want to be told what works, because it does not need their attention. The purpose of the process is not to form a cheering section, but to gain productive feedback that will ultimately lead them as close to perfection as any of us is capable of. They already possess the confidence needed to succeed; what they need is an outside and objective perspective to hone their work to publishable quality.

The Community. This Writer's Group is about more than just honing skills, it is also about support and encouragement, celebrating successes and commiserating about rejections. This is a writing community that shares its knowledge of both publishing opportunities and the wisdom gained by experience, where topics generally gravitate around writing, though socializing and tangential conversations are not unheard of. A well-rounded environment that is writing-oriented but not narrow focused. The work is looked at as a whole: what works is praised and what doesn't is addressed. This is the middle ground between the two groups we have already discussed. It is for people becoming more serious about their writing, but lacking the knowledge, experience, or perhaps the confidence in their own work to take it to the next level. The community is about nurturing.

How Shall We Meet Again?

Generally there are three methods by which Writer's Groups are conducted: In-person, on-line, and by correspondence. These three methods are also known to cascade into numerous variations on the theme when put into practice, tailored to fit a group's particular needs. The structure of the group decides when and how often "meetings" take place.

In-person groups take place just about anywhere: members' homes, libraries, bookstores, diners… the possibilities are, as they say, endless. Depending on the venue, and the availability of the members, these groups generally meet weekly or monthly. To connect with one, visit the local community bulletin board or website, check the classifieds of the local weekly paper, or ask at the college campus, bookstore, or library nearest you.

One of the drawbacks of these groups is the experience level is generally uniform across the board, with everyone having very little knowledge about the technique of writing or experience with actually being published, or grossly unbalanced with the majority of members having little or no experience and one or two people being more advanced. In the first case the majority of the feedback received is going to be subjective, based on the readers' tastes, rather than on any firm understanding of why something works or what the industry is looking for. In most instances, critiques are vague and unproductive. In the second case, those who have little experience will benefit more from the feedback of those who have achieved some level of proficiency, while those with more experience will not get as much out of the group.

On-line groups are the most fluid. Conducted by means of message boards, live journals, blogs, newsgroups, list-serves, email, or any combination therein, their activity — while dependent on the participation of the members — is for the most part continuous. Its flexibility is in being able to participate when it suits your schedule. Also, because the web is far reaching, the experience levels are more divergent so everyone generally finds something of use in their own efforts.

Because of the diversity of the medium, the resources available to such groups can be more valuable than the member interaction itself. With endless links for writer's resources and submission sites and research pages easily passed from member to member for immediate access, this avenue of meeting has revolutionized Writer's Groups.

Also, the method in which you interact with the group can be chosen for the way that most suits you. Message boards, live journals, and blogs have features that can send an email alert to let you know when there has been activity on a particular topic, and newsgroups allow you to tailor your user preferences so that you receive posts by email as they are made, once a day by digest, or none at all, in which case you access them at your leisure via the newsgroup home page.

These are also the easiest to find, though you will have to try out a few before you find one that is a good fit. Check out the classified section of your favorite writers' magazine or run a web search on Writer's Groups. You will find literally millions of hits. All you will have to do is decide if you want one for writers in general, or one tailored to a specific genre or style that you write in. There are benefits to both.

The flaw of this method is volume. There are so many groups to choose from that it might be difficult at first to pin down one that suits both your needs and your personality. With some internet groups and boards activity is sporadic and not always helpful, with others the members participate with such enthusiasm your mailbox will literally overflow each day. Such can clearly be overwhelming, even if the dialogue is stimulating and resourceful. For the most part it is just a matter of moving on to another group until you find something you are comfortable with, but after a time the registering processes some groups require can be tedious and off-putting.

Once you have found your group, the next great hurdle is conflict among the members. Sometimes that can be more brutal in the faceless realm of the internet where typed words can be misinterpreted or filled with venom to a degree that would not necessarily happen in a face to face encounter. Such occurrences are inevitable; the mark of a good group is when they are the exception rather than the rule, and they are promptly defused by those running the show.

Correspondence groups are in a way a more personal interaction. Conducted by conventional mail, they can be an exchange between yourself and one other person, or a handful of people, but for the most part groups such as this are small and selective. This method most benefits those who are, for one reason or another, unable to travel to an in-person group and do not have readily available or dependable internet access.

Interaction in this case is restricted by delivery time. The frequency of exchange is determined by how quickly you receive and review the work, and how dependable the postal service is in returning it. (In theory, it would also be possible to use a fax to go back and forth in this method of "meeting," but given the variable quality of fax print-outs, this may or may not be a good idea.) This method can be supplemented by phone conversations, though depending on the distance, this can grow costly.

To find others who are interested in such an exchange, look to friends, family, or the classified portion of writers' magazines. Whichever of these methods you choose to employ, take care to protect your work. Any time you exchange ideas or material with an acquaintance you are taking a risk. Whether you know the individual or not, there are those who have no qualms against claiming work or ideas that are not their own. It is horrible, but true.

The Creative Approach:
Alternatives to Structured Writing Groups

As I touched upon earlier, for some of you, where you live, the type of equipment you have, or other physical or time constraints may prevent you from taking advantage of the more standard Writer's Group options, which are, as discussed, in-person and via the internet website or news group. One alternative I've already mentioned is critiquing by correspondence. Now I will review a few more supplementary options.

Writers' Seminars or Workshops

Run a search on the internet, or pick up a writers' magazine, and you will find pages and pages of sites or ads for Writers' Seminars and Workshops, ranging from anywhere to a weekend or several weeks in length. Some are extremely discriminating, others are open to all. Almost all of them have a hefty participation fee.

Programs such as Clarion, which holds workshops around the nation and even in Europe, and Odyssey, the annual Fantasy Writing Workshop run by Jeanne Calevos — former senior editor with Bantam Doubleday Dell — in Manchester, New Hampshire, are by acceptance only. Think of them as literary boot camp. Or crash-course inductions into the professional literary world. These are intensive programs organized and run by industry professionals to prepare those whose work is almost, but not quite publishing quality. There are only a limited number of openings and they are allotted for those whose sights are set on a literary career. Your work is evaluated and you are then allowed into the program, or refused. These workshops can be brutal and costly in both time and money, but they also provide an intense writing evaluation and seminar geared toward honing your talent. They will take your work and tear it down to the ground, and then show you how to put it back together stronger than it was before. Courses are taught by established authors and experienced editors, those who already have an intimate knowledge of the field you are attempting to break into. Courses such as these will not coddle you, but if you let them, they will improve your abilities and understanding of what it is to be a published author.

For those who view their writing as a more casual passion, there are numerous other workshops where the process of admittance is less stringent, where those with the fee and a desire to improve their writing are welcome. The structure of such workshops is more discussion panels and mini-seminars that for the most part do not need to be signed up for—though there are exceptions to this. Such workshops are generally a weekend, or perhaps a week in length, and attendees set their own schedule based on the topics on offer and which they think they will most benefit from. Again, presenters and lecturers are professionals in the field, established authors, editors, publicists and such.

Another draw of these writers' workshops is the networking opportunities. The organizers not only set up programming to help writers polish their work, but they also arrange formal pitch sessions and meet-and-greet receptions.

Literary Conventions

I'm going to include something under this venue that might have some of you looking at me cockeyed, but among the ranks of Writer's Groups I include the literary convention. On mostly any given weekend of the year there is a literary convention taking place somewhere in the world and, in the world of fandom there are convention gypsies. Though not every panel discussion at such conventions is about the craft of writing, enough of them are that they would be a benefit to someone wanting to polish their abilities. There is a lot to be gained from listening to your favorite authors explain how they approach their craft.

In addition to such panels, some conventions have actual writers workshops, which can take two different tacks: A panel of established authors and editors evaluating pre-submitted works, pointing out the strengths and weaknesses and offering constructive criticism on how to improve the story; or, an informal panel where the moderator has prepared a series of mini-exercises to show ways to advance your writing. While the duration of such workshops is generally only two to three hours, the benefits can be innumerable. Most weekly and monthly writers groups do not offer the feedback of professionals in the field, especially editors, the very people you most notably need to reach and please.

Who Am I to Talk? Let Me Tell You...

You may ask what qualified me to write on this topic, to educate you on this phenomenon. Well, at the time I am writing this, I am a part of no less than five on-line Writer's Groups, all of them some variation of what I've outlined above. Most notably, though is the fact that I founded and have been running for the past eight years Yesterday's Dreamers, a Writer's Group on Yahoo! Groups, While there is absolutely no way I've seen it all, I've seen a lot!

For those of you who have tried what I have mentioned above and met with little success, or those whose situations make it difficult to take advantage of my advice, I would make one more suggestion: start your own Writer's Group. Decide what you are looking for and find others of a like interest. This isn't easy, but it can be done. For myself, I was already a published author before I even knew what a newsgroup was. I discovered them as a useful tool during a literary convention when I was promoting my work. That made getting started easy for me; all I had to do was set out a sign-up sheet. People interested in me and what I had to say put down their email address and they received an invitation to the newsgroup. Using this method I have gathered people around me not only interested in writing, but also interested in fantasy and science fiction, which is what I primarily write. On top of that, I also had the benefit of starting the initial relationship with about ninety percent of my members in person. Because we met through conventions, we even occasionally reunite in real time.

Not everyone is going to have such an opportunity for start-up. What you can do is begin with people you already know that share your interest and desire to improve, then move from there to place one of those ads I've been mentioning in either the local paper or writers' magazines.

When starting your own group—on-line or in person—keep in mind that structure, organization, and discipline will be the key to smooth operation. Not only does my group's home page clearly state my intentions for the group, but each time we have a new member join I formally greet them and outline how the group works. We are currently up to sixty-eight members, many of whom are only lurkers (silent and don't generally contribute, but as they haven't quit, they must get something out of the group). There is a core of about twenty to twenty-five members who regularly contribute to discussions and a handful more who occasionally comment on a topic. Because the majority signed up at literary conventions we have a nice mix of experience levels and everyone benefits.

Decide what you want for yourself and what kind of group you would like to have. For an in-person group, approach a local library, bookstore, school, or diner, any quiet place where there is space, chairs, and someone in charge willing to work out the details with you, and gather your group.

If you are going for an on-line group, there are plenty of list-serves, newsgroup servers, and message boards to choose from. All require some form of registration, and naturally some are better organized than others. Look for one that does not clutter your posts with ads, and that has a dependable reputation.

Once you pick your method of meeting, decide on a schedule (if applicable) and what your objectives are. For me, I intended that my newsgroup would be mainly a support structure; a place where writers could share opportunities and successes, and ask specific questions regarding the mechanics of writing generally related to snags they have hit in their own work. This has served us well and has kept most people interested, without bogging everyone down with stories to read.

Because some people needed a fresh perspective on their work, and feedback based on experience, we also run a critique group by email, separate, but still linked to the newsgroup. The precept for that is simple: everyone submits a story, the names are stripped off, the anonymous selections are sent to everyone participating that round, and everyone is free to comment without being self-conscious about commenting on a friend's story or worrying about everyone else knowing which one is theirs. The only guidelines they are given is to be positive and constructive in their comments, pointing out both the strengths and weaknesses in a piece. The group takes a month and half to read through all of the submissions before sending in their feedback, and then the cycle starts again.

In this way my Writer's Group has the flexibility that those who want or need feedback receive it, and those who just require a sounding board can sit back and enjoy the discussions.

Everything in Moderation

Whether you are joining someone else's group, or starting your own, policing the members is very important. Knowing when to speak up and when to sit back and let a situation fade on its own isn't easy, but it is going to come up. Any time you bring two or more people together there is potential for disagreement, especially in a group as opinionated as writers. Add ego to that and eventually worlds will collide. If you are moderating or just caught in the crossfire, tact is your most powerful weapon. Redirect the conversation, or intercede in a way that reminds the combatants that everything is a matter of opinion and the important thing is not to confuse different with wrong. If diplomacy doesn't work, take the offenders off to the side (physically or metaphorically) and explain that if they cannot come to an agreement they need to restrict themselves to commenting peaceably on topics unrelated to the disagreement and take the argument outside the group. Anyone who continues to be a disruptive force ultimately must be asked to leave. It is harsh, but necessary at times.

Remember, regardless of the type of group you are in Writer's Groups are about connecting, support, sharing, and improving your ability. Politics are best left by the wayside.

Anthologies
The New Magazines

Well, not really, but in the scheme of a writer's career, they serve the same purpose. See, it takes a long time to write a novel. Takes even longer to get it published, unless you are very lucky — or not very picky. That can be a problem when it comes to keeping your name in the public eye. Supplementing your efforts with short fiction is the way around that, assuming you are comfortable writing short, not everyone is. It is a skill worth cultivating if you are serious about being a published author.

In the heyday of magazines, a writer could build and sustain a respectable career, not to mention a steady pay check by submitting to that market. Unfortunately, the market is shrinking. There just isn't enough audience for all of the subscription publications out there, particularly when there is so much of their content available via the web. Anthologies have become more prevalent, filling both the readership's desire for a ready source of portable short fiction, and the writer's need for a market of such.

A Brief Primer

As with magazines, anthologies come in many varieties. Some are themed, others cater to a particular audience, and yet others feature the best of… well, whatever. Let's look at what all of that means:

Unthemed. Writers submit on any topic and there is no unifying factor from story to story, other than that they are in the same collection. This means freedom for the writer, as they are not restricted in what they submit, but not as appealing to the reader because there is the real possibility they will not be interested in all the stories. With unthemed, the audience is more likely to be influenced by the names in the book.

Themed. Well, this is pretty self-explanatory. This is a collection of stories that have an overall theme connecting them. The theme can be broad, or very, very specific, but it serves to unify the content so that it is targeting a particular market with which that theme is popular. Basically, it means the reader is more likely to pick it up because they know what to expect, in general, from each story. Examples of themes are Love-At-First-Sight, Vampires, Pirates and Magic. Yeah, pretty much anything. The benefit of this type of anthology is that readers may be drawn by the topic, even if they are unfamiliar with the authors.

Shared Universe. I know… *what*? This is a kind of very specific themed anthology where the author must write in someone else's established universe. Mostly you see these as media tie-ins (universes based on television or movie franchises), but occasionally you will see them based on gaming systems or popular novels by other authors. These collections are most likely — but not always — invitation-only and require the author to either already be conversant with the universe, or adherence to a series bible that familiarizes the writer with the relevant details before they start writing. Basically, you are playing in someone else's playground. It can be good for getting your name out there, but can also limit you when it comes to writing your own original work, which may not be as well received if the readership has come to expect other material from you.

Best Of. Mostly this is here just so I know I'm doing a thorough job. We all hope to be included in one of these someday. Someone else generally decides. Whoever is putting the collection together decides on their source and the parameters of the collection and then they comb through all the works published that fit those guidelines. It might be the best of the year, the best of a particular magazine or genre, or the best of a particular author. Consequently, this is a reprint type of anthology. In some cases the editors find the material on their own; in others you or your publisher might have the opportunity to send in a collection that contains your work for consideration. Mostly, you have no control over this one, but yes… we can all dream!

Now all of this only covers content. With anthologies there is another way of classifying them that we should look at. That deals with the terms of submitting.

Open Submissions. This is where a call is made public and anyone can submit as long as they follow the parameters set out by those putting the collection together. There is a lot of competition from hopefuls like yourself.

Semi-Open Submissions. The editors make a limited public announcement being very specific where it appears. Less competition, but also potentially less opportunity.

Invitation Only. Well yeah, it's just what it says. The editors hand-select specific writers they would like to include in the collection — or have writers recommended to them. With this type it is about who you know… or who knows (of) you. Acceptance is not guaranteed, but is more likely, depending on the editor and if they have ordered exactly enough writers for the number of stories they want to include, or if they invited more than needed and must select from among them.

Reprint. This is generally a variation on both Invitation Only and Themed combined. Basically an editor or publisher decides they want to publish a particular collection (say, on Lovecraftian Horror or Dog stories… just saying). They will go through a bunch of published fiction that fits their chosen parameters and then attempt to secure the reprint rights from the author or the previous publisher, depending on who holds the rights (assuming the story isn't in the public domain, which is quite possible).

Competition. These may or may not have an entry fee. I tend to stay away from those that do, just because there are enough out there without them that I figure, why pay? Competition collections are usually incidental to a particular writing contest. Meaning, you enter the contest to win the prize — usually monetary — and the anthology is just a small part of that prize. Competitions are generally governed by theme or genre and often have restrictions as to who can submit based on experience level. In other words, if you have too many pro credits, you might be excluded, so check all of the contest guidelines carefully. However, if you haven't made a break into the industry, this might be a good way to do it as many of the contests are high-profile and can serve to quickly propel you out of obscurity... at least initially. (After that it is up to you to make sure you stay visible.)

How to Find Them

This is the easy part, believe it or not. These days it seems everyone is putting together anthologies, particularly in the small press markets, but even with the major houses.

Why? Well, to capitalize on the market. If you are trying to draw an audience it is much more productive to tap the fan base of multiple writers than just one or two.

It used to be anthologies were either school books, best of, or reprint collections, and there were relatively few of them. These days they abound. Just go to the internet and you will find hundreds of prospects... and those are just the ones open to everyone. There are various websites that specialize in listing anthology and other publishing opportunities. Most notable is www.ralan.com, but there are others out there.

Whatever you do, be cautious and research publishers you are considering submitting to. Be sure you know their reputation, what they offer, and what rights they are requiring. I also recommend looking for other books they have done to see the quality of both the writing and the production.

Another option — presuming you have contacts in the editing/publishing world — ask. I know... seems obvious, but did you think of it? Not everyone would. Asking around though, can't hurt, and it might just get you an opportunity to submit to collections that aren't necessarily open to the general public.

Summing Up

I could go on and on about anthologies. After all, I've barely touched on them here, but the truth is, I could — and likely will — write a book on the topic. For now, though, this is just to introduce you to the possibilities.

In the time of the vanishing, or at best, uncertain magazine market, anthologies are a gold-mine of opportunity. They get your name out into the public eye, and — with hope — keep it there while you are working on longer works of fiction. They serve as both career-building and promotional tools, as well as another source of periodic income — again, with hope. If short fiction is a part of your skill-set, by all means, this is a venue you should consider pursuing.

On the Size of Fishes and Ponds
Your Place in the Publishing World

I have to tell you—though I probably don't *need* to—that you have not picked an easy passion. Or a solitary one, for that matter. You are in plentiful company in your desire to be published. (Let's face it, if you only wanted to write you wouldn't be reading this book.) The important part of this conversation is that the proportions of hopeful writers to publishing opportunities are not very favorable. Given that, I think we should talk options.

Yes. You have options. You might not like all of them, but then, that's another conversation entirely.

Option 1: Write just to write. (I know… most of you are saying, *what's the point?*) Getting published takes a combination of things: skill, patience, perseverance, connections, and pure, dumb luck are the primary ones. Your potential for getting published decreases exponentially the more of those you have missing from your toolbox. If you are not prepared to be dedicated to the proposition, don't set your goal on seeing your name in print. Getting your clichéd foot in the door (and keeping it there) takes a lot of time, effort, and frustration. Be ready for that or don't even bother to knock.

Option 2: Self-publishing. (Here's where I say, *what's the point? No… really, it is.*) You have to ask yourself what the true focus of your goal is. If you want to be published just so you can have a book with your name on it to put on your shelf or give out at Christmas, okay, this may be a viable option for you. If you want to have a career in publishing, consider carefully if this is the best way for you to go. It could work great for you, or it could be literary suicide.

Want to know why I say this? Might as well, since we are here. Most publishing professionals will not give serious consideration to a work that has been self-published. Yes, there are exceptions, but those are precisely that. The majority of fiction that is produced by self-publishing is not of professional quality: either the writing or the book production. The reason for this? Most writers do not have the skills or knowledge to put together a professional quality book. When you go to a vanity press one of the ways they make money is to get the author to do the majority of the work. They make it seem like they are giving you creative control, but in truth they are working every angle they can to get you to do the job you are paying them to do. Unless you work in publishing or a similar field you just don't have the skill set to know what makes good cover art, or back cover copy; you probably wouldn't recognize poor design or indifferent editing. These are all characteristics endemic of self-published books.

Now that is just looking at the technical aspects of publishing your book. There is a more fundamental reason why self-publishing could hurt you. It is the matter of paying your dues. No. Not talking about a pro organization here or anything like that, but self-publishing can send the message that you are impatient enough not to try your luck with everyone else that has had to claw their way into the industry based on merit. Some would see it as a lack of dedication. If it was too much effort for you to go through conventional methods, it implies you either couldn't be bothered to earn your place among the ranks of published authors, or you weren't good enough to. Now whether or not either of those opinions are valid is irrelevant, we're talking implications here, not facts. Bare bones, it's going to look like you bought your way into the game.

There are some specific exceptions to this. It is unfortunate, but this stigma seems to apply predominantly to adult fiction. When it comes to picture books, comics, graphic novels, and role-playing games it is virtually expected you will self-publish until you have proven yourself a viable commodity. There are also cases of established authors self-publishing their backlist once rights have reverted to keep the titles alive.

I am not saying self-publishing isn't a viable way to go... but I am saying consider everything carefully, do your homework, be ready to put in time, effort, and/or cash to make that dream happen if you go it on your own. Not only will you need to do — or hire out — all the production work, but also manage the business and promotional side. It isn't enough to produce a book, you have to have a plan for how to distribute and market it.

Option 3: Online. Often there isn't any money in it, but publishing via online markets can be a way past the dreaded slush pile. This venue offers online magazines, eBooks, and articles or fiction for dedicated websites featuring such things. Some pay, some don't. When there is money involved it is usually just a token, so you have to decide what the publishing credit is worth for you. The standards for this venue are not lower, but the opportunities are more plentiful and less market-driven. Online is a good way to build a personal bibliography that may just get you a bit more notice in more traditional markets, depending on the site where you are published.

Option 4: Magazines. Some people write strictly short fiction. The typical market for such things has in the past been magazines. They reach — one would hope — a wide and dedicated audience generally anywhere from one to twelve times a year, depending on the magazine circulation. Magazines are good for reaching a target audience, as well as for increasing the visibility of your name. In addition to that, the high-level magazines at least are automatically sifted for award nominations for the major genre awards each year, as well as best-of collections, whereas most anthologies only come to the attention of the nominating board or best-of editors if a copy is sent to them by the publisher.

Unfortunately, most magazines lately, even those well-established and considered major publications, are an unstable market. With the internet affecting subscription and sales numbers many of the smaller and even some of the larger magazines have gone under. Because of this, competition is fierce, making it difficult to get an acceptance. Of course, that means rejection turn-around time is generally swift. You can make a name for yourself publishing strictly in magazines, but there will be a lot of effort and waiting.

It bears noting for the novelists out there, some magazines have been known to run longer works as serials. Not as prevalent these days, but something to look into.

Option 5: Small Press. By far this is the market where most authors find recognition for their work. The primary reason for this? There are a greater number of small presses than there are major publishing houses, and small press is more driven by niche markets rather than marketing (sales) trends. This is a relatively new development in the publishing industry, mostly in the past ten to fifteen years, mostly made possible by the advent of POD — or print on demand technology. Because of this development it became possible for the smaller publishers to build their catalogue without the expense of printing and storing masses of books. This gives them the luxury of putting more titles in print and leaving them there for longer, taking the long view on profitability.

The primary draw-back of small press? The 'small' applies to virtually every aspect of the business: staff, profit, promotions, budget, etc. Since the money is not there, normal production tasks like editing, design, and proofreading are often handled by one person, or freelancers. This can introduce a variable quality to the finished product, as well as an unpredictable publication schedule. (Remember what I said about patience and dedication.) In addition to that, there is virtually no budget for marketing. With a small press it is a guarantee that the author will have to take a very active part in promoting the work; of course, in my experience, it doesn't matter what size your publisher is, you should put maximum effort behind promoting your book any-way. Even assuming the publisher has a marketing campaign, who has a more vested interest in your work? The answer certainly isn't the person in charge of promotions. Still, a writer can do very well in the small press market, often having a longer publication life and more flexibility in content than would be found in more traditional publishing.

Option 6: Major Houses. What do they say? Go for the gold? Maybe. Or maybe not. As is most often the case, even if you are fortunate enough to be picked up by a major publisher, you end up with gold leaf, not bullion.

Why? They gamble, but only penny ante. They take a chance on a small portion of new authors, but the majority of their lists are comprised of proven money makers. How? Well, say you sold your book to a major house. You are an unknown quantity. Most likely your writing was decent and you had the solid luck of landing on the editor's desk with a story line that hit the current marketing trend. They put minimal budget behind your book, set you up with the bare basics on promotions, and then they sit back and see how you sell. If you do, you've dodged the bullet. If you do but not to the standard they are looking for, you get cut, your book goes out of print, and they likely won't accept another manuscript.

So, why do people aspire to this? Well, it helps to have a big, established name behind you, even if they don't do very much; there is the chance that you will be that break-out hit; and what-ever else they do or do not have, major houses have distribution. Face it, if you are going to hit it big it is more likely to happen with a major publisher; but if you are more interested in longevity and the opportunity to build your name, this might not be the place for you.

Summing Up

Basically, when it comes down to it, you have to decide what you want out of this dedicated hobby you've chosen. How much effort is it worth to you? What are you willing to gamble? No matter which publishing option you choose—with the exception of the first one—it is going to take time, effort, patience, and dedication on your part. My best advice: don't sit back and wait for anything to happen. Figure out what you want and work toward that. No one else is going to do it for you. If you don't want it bad enough... you never really wanted it at all.

Something More Than a Thick Skin

You know, many beginning writers, once they've reached the stage of having something to push — yes, I said push, because you better believe that all of us who aspire to or have accomplished that vaunted goal of "published," seek to addict the masses to our particular works; but back to my point — many of those just getting started believe the worst thing writers must defend themselves against is the brutality of rejection and the tedium of waiting. I wish I could tell you they were right.

Publishing is a business.

Businesses are fraught with pitfalls. Shall we take a look at some of those you should look out for?

In the Market for a Bridge?

No one likes to think they might be taken advantage of (I know, common sense), but if you aren't familiar with publishing it is way too easy for this to happen. Heck, there are even a plethora of ways for this to happen.

Theft of Intellectual Property. Once you develop an idea it is yours. Unfortunately, the moment anyone else becomes aware of that idea, there is the potential of it being stolen. If the idea is in your head, there isn't much you can do about it. If you have the idea down on paper you might be able to make a legal case — *might*. Assuming the idea in question — or more to the point, the other person's success with your idea — is worth the prospect of a court battle you will need to establish (or try to, anyway) that the original concept was yours. Sadly, even with documentation, this is not always possible and the best you can often hope for is to reach a settlement… and walk away from your idea. To protect yourself against this, limit where, how, and with whom you share your concept. Among family and close friends you are *most likely* safe, but online and among casual acquaintances you might want to refrain from discussion.

Plagiarism. This is pretty much the same as above, only it generally refers to when someone tries to pass off as their own, in whole or in part, the published works of another person. The first step in protecting yourself against this possibility is to file your works with the copyright office. This can easily be done on line and is not very expensive. Another method of questionable effectiveness is what is called a poor man's copyright. This is when you mail yourself a copy of your manuscript by federal mail and file the unopened package away. In theory, the date stamp of the cancelled postage establishes an irrefutable point of ownership. As I said, it is a theory. I am told this is not ironclad, but it helps, particularly if you also have research and development notes.

Unfortunately, there is not much else you can do to guard against this; it is more a matter of watching for it once it becomes a potential threat. With shorter works it would likely be your responsibility to pursue action against this manner of theft; with novels and such, the publisher — and their lawyer — is the one to bring action, on your behalf, against the party in question as it is their commodity as long as they hold the rights.

Vanity/Subsidy Press. I've already talked about this some. Basically, these people are out to make money. They don't care about the quality of the book so much as the quantity of the titles they can produce… and how much of your money they can extract from you and the other hopefuls (and/or impatients). At best they will charge you every step of the way for every service, even those they manage to get you to do for them. At worse they will bind you in a contract—yes, they have contracts—that will tie up your rights for as much as the next ten years!

If you go this route, do your research. Not just into the press you are considering giving your money to, but also into the production process. Learn how to put a good, professional book together so that you can tell if you are getting your money's worth. And if there is a contract, be sure to have it looked at by someone knowledgeable (preferably a lawyer, but if not, at least someone familiar with publishing contracts).

As a side note, for those who write short fiction or poetry; if someone accepts your work for inclusion in a collection and 1) does not offer payment for the work, and 2) requires you to buy your personal copy, that is also vanity press.

When the Professionals Aren't

Now, the previous section just touches on those people consciously attempting to rip you off. Sadly, that is not all we risk in this venture. You need to educate yourself, which I presume you are more than willing to do considering you not only purchased this book... but you've read it this far!

In the days before the internet this was much harder for writers to do. There were a few books, and word of mouth, but mostly everyone took their chances and learned things the hard way. No excuse for that now. On the internet you can find virtually anything about anyone, pun intended. Before you approach any prospective publisher—or editors, agents or publicists, for that matter—do your homework! Run a search on the company name, look for individuals that have done business with them, see if there are any gripes against them. How visible are they on the internet? How professional is their presence? Do they have a reputation?

One of the best sites on the web for this is Preditors and Editors (http://pred-ed.com/) a free website that maintains an extensive listing of publishers and individuals/businesses related to the industry. Mostly only the basics are included: the publisher's address, what they publish, if they are still a viable market, and if they are recommended or not. However, the older entries can be somewhat extensive as they are continually updated as information is submitted to those that maintain the site, but generally they are a paragraph long or less. If anyone reports problems such as matters of ethics, payment, or communication, all of that is listed as well. There are also a variety of similar sites run by individuals, authors, and professional organizations, so be sure to check several sources for as complete an understanding as possible.

In addition to third-party sources, be sure to visit the publisher's website. It can tell you a lot about how professional they are. Also, if possible, take a look at the books they produce: the cover art, the interior design, the quality of the writing. Ask yourself if you would be pleased to have your name on the finished product. Look for information on distribution, where applicable, and terms.

Things to Look For In a Publisher

What is their distribution? A good publisher will be carried by at least one of the major distributors, which for fiction are Ingram and Baker and Taylor. Now, it is important to know that there are two types of accounts publishers can have with either of these companies: distribution, which means third parties can order stock through the distributor; and wholesale; which means the distributor will warehouse stock of the publisher's titles and supply them to the major chains. Small press generally only have distributor accounts.

Do they publish what you write? This is common sense; you don't go to an erotica/romance publisher if you are selling a cookbook and you don't try and interest a young adult publisher in an adult military science fiction.

What are their terms? I cover this more in depth in the next section, but basically check out the websites for the professional writers organizations for an idea of what standard terms are so you can tell if the publisher you are considering offers fair terms. They should not be too restrictive and there should be no concessions to the publisher after rights revert.

Does the publisher have a visible and professional presence on the web and in the market place? My first publisher was hardly even known by their authors, let alone the public. Small isn't necessarily bad, but visible is important. At the very least you should be able to find their titles on the major third-party internet sales sites like Amazon and Barnes and Noble.

Does the publisher promote and market their titles, beyond maintaining their own website? Now I've already mentioned that the author cannot and should not depend on this even if a publisher does have a marketing department, but it is important to know that they actively stand behind their product and make some effort to promote. You can tell if they do by checking their staff listing on their website or calling up their office and asking to speak to someone in the promotions department. You can also search for ads, listings, and such on the web or in magazines.

Is the product the publisher produces professional? You might have to invest in a book or two, but it is worth it to see if the publisher takes pride in the quality of their books or is just trying to get as many titles out as possible so they can make an accumulative profit.

Are their authors happy? Hard to know without talking with them, unless the recommended web search turns up any dirt, but something to consider.

Things to Look For in a Contract

What rights are they requesting? Industry standard is print (paperback, hardcover, or both), electronic, and worldwide English language rights. Any other rights you grant the publisher (audio, media, foreign language, etc) are at your discretion and should include a provision for what you would be paid should those rights come into play. You do have the right to request certain rights be removed from the contract, or to negotiate the terms by which they might be granted.

Are the rights exclusive, nonexclusive, or a mix of the two? Industry standard for novels is three years exclusive, with rights reverting upon written request, generally within 30 to 90 days of notice. This allows the publisher to recoup their production costs and sell any remaining stock before the rights revert. (They will often offer the author the opportunity to purchase any remaining copies themselves at a discount.) For short fiction, the publisher might request either one-year exclusive, followed by a period of nonexclusive rights for the above same reasons, depending on if the venue is a collection or a magazine. For reprinted material the terms should always be nonexclusive, as the work has already been previously published.

What payment is offered? There is no industry standard here. Possible payment methods depend on the level of the publisher and the type of publication. You can expect to see any combination of the following: advance (against estimated royalties), royalties, flat-fee, per-word, contributors' copies, and author discount (anywhere from 40 to 60%, generally). If a print and electronic version of the work is produced, the royalty rate on the electronic version is usually higher than the print version due to lower production costs.

What is the payment schedule? Industry standard is every six months to a year, with royalty statements provided quarterly, though there is as much variation here as there is in the actual form the payment takes. Some publishers even report and pay royalties monthly, though this is rare. With short fiction, depending on the type of publication, payment is either made in advance, upon publication, or as a royalty per above if the work is appearing in an anthology.

What terms have been laid out for rights reversion? As mentioned above, rights revert after a set number of days from receipt of the written request once the time obligation outlined in the contract has been met. It is up to the publisher's discretion if they will allow early rights revision before the obligation has been met.

Summing Up

Now I'm sure you know what I'll say right now... there is no way I've covered *everything* you need to know here. Not only would it fill a book all on its own, but I'm also sure that I haven't encountered every single stumbling block there is. The best I can tell you is to educate yourself in every way you can. Ask questions — of people or on the net — do research, and pay attention! There are good publishers, okay publishers, bad publishers, crooked publishers, and just plain incompetent ones, try and figure out which is which *before* you commit!

Unfortunately, there are plenty of things you are likely not going to find out until you start working with the publisher one-on-one. Things like, do they communicate in a timely manner? Do they pay royalties on schedule? Do they meet publication schedules? Do they remember details of agreements made post-contract? No publisher is going to be perfect; the best you can do is avoid the bad ones where you can and try someone else when the time comes if you can't.

Promoting For the Beginner

(Originally published as Let the World Know You're There:
Promoting For The Beginning Author in The Graveline,
the newsletter of the Garden State Horror Writers)

I've written and talked about this many times, but it bears repeating: finishing the book is not the end of an author's job. Neither is getting it under contract… or receiving your print or eBook copies. Unless, of course, that was your only goal.

Ask yourself what are you in this for? Is it just to add "author" to your list of accomplishments? Is it to have a display piece for your shelf? Maybe for some… but not generally. You want to share your stories, you want people to know your name, you want—as we all can't help but want to some degree—to hit the bestseller list and reap the lovely check that entails.

Word of advice… DON'T do it for the money. Maybe it will come, maybe it won't, but it will definitely demoralize you starting out if you expect four-figure checks. I've gotten those… there's always a decimal point in the middle.

I'm not saying it isn't possible for your writing to be lucrative and successful.

I'm saying it takes a lot of hard work… and not a little luck.

I've been a published author for nine years, I've graduated to five figure checks… if you count the two after the decimal. And excuse my frankness, but I've worked my ass off to get here. It's isn't easy.

Whether your credits are print, eBook, novels, anthology, or magazine contributions, it is your responsibility as an author to promote that work. You can't assume anyone else will. It would be nice, but the reality is usually otherwise. Who gets the most attention? The person standing on the sidelines watching and waiting quietly, or the loudmouth waving and jumping around?

Okay… maybe you don't want to be the loudmouth, either… but you can toot that horn and sing your praises — within reason — without making an annoyance out of yourself. How will people know to look for your work if they've never heard a thing about it?

My second bit of advice… promote yourself as an author, rather than just focusing on any one work. Books are transitory, they go out of print, they are overshadowed by new books in the audience's attention; magazines are fleeting as well, with another issue out relatively soon after. What you want if you are building a literary career is for the audience to know YOUR name, the rest will come after… if you do your job right.

The internet alone is a wealth of promotional opportunities, mostly free but for a little time, so I'll focus there for now.

Blogs. Just about everyone has a blog these days. They talk about what they ate, where they went, and what pissed them off that day. And people read it. Just think how productive your own efforts could be if just one day a week you posted news about your releases, your upcoming appearances, your writing process… You never know who will read that and go to check out what you've done.

Official Websites. As soon as you have credits to your name start one. Simple, but professional. There are programs you can use to create your own site, or freelancers out there who can put one together for you for a fee. Showcase yourself, post news, update as frequently as possible with author appearances or new releases, but have a presence.

Social Media. Twitter, Facebook, etcetera, etcetera, etcetera... there are tons of new and established social media venues from the general to the specific that you can utilize to reach your target audience. Once you're set up, most of them are relatively easy to maintain. The cool thing from a promotional standpoint... most of these can be linked with Twitter or your blog so that you get three times the exposure for one posting, and in theory you are reaching a different audience with each one.

Book Sites. As with the social media, there are a bunch of sites that cater to book-readers, and most if not all of them have some feature you can activate that give you extra *umph* as an author. Even if you don't frequent these sites make sure you establish some kind of presence.

Network. Whether in person or via online groups, this is vital. Make an effort to meet professionals in the industry. I belong to the New Jersey Authors Network, the Garden State Horror Writers, and Broad Universe. Each one has something different to offer me as an author. Doesn't matter which group you join as long as it is active, productive, and you can meet others like yourself who are trying to get started, those with the same interests. Share what you've learned, listen to what they have figured out, and keep your ear open to publishing and promoting opportunities. Conventions are a great opportunity for this, as are local book festivals. Not a whole lot of sales given the mixed nature of the audience and the abundance of authors, but relationships are established that pave the way for future events. Most important, though... these offer the opportunity to connect directly with the fans. By making a direct connection with them you become more than a name on a cover or page.

As authors we may start out solitary, in a dark room with a computer and a cup of coffee, but to succeed we must venture out. Immerse ourselves in the world and remind them over and over that we are here.

General Publishing Terms

(By no means a comprehensive list, but it is a good selection of common terms.
It was compiled for an Anthology seminar I presented at a monthly meeting
of The Garden State Horror Writers)

Advance – fee paid to authors upon acceptance of their work drawn against future royalties.

Anthologist – one who creates anthologies from concept to finished manuscript; also called a Packager.

Copyeditor – the person responsible for correcting technical aspects of a manuscript, such as grammar, spelling, and typos.

Copyright – the legal protection declaring your intellectual property yours.

Cover Art – artwork designed, commissioned, or licensed for use on the front cover.

Cover Template – a guide used when typesetting the cover to ensure all relevant data is properly positioned so that no important information is trimmed off during binding.

Critique – offering feedback on a story, making recommendations to strengthen, correct, or improve the writing, noting technical errors and querying points that are unclear. It is up to the author if they utilize the recommendations.

Deadline – the date by which a work must be delivered or a stage in the process completed.

Design – selecting the artistic style, fonts, and layout for the finished book.

Editor – the person responsible for accepting or rejecting submissions and determining the print order of the book; also called a series or project editor.

Edits – corrections or queries the editors require to be addressed in a story before publication.

F&Gs – Stands for folded and gathered signatures (book blocks). The printed text pages of the book sent as a sample of the finished product. Basically a proof copy of the book block, only there is no opportunity to make corrections. However, it does allow you to catch production problems before the printer binds the books.

Flat Fee – payment made to authors in lieu of royalties, generally per word or a set dollar amount.

Galleys – electronic or print copies of the finished manuscript used for the authors and editors to look for any last errors in writing or typesetting so they can be corrected before the book goes to print.

Illustration – black and white line art, halftones, or color images included in the book based on or complementary to the story.

Line Editor – the person responsible for improving the style, plot, and continuity of a story line.

Outline – A bullet list of the major points in the storyline that an author uses to plot out a book. Sometimes a publisher will request to see this before asking for the full manuscript, depending on the publisher.

POD – Print on demand. A digital technology that allows publishers to produce books in low quantity. Often confused with being synonymous with vanity press since they were among the first to make use of the innovation.

Proof – a printed version of the book provided by the printer as a last opportunity to ensure the book is printed properly and there are no major errors.

Proofreader – traditionally, someone who compares typeset pages to the original manuscript looking for errors; in more modern terms, someone who reviews a manuscript for typos but not content.

Proposal – a brief description of the basic story an author intends to submit, also called a synopsis.

Royalties – a percentage paid to the author/contributors for publication of their work. It is generally based upon the net sales price per book sold.

Submission – full-length fiction, or a story offered for potential inclusion in an anthology.

Standard Formatting – double-spaced, first-line indented, standard font (Courier or Times New Roman) with underline representing italics and a tab used for the indent.

Synopsis – A concise description of the plot of the book, something like a book report, only written by the author and submitted, when requested, to the publisher so they can determine if they are interested in seeing the full manuscript. Should not be a tease, but hit on all the major points of the book.

Theme – the unifying topic for a collection.

Typesetting – taking the completed manuscript and formatting it for print.

Work-For-Hire – any art or writing you do as a specific commission for a publisher or corporation for which they retain the copyright or are legally considered the owner of the creative content.

Summing Up

I once saw a squirrel purposely do back flips in an effort to part me from a portion of my lunch. He would flip, stop expectantly, then flip again, gradually getting a little closer. It worked (though I have to admit, he was not much pleased with what I had to offer. He frankly looked a little disgusted that he had gone through such effort.)

I often feel like that squirrel (the flipping part, not the disgust).

As writers, our words seem only to mean half as much until they are read and appreciated by others. Achieving that can require more effort than the writing itself. It really can. But you know what, if you want more than just a book on the shelf, you have to put out that effort. Now I know this can be difficult given that I know more introverted writers than extraverted, but getting out from behind your keyboard and into the public eye is a necessary step to bring attention to your work.

For about nine years now I have been driving up and down the East Coast on the convention circuit and to various author events I have arranged. I can't tell you how many more friends I have, let alone fans of my work due to these efforts. But don't mistake me. This isn't just about waving your work around until someone buys it, author events (well, the successful ones, anyway) go a long way to revitalizing your passion as a writer. At least it does for me. Whether I spend a few minutes or a few hours talking to one person or a room of people about my process and various works I walk away with an energy boost like you wouldn't believe. Some of my best writing is done after such events.

It's about reconnecting with yourself, your passion, and your audience. It is often mistakenly construed that writing is a solitary venture. In truth, the real life of your writing is found in your interactions with others. I get a little scary, I think, when I am talking to a writer just getting started about how and why I did various things in my stories. I have benefited by the reminder of why I love what I do. Sometimes we forget what it's all about... until we see our excitement reflected in the eyes of our readers.

Some authors forget this. Some get caught up in their own importance, distancing themselves from their audience, alienating others in the profession. I strive to remember that the only measure of my success is how connected I am with the reader. The only place prima donnas belong is ballet.

Ty Drago

Ty Drago is a full-time writer and the author of nine published novels, including his five-book *Undertakers* series, the first of which has been optioned for a feature film. *Torq*, a dystopian YA superhero adventure, was released by Swallow's End Publishing in 2018. And his science fiction novel *Dragons* will release through eSpec Books in 2021. Add to these one novelette, myriad short stories and articles, and appearances in two anthologies. He's also the founder, publisher, and managing editor of ALLEGORY (www.allegoryezine.com), a highly successful online magazine that, for more than twenty years, has featured speculative fiction by new and established authors worldwide.

Ty currently just completed The New Americans, a work of historical fiction and a collaborative effort with his father, who passed away in 1992. If that last sentence leaves you with questions, check out his podcast, "Legacy: The Novel Writing Experience," to get the whole story.

He lives in New Jersey with his wife Helene, plus one cat and one dog.

The Literary Handyman

More Tips
From the Handyman

Dedication

To those with the courage not only to spill your hearts onto the page, but to show it to the world.

Contents

Honing Your Craft

Getting Down to Business

A Quick Note from the Handyman

Hello, and welcome! Or, should I say, my condolences… ?

Two points before I begin — three, if you need informing that I'm not actually a handy*man*, but then, I think for most of you, the cover will have given that away.

Point one: This series is and always has been a helping hand to those just beginning their exploration of writing and publishing. It will cover topics established authors will likely consider very basic. I tell you this upfront so that you are not disappointed with this book for being exactly what it was intended to be.

Point two: This is not an instructional guide. These are tips I share with you from the far side of nearly thirty years' experience working in publishing and nearly twenty years' experience as a published author. I am not a teacher, and this is not a textbook. It is my hope that the topics I do cover here will help you polish your craft and gain insight into the world of publishing without having to go through all the intervening years that I did. Because these are articles that have been written across a period of years, there will be some repetition, but each article does cover a separate — if at times related — topic. I come from a speculative fiction background, but most of what I have written here will apply to any genre.

This venture you are about to embark on will be filled with joy and wonder, but with an equal — or disproportionate amount of frustration, as the case may be. Really, it depends on your luck. Not saying that to discourage you, just to brace you for the hard, realistic facts. Aspiring to be an author is not an easy dream, but it can be a fulfilling one.

I will share with you the advice I gave in the first *Literary Handyman* book: consider this a dedicated hobby, that way, when success hits, you are pleasantly surprised, and if that takes a while, you are not bitterly disappointed.

As with most things in life, success is not solely based on skill and hard work but also on luck and opportunity. But remember, if you give up, you have guaranteed failure.

On that cheery note… shall we begin?

Dream Big!

Danielle Ackley-McPhail

Honing Your Craft

The Author's Opening Salvo: Book Titles

You know, there are a hell of a lot of books out there.

(Yeah, I know... *Duh!*)

So, sarcasm aside, how do we keep them all straight? There is so much information associated with a book: the author's name, the publisher, the ISBN, but first and foremost is the title. In most cases, that is the first and maybe only bit of information your audience is going to know.

Guess it better be good, right?

This article was inspired by comments I received on an article from *The Literary Handyman*, "The Naming of Names," where I go in-depth on naming characters. Well, books are a writer's children just as much as any born from their loins — or imagination — and should garner a similar level of thought in naming, so let's get down to it, shall we?

Getting it Right

You know, some parents will be outraged at this next comment, but I dare say it is more critical to get the name of your book right than it is those of your children. Why? Well... a child might hate their name, but there is always the option of a nickname, or should you truly cock it up, legal name changes. Basically, your children have options. Your books, not so much... Once you release a book, it is very unlikely any significant change will ever be made in the title (unlikely, not impossible, before you protest, but I'll get to that later.) Why do I assume that the title is the first — and possibly only — aspect of your book your audience will encounter? Well, if you should be fortunate enough to have your book shelved on a physical bookstore shelf, the majority of books are spine out. If you don't make it into a brick-and-mortar store, you have to consider that many internet or database searches do not always display with images, or when book sites do return images, they are often of a size that doesn't really do justice to the cover. That makes a good title even more vital. Because of this, the name of your book must stand and represent. Here are some points you need to consider when thinking about potential titles:

- *Is it catchy?* The best corollary to a book title is a jingle from a commercial. Short, sweet, and clever ones tend to linger in a person's memory. Because of this, many (but not all) titles tend to be four or less words (counting articles), and they tend to "pop" as they say in the industry, for example: White Trash Zombie, Bad-Ass Faeries, A Series of Unfortunate Events (Lemony Snicket). All of those are attention-getters or have some sort of shock value that imprints them on people's brains.

- *Is it easy to remember?* Titles shouldn't be too complicated or long because those aspects increase the potential for a person to either forget them or remember them incorrectly. Because many of us depend on word-of-mouth to expand our audiences, it is vital to facilitate those talking about a book getting the title correct.

- *Is it relevant?* What does the title say about the book? You have to think about the title as your one-floor elevator pitch. It needs to catch your audience's attention, catch it quickly, and hold it. If the title doesn't intrigue the audience, you have lost your first, best opportunity to inspire them to consider the book further. You want them curious enough to pick it up and read the back, or in the case of the internet, click on the link to read further. To that end, the title should reflect something of the tone and subject matter of the book. It doesn't have to be overt... sometimes subtle works really well in making a book intriguing... however, there can be an extremely fine line between intriguing and confusing. (Make sure you know which side of the line you're on.)

- *Is it distinct?* As I mentioned, there are many different identifiers for a book that should make it simple for a reader to be sure they have the one they are after — preferably yours. However, you can't assume your audience will have all those details when trying to find your book. After all, we depend on human memory here, in many cases, or idle references made on internet blogs or such, where those making the post may not see a need to be thorough with including certain details.

What's In A Title?

So... I know what you're saying now. How the heck does that help me come up with titles? Fair enough. Believe me, these points are relevant once you have a few ideas on the table, so to speak. Just keep them in the back of your mind while I go into some of the approaches you can take to the task.

Theme – Determine the theme of your work and try to incorporate that into a title. For my first novel, *Yesterday's Dreams*, sacrifice and self-discovery were two overriding themes for the book. The title referred to a key location in the book, a pawnshop, but it also referred to the sacrifices the main character makes for her family as she gives up first a career as a concert violinist and then her prized violin. That is the first relevance. It also refers to the character coming into her own when she feared there was nothing left for her. So dreams let go and dreams achieved.

Another example from my work is the series *Bad-Ass Faeries*. This meets all of the above bullet points quite handily, but in relation to the theme, we started the series to bring the popular perception of faeries back to the roots of the legends where the fae were malevolent, mischievous, or warriors... not cute and fluffy. When you read the title, you know you aren't going to be reading about <insert major franchise here> faerie princesses... unless they are also warriors.

Genre – which one are you writing in? This is relevant for two reasons. One: if you are writing genre, you are generally writing to a very narrow target audience and there are often certain conventions in titles you might want to take into account. Doesn't mean you have to follow them, but you should be aware. Two: genre writing has distinct characteristics that the title should reflect so the potential reader is more likely to recognize that your work is what they are looking for. My example for this is *In An Iron Cage: The Magic of Steampunk,* an anthology I once edited. This one we have to pick apart a bit. The "In An Iron Cage" part is catchy and intriguing but doesn't really tell you what the collection is about. The subtitle "The Magic of Steampunk" clarifies this is a steampunk anthology and that the stories include magical elements, which identifies the book as both steampunk and fantasy.

Tone – Is your story or book serious or humorous? Is it full of drama or romance? It seems obvious enough, but this is very important to sort out. After all, you don't want a joke title on a serious book because the audience will expect the title to reflect what they are going to read. For example: *The Hitchhiker's Guide to the Galaxy* by Douglass Adams. With a title like that, you expect the contents of the book to be humorous. By contrast, *The Amityville Horror* by Jay Anson (yeah... I had to look it up too...) tells you right up front that the story is frightening.

Concept – is there some defining idea in the book that would be interesting to the reader that you can allude to in the title? I'm working on a science fiction story at the moment that involves theoretical travel beyond known space. In doing my research, I ran into a bit of information in a Dark Matter article about a reference ancient mapmakers use to place on their maps for unknown areas: Terra Incognita. That was a fun fact, and given the concept of my story and the fact that it had to deal with space travel, I had to name the story *Astra Incognita*. Not everyone will get the historical reference I'm alluding to, but they will—I hope—be intrigued enough to read on! And hey, for those who do get the reference, they will be thrilled and feel like they are in on a secret, and again—I hope—eager to see where I'm going with it.

Play on Words – I develop a lot of anthologies from concept to completion. I often start with just an idea or a title, or sometimes a piece of art that inspires a title. One of those collections is *Dragon's Lure*. See, I have a couple of books to my credit with dragons on the cover, but no dragons in the stories (don't ask), much to the disappointment of dragon fans. That made me realize I had a market for a dragon book if I could come up with an idea. For something different, I figured it would be good to explore the concept of why world mythology attributes certain things as lures for dragons... like virgins and the moon or nests of gems. So the book is both about dragon lore and dragon lures, thus the title. Now, like I said, I started out with the title in that case, so it's kind of a cheat as an example, but you get what I mean, right?

Now I am sure that there are other things you could consider, but rather than go on and on, it's time to cover some other relevant points.

The Business Side of Titles

Working titles. A lot of writers have what they call a working title in the beginning. It's not really what they want for a final name, but it gives them something to reference when talking about it and something to name the file on their computer. It's kind of like calling a baby or a pet "sweetie" or something cute like that until you get around to no longer bickering over what to call them. (unfortunately... my cat, Baby, got stuck with his pre-name). Of course, you might decide that you're comfortable with your working title by the time you are done... or conversely, your publisher, in the end, may consider your *final title* the working title and proceed to tell you what it's actually going to be.

Will the Real Book Title Please Stand Up

Names repeat, whether they are for children, characters, or books. It just happens, hard to avoid with the combined volume of all three in the world. Of course, with books, you have a hope of minimizing any overlap. Nothing says two books can't have the same title, but you want to be cautious and think through the ramifications. Do some research and see if there are other books out there with the same title. If it is an older title, I wouldn't be too concerned, the way I would if it was a recent release. I definitely would think twice if the other book (or books) are in the same genre or have the same topic as yours because that is just asking for confusion among the reading audience... like I said, sometimes all they have is a title to go on so if you have two books with the same title and different authors, there is only a 50-50 chance they'll pick the right one if they are after yours. The odds get exponentially worse if there is more than one already out there. I have a friend, L. Jagi Lamplighter, who ran into this problem. Her manuscript—which she had been working on for something like ten years—was titled Prospero's Daughter. Somewhere in the middle of her working on the manuscript, someone else released a book with her title. Both are fantasies. My friend eventually sold and released her book, and while the publisher wasn't too concerned about the title issue, my friend was uncomfortable with it and changed the name to *Prospero Lost*. Two more sequels have since released in this series... which brings me to my next topic.

Series Titles

Like subtitles, series titles help tell a bit more about books that are linked, if nothing else, identifying that they go together. In the case of Ms. Lamplighter's books, her original title, *Prospero's Daughter*, became her series title, thus allowing her to retain the title she liked and providing more information on the series, which are all from Miranda's perspective (the books are based on the characters from Shakespeare's *Tempest*).

I have several series that I am associated with in one capacity or another, and the fact that there is a series title lets the reader know there are more books out there. For instance, *Yesterday's Dreams* is book one in the *Eternal Cycle* series (followed by *Tomorrow's Memories* and *Today's Promise*). I have another novel, *The Halfling's Court: A Bad-Ass Faerie Tale*. In this instance, the subtitle is also the series title, as subsequent books in the series will have the same subtitle. In addition to identifying them as a part of a series, it also links the books to their origins, the *Bad-Ass Faeries* anthologies.

Basically, creating a series is creating a brand. All the above applies, only it has relevance for all the books under that series title, so some forethought needs to go into the process. Of course, sometimes you don't realize you are writing a series until after the fact, sometimes after the first book is already published. That's when you roll with it and hope the publisher is willing to submit a corrected cover after the fact; otherwise, your only recourse (short of getting a new publisher) is to link the books as a series on the internet so that a search of the first book turns up information on the subsequent books.

Summing Up

I could say more, but I am afraid it would be difficult to cover everything in a reasonable space and time (besides... my lunch hour is over), so I'll end it here and leave something to talk about another time...

This article was a little hard for me to write. Coming up with titles is fairly easy for me. I discovered that *explaining* how to come up with titles is not. There are so many aspects that go into naming a book or story, and it is such a personal process. I hope this advice gave you something to think about and at least a direction to forge in to allow you to sort this out for yourself. There is no one right way, after all.

Keeping It Short – When the Words Count

In writing, as in everything else, most of us have a natural range. Some people are right-handed, some people left, and just to screw up the curve, some can use either hand interchangeably. You have sopranos... tenors... basses, and the rare vocalist who can manage to bounce all along the range. In writing, it is a touch simpler.

Some people excel at novels, others at short fiction. (We don't talk about those who can do either one with ease... they tend to get a lot of dirty looks from other writers.) Now, just because you have an innate length doesn't mean you can't hone your ability to write longer or shorter. It's all about scope and scale. If you can get a handle on those, you can run up and down the word-count range with the best of them, no matter your natural impulses.

Think of a short story as what you see through a telephoto lens. You zoom in right on a narrow image and capture it. You go for the crisp, tight detail, and it's all about that. Short stories capture an instant, a single thread. There are generally only a few characters dealing with one event or goal. The action/tension comes fast, and every word leads toward the resolution, with little to no wandering. It is more about what is happening than who it is happening to. Don't get me wrong... this doesn't mean you get a free pass on characterization. What it does mean is that in short fiction, character details tend to be the type that move the plot forward, whereas, in longer works, the author has more room to explore the character's depths for their own sake and not for what they offer toward resolving the plot.

Now, nothing is universal. There are always exceptions, but for the purpose of discussion, I have outlined some of the usual differences between short fiction and novels. Just know... if there is a "rule" somewhere, writers will break it...

Short Story	Novel
• Detail relevant to the plot	• Detail relevant to the plot
	• Detail that builds the characters and universe
• Brief build-up with limited action/tension leading to the resolution	• Detailed build-up with multiple actions/tension leading to the resolution
• Single thread of action	• Multiple action threads
• Single character Point of View	• One or more character Points of View
	• Secondary, tertiary, and background characters
• Scale is equivalent to a scene or an episode	• Scale is equivalent to a movie or series season.

Establishing Character in Short Fiction

Short stories have a limit. Go past that limit, and they are no longer short stories. This is a fundamental fact many writers have trouble grasping (says the editor who has received 15,000-word "short" stories). So, how do you keep the words reined in and still have a distinct, recognizable character? You cherry-pick details. Find one or two elements that make your character unique and introduce them early, then find ways to reinforce those elements throughout the story without going into great detail. For example, I have a character named Scotch. He's a wiseass. Most of the time, this does not come into play, but once in a while, a natural progression in the dialogue will leave an opening for a smart-ass comment. Scotch never misses an opportunity to jump in. It is always brief and always about what is already happening, but it is enough to set this character off from Kat, his sarcastic, "straight-man" companion. Now for Kat, I use two things to distinguish her... at random times, the events happening inspire thoughts of her PawPaw that somehow tie into what is happening, and when she is tense, her gun is like her security blanket. Those aren't a lot to go on when defining who a person is, but they are distinct enough details that you feel you know them and care what happens to them when I keep dealing them blow after blow on the way to the climactic ending.

Keep Your Eye on the Goal

As a short story writer, you have one goal: Keep it short. That means your characters have one goal. Stick to that one goal, and you can write a short story. Start pulling in multiple threads and get ready to find beta readers for another novel. In a short story, everything that happens should have the express purpose of taking you one step closer to the story's resolution. Anything that doesn't do that has to go. Okay... most of everything that doesn't do that has to go. (Like I said... writers... rules... things are going to break.)

Doing a 180

Not going to spend too much time on this, but I wanted to at least touch on it, because, you know, some people have the opposite problem. How do you move past short to novel-length? It helps if you think of a novel as a series of short stories all headed in the same direction, only not in an orderly fashion. They jumble together, touch, and even trample across each other's paths until threads get tangled, but in the end... if you do your job right... it all makes satisfying sense. The difference in a novel is that some of these "stories" are the getting-to-know-you kind, while others are the action-packed rush. The key is that each one builds on the next, with all the little sub-threads coming together for an overall goal.

Summing Up

So… have short stories frustrated you in the past? Feel there is always more story to tell until suddenly you have a book? If you want to keep it short, keep it tight. Ease your way in. Maybe try writing one encapsulated scene. Pick a character. Pick one goal. Pick one conflict. Pick one opponent. Find a twist. Find a solution. Do that over and over. Make it complete. Don't worry about if it is a full story. Just get used to dealing with one goal. Make it interesting, make it intense, either with action or emotion. When you are done, take a look and see what things look like under a microscope. It doesn't matter if there is more story to tell as long as you resolved your scene's primary objective. After all, nothing says you can't just write another story!

Serial Tendencies –
Why Some Writers Are More Than A Little Mad

(Originally published in The Writer's Toolbox, Allegory Magazine.)

Well, as you might have noticed... the world did, in fact, not end.

Hard to believe, I know, but there it is. That makes this now "The Rest of Your Life, Part II." Rather appropriate as I'm in the mood to talk about the insanity of series writing.

Even if you haven't finished writing your first book, don't start thinking this article will be of no use to you. Not only might you be taken with the feverish desire to write a series someday, but in the here-and-now, a lot of what I'm going to recommend may come in handy with a stand-alone novel as well, or for those of you who write serial short fiction.

So... you. Sit back down and start reading!

A Matter of Focus

This is the difference, really. Writing is writing, but the scale determines the type of focus a writer needs to have. To give you an idea of what I'm talking about, I will give you a brief outlook on each of the different types of fiction writing first, as they relate to focus. (Keep in mind, nothing is absolute. These are just what are most common. The focus terms are mine just for the purpose of this article, not something established.)

MicroFiction: Pinpoint focus – These stories are called many other things, but this is the name I use. It is a story that is

184 More Tips From the Handyman

somewhere between 1 and 99 words, an insane number. A brief interaction where economy of words forces the reader to infer the greater story represented. Think sound bite.

Flash: Tight focus – A story between 100 and 1500 words. One scene generally, with little attention paid to the background or characters beyond the literary equivalent of an establishing shot. The story deals with one point in time and one goal. Think commercial.

Short: Individual focus – A story between 1500 and 10,000 words. To simplify, think of these as A-Day-In-The-Life type stories. That doesn't mean it literally is only one day, but the plot generally deals with one character or group in a specific situation. One storyline. Think television episode.

Novel: Communal focus – A story between 10,000 and beyond, including Novelettes and Novellas. More intricate than all the others mentioned, this deals with the broader environment for a character, group of characters, or community. There is generally a primary plot and several related subplots woven together to reach a central goal. The setting and community are more developed, as is the back story, but generally in the context of the plot, with collateral details there but less developed. Think miniseries.

Series/Shared Universe: World focus – A collection of linked short stories or novels against a common backdrop, written by the same author, or by various authors following the same world bible. Sometimes with an ongoing overall storyline, sometimes not. Not only are there multiple plotlines, a whole cast of characters, and the greater backdrop of community, world, and even universe, but there is a depth of detail that turns the backdrop into a major character in its own right. The writer needs to know how things interact or could interact if a given situation were to occur, even if it never does. This is an intricate tapestry of characters, settings, and events. Think long-running series.

The Insanity of Series Writing

It's hard enough to write a novel, right? Making sure your primary characters are well-developed, that the setting is established and makes sense, and that subplots and the primary plot are resolved by the last page. Depending on how complex your novel is, that can be a lot of detail to keep straight. Imagine doing that for a series, where continuity needs to be maintained from book to book, and the primary plotline is not generally resolved until the very end... whenever that might be.

Pulling a series off well takes coordination. Now, I'm not just talking things like outlines and synopses, particularly as not everyone works well with those. But there are several other tricks you can use to keep things in order.

Character Sheets - You can get elaborate and create an actual sheet, like gamers use, or you can just keep note cards (physical or virtual) on each character. There are also writing programs — like Scrivener — that have a built-in system for tracking your characters. Whatever method you choose, here is some of the basic information you should track and update as needed: hair, eyes, build, scars, distinguishing features/behaviors, relationships, habits, skills, experience. Not only does this information help you to depict the character accurately as you write the series, but it also helps you to understand who they are. You want to include deeper background on primary characters even if the information doesn't appear in the book(s) because this is the type of information that affects your characters' decisions when confronted with a situation. Additionally, it can help you track how they have become who they are through the progression of the series. This can be important if you find that they are coming off the wrong way or too one-note.

Timeline - These can get real complicated, depending on your story and how many characters you have. They not only help to keep track of when things happen, but who they happen to and how that affects other events elsewhere in the story. By maintaining timelines, you can weave things more tightly together. If you have a very complex series, you will want to consider several different timelines. One for each primary or even secondary character, and a combined timeline of everything that happens. Not only does this help you keep things straight, but it also is a tool you can use if you need to backtrack and add an unplanned scene. The timeline will give you a better understanding of where that information needs to go depending on what has to happen before and after and which characters you need to involve in the scene.

Story Board - Even if you don't outline, chances are you have some idea of the major points you have to hit to get where you are going. Using sketches or note cards, you can create a visual timeline that is easy to rearrange as needed. It gives you flexibility and also helps you to see where you need to fill in gaps. You can also track individual story arcs by color coding or marking in some other distinct way so that you can keep things straight no matter how complex.

Focus - This differs from the focus mentioned above. This focus is about keeping your eye on the goal, to digress into cliché. When writing a series—primarily the -logy (duology, trilogy, etc.)—you have to always keep in mind where you want/need to end up. This is often complicated because it can be a long time between the first and subsequent novels. It's sometimes easy to forget where you are going when the journey can take years to complete. Beyond that, each individual book must have a focus of its own, a subplot that will make it a satisfying read in and of itself beyond the overall story arc. This is important because (1) you want to end up where you're supposed to, and (2) you don't want the series to have too many unrelated tangents to confuse matters. See, when you start to develop something that ends up going nowhere, it can really piss off the fans.

Why We Do It

Why would we, as writers, invite such a headache? Why would we live years with so many personalities crammed into our brains waiting to come out? There are several reasons for this.

First, sometimes a story is just too big to tell in one book. That happened with my Eternal Cycle trilogy — *Yesterday's Dreams, Tomorrow's Memories*, and *Today's Promise*. The story started out as a young girl sacrificing her heirloom — an enchanted violin — to save her family's home. She discovers she is something more than human, can do magic, and that both the good and evil figures of mythology are real beings who want to either protect or use her. In my research, I discovered a myth of Carman and her three sons. They terrorized ancient Ireland until they were destroyed by the Sidhe (Celtic Elves). As the Sidhe were my good magical creatures, Carman and her sons were the perfect counterpoints. Unfortunately, trying to deal with all those characters at once would have been too complex for my first novel, so I dealt with one son at a time and built on the storyline as I went along. This allowed me to work with manageable subplots while building to the primary plot. It also let me explore the various locations, cultures, and characters involved. I am that writer who has taken ten years to complete a series. It is a very difficult undertaking when spread out over that amount of time. Not only is it easy to forget what threads are still dangling, but my writing style and ability changed significantly over those ten years. That makes it a challenge to maintain the series "voice."

Another reason for writing a series is "branding." Whether at the publisher's motivation or as a personal choice, writers develop series or universes to play in because they develop a following. The more opportunity you offer the reader to immerse themselves in a world they are familiar with, the more they seem to want of that world. The characters become cherished friends or mesmerizing foes. The setting becomes comfortable, and true fans thirst for a deeper understanding or greater detail. If the writer has done their job, the world becomes real, and people want more—readers because they have invested interest, the publishers because they want to capitalize on that interest.

The Difference between Series and Shared World

Both of these have existed for some time and have similar characteristics and methods of development. But let's look at some of the fundamental differences.

Series are often a natural development. A writer will either start out with a series in mind, or the story will grow beyond one book. (In some instances, the publisher decides one book should be broken into several, or that they want continuations of a solo book to create a series, but that is a marketing decision brought on by the bottom line.)

Shared Worlds are crafted specifically to establish a universe that an author or several authors can play in. It has many of the characteristics of a series except that the world's development generally comes from multiple sources. Again, this is for branding purposes. If multiple authors write in the same universe, it increases everyone's visibility, develops content quicker, and makes for a rich and varied backdrop for endless story possibilities. Novels and short stories often come out of such efforts, with everyone taking part in the profit based on their level of involvement or what content they developed that was utilized. This is a way to build a body of work and recognition without the level of effort a series by a solo author would take. If a shared world becomes popular, it can build an author's career.

The Dangers of Series Writing

Yeah, there is always a drawback, right? In this case, several...

Early Termination. If an author plans on a series, they invest time and effort in multiple volumes. Unfortunately, several things might happen to prevent all the books from being published, or even written.

- The publisher might elect not to publish subsequent books if those published did not do as well as they anticipated, but they still retain the rights, preventing the author from seeking publication for the full series elsewhere.

- The publisher might cease operation as a business.

- Due to some life event, the author does not complete all of the volumes in the series.

Creative Burnout. An author by choice or at the motivation of the publisher takes on a series project and, at some point, loses focus or inspiration, resulting in a rambling collection of stories that are linked but lose cohesion. Typically, this applies to the massive bodies of work that go beyond the number of volumes you can count on one hand. (An exception to this are those authors who break their series into groupings, smaller -logies set in the overall storyline and universe, but with their own personal story arcs.)

Boredom. An author finds themselves stuck when a series becomes popular enough that that is all anyone — publisher or reader — wants from them. They are so caught up in meeting the demand that they find it difficult to explore other, unrelated ideas they might have. At best, the author just doesn't want to do what they are doing anymore and stops. At worst, they keep going until it becomes obvious they don't want to do what they are doing anymore, reflecting in their writing.

The unfortunate result of all the above: the reader is left frustrated or disappointed. There is either a lack of closure when a series prematurely terminates, or a lack of love when one goes on too long.

Summing Up

Series can be fun, productive, and lucrative. They can also be a trap. Play, explore, milk it for all it's worth, but in doing so, don't sacrifice your creativity and the variety that makes what we do exciting. If you are going to do this, do it well, be organized and thorough, or stick with solo works where continuity is only relevant for the book's duration.

Above all, we do this to fulfill our passion. Nothing kills passion like an obligation. If you have a passion for a series or a shared world, by all means, pursue it, but be prepared to put in the effort it takes to do it justice. And therein lies the madness...

Laundry Lists and Info Dumps

(Originally published in The Writer's Toolbox, Allegory Magazine)

In gaming, there is a rule…

(Hey, pay attention. I am going somewhere here.)

There is a rule in gaming: If the GM didn't hear it, it didn't happen. This works pretty well in gaming. It keeps the players honest, makes them precise, and failing that, gives the GM something to work with to add a little excitement to a campaign as things tend to go not as expected when players are sloppy with their declarations.

Unfortunately, while applicable, the same rule doesn't work as well in writing all the time. Writers need to remember that when conveying information, it needs to be fluid, dynamic, and interesting enough to hold the reader's attention. Unlike in gaming, where it is necessary to give a concise list of steps involved in an action.

There are two ways that writers do their work a disservice when adding detail to their story. (Okay, there's probably way more than two, but these are the ones I'm concerned with today.)

Laundry Lists

Don't leave out steps. We've all been told that at one point or another, right? If you leave out steps, you end up with characters that put down a coffee cup they never picked up to begin with or some other confusing stumbling block to the logic and flow of your story. Of course, in their eagerness to not miss a step, some authors fall into the trap of the Laundry List. As far as I know, this is my term, so don't look at me cross-eyed if it's not familiar to you.

Now, let me explain. A Laundry List is when a writer gives a point-by-point account of the steps a character goes through in completing an action in a paragraph or even one sentence. Think of it as a bullet list. For example:

> Katy reached for the knob, turned it, and pulled the door open.

There is nothing wrong with this sentence, *per se*, but it is dry, slow reading, particularly if the author makes a habit of using this style throughout their work. Not only that, but it can create an uncomfortable pattern in the pacing. In this particular instance, it certainly makes more sense to say simply that Katy opened the door.

Now, this was just an example of a simple action. There are times when you want to expand on a series of related actions instead of contracting them. For example:

> Devin opened the car door, slipped inside, put his key in the ignition, and started the car.

In an instance like this, you could just contract:

> Devin got into the car and started the engine.

See, all the other steps are implied in the two actions you condensed to. Simple, not very interesting, but it gets the point across so you can move on to more important things. However, what if this *is* a pivotal point in the action. That is when you want to invoke an emotional response; you want to build the tension. In instances like that, you want to go for more, not less.

> Devin hurried toward the car. His gut clenched as he attempted to slide his key into the lock. It took three tries with the way his hand shook. He stopped and took a deep breath, then forced his hand to still. This time the key slid into the lock. As he got into the car and started the engine,

his mind already raced ahead to Cooper General, where they had taken Kara.

In this example, I have added more steps, but I also peppered it with physical and emotional responses and added details that made the excerpt a point of interest, which moves the plot forward.

Info-Dumps

Now I know everyone has heard of these. Heck, everyone is guilty of these! But do you know how to recognize one? For me, an info dump is when the author steps back from the story itself to provide a load of details or information. It can be about the setting or the society or pretty much anything, but it is provided in a solid block and generally in an omniscient perspective, rather than from your POV character's perspective. Usually, it is detail relevant to the story and that the reader needs to know, but it is presented in a way that interrupts the story instead of flowing with it. That means it's taking the reader out of the story as well. They lose the thread of the action to partake in a mini (or not so mini) lecture. You don't want that. When you break the pacing like that, you are increasing your chances of losing the reader. Info dumps are boring. They are like the commercial that interrupts the action scene in a television show.

> Simon galloped across the fields aiming for the secret pass leading through the hills. His gelding screamed defiantly at their pursuers. In response, the mounted archers loosed a volley of arrows.
>
> One creased Simon's shoulder, and he crouched lower, giving Duro the signal to run faster. The horse leveled out with a clatter of hooves until the distance between them and the king's men lengthened. They crested the hill well in advance of the enemy.
>
> On the far side of the crest spread the land of Trinnon. An independent state holding only uneasy neutrality toward King Grant's realm. Deceptively peaceful, the

land had all manner of protections woven into the very landscape. What appeared now as peaceful, windswept wheat fields could very well drain an intruder of every ounce of blood simply with the lashing of those stalks against unprotected skin. Even the ground itself, gently rolling as it seemed, was known to rise up and crush a man beneath its folds, were he not there with honest intent.

Okay… a pretty long example, but what can I say… hazard of being a writer.

The first two paragraphs are active and full of tension. Something is happening, and we really want to know if he gets safely away. Then BOOM! Info Dump. See, we need to know this information, but this really isn't the way to do it. The third paragraph just kills all the lovely tension we've built up, and it takes the reader out of the action. Not good.

There are two ways you can handle this. One, introduce this information sooner in the story, then just allude to what the reader already knows. As so:

> Simon had to reach Trinnon, where the enchanted land itself would rise against the intruders following him.

This assumes the reader already knows what the land is capable of. If that hasn't been set up yet in the story, you could handle it this way as well.

> They crested the hill well in advance of the enemy.
> On the far side of the mound spread the land of Trinnon. Simon did not relax as he entered the enchanted land from which his mother had come. He watched closely for the signs she had warned him of. Signs that the land prepared to attack. With care, he guided Duro around the fields of wheat, not out of care for the farmer's bounty, but knowing that should Trinnon decide he trespassed, those sheaves would slice his skin to the bone. Though their pace continued slow, Simon's gut clenched tighter as he watched the ground for signs it would rise up and swallow them whole, all the while wishing he could gallop clear

before the soldiers drew near enough to spy them. His shoulders tightened at the thought. His mother never said what Trinnon would do against an arrow.

He tightened his grip on Duro's sides and risked a bit more speed, praying to be out of bow range before the enemy caught up.

So… it took me more time and words to convey the same information, but I did it in such a way that the reader learned what I wanted them to know while still maintaining the tension of the scene and moving the plot forward. The best way to both spot and avoid an info dump is to stay in your character's head. Once you leave that place, it's like hitting the pause button on the story. Find a way to integrate the necessary information into the action. If a paragraph is nothing but information, you know you've lost the thread. Your POV character should be the filter through which all information is fed.

Summing Up

Fiction should be a tapestry of emotion, action, details, and dialogue… all woven together to create a whole (hopefully pleasing) picture. To accomplish that, you need to integrate things seamlessly and maintain the proper tension and flow for the type of scene you are writing. This is why you need to be aware of any Laundry Lists or Info Dumps and work toward transforming them, integrating the details they convey into the story instead of letting them act as interruptions. Now, there will be times when you just want to acknowledge an action that has taken place and move on, but always remember to keep it interesting for the reader, keep them immersed in the story, and keep the details integrated. Most importantly, everything that takes place or that the reader learns about should be filtered through a character's point of view. This immerses the reader in the story in a way random exposition cannot accomplish.

Our Tawdry Love Affair
with Language

Don't deny it. Don't pretend. We are all in love with words. Sometimes we are transported. Sometimes delighted, and yes, sometimes carried away.

It's easy to lose control when you are having such fun. The elegance of a phrase can easily blind us to what is and is not good prose. Unfortunately, at times, while we are having fun with language, the reader just wants to know what the heck is going on.

(Oh, stop pouting!)

There is a time for letting go and a time for reining yourself in. Your job: figure out when is when. Let me help you out. There are several questions you can ask yourself when you are reviewing what you have written:

- *Does it say what needs to be said?* Exercising your vocabulary is all well and good, but you have to keep in mind the objective of a scene and make sure you have chosen the right words for what you want to say and don't lose track of what you want to convey, to begin with. (In other words, make sure the words mean what you think they do, and don't forget to get to the point.)

- *Is it clear?* When we get grand with our words, there is a danger. We know what we had in mind, but if the flourishes are too grand, the reader might not be able to follow. When using words that are likely to be less familiar to the reader, make sure that you help define them through contextual references. If they missed the important point, all those pretty words were wasted, as was the scene. For instance, kine is a cool word for a cow, but if you don't make that clear, the reader is left wondering what that strange animal on the hill is rather than paying attention to the dragon swooping down to eat it.

- *Does it distract the reader from what is going on?* What is it you are trying to get across? Are you trying to immerse the reader in your world, or are you trying to give them the information they need to advance the story? When you are just setting a scene or building a character, your allotment of frivolous words increases; when a scene has a more specific purpose, you want to be a bit more stingy because the more emphasis you put on something, the more important the reader thinks it is so they might not pay attention where you want them to if there are too many things going on.

- *Does it slow down the pacing?* Fancy phrasing is not compact... you need time and space to be eloquent. The pace of a scene will slow down significantly the more intricate your prose becomes. Basically, you have two choices: relaxed or tense. The more words you use to say something, the less hurried the reader feels. So... describing a battlefield after the battle, explore every nuance you want; gearing up for the battle itself, keep the pacing — and the wordage — tighter than a miser's fist. The action has the wrong kind of impact if you don't build up to it, so pacing is an important part of literary tension. You want the reader to anticipate what is coming and feel the tension the characters do, so background details that are not relevant fade away, sentences get short and to the point so that while the reader is reading faster, they feel like they are rushing head-on into the action.

- *Is it appropriate?* What type of setting are you writing about? What are the characters like? If you get all fancy with the language when you are writing a story about street kids in East L.A., the poetry of your words is going to jar against what should be gritty images and settings. Let your vocabulary out to play, but make sure it gets along with your topic. Otherwise, the tone of your story is going to contradict the content.

Reality Check

After you are done evaluating your work against the above checklist, you have one more thing you can do to make sure your piece in harmony with itself and achieving its objective. Read it. Yes, read it… out loud!

(Okay, now you're just whining…)

The best way to catch conflicts in your own work is to read it out loud because you can hear the language and because it forces you to slow down and actually think about the words. Reading silently doesn't cut it because everything sounds perfect in your brain and your memory helpfully supplies any details you missed adding to the page. If you read aloud, it will emphasize those places where information is missing or where there is some disconnect between the language and the content, particularly in the dialogue. If a character is talking and you feel silly saying the words out loud, it is much worse than if the narrative sounds a little hokey.

Not comfortable reading yourself a story out loud? There are programs that can do it for you. Some of them might even already be on your computer, tablet, or smartphone.

Summing Up

Words can be wonderful, glorious, and a lot of fun to play with. They can evoke emotion, they can transport imaginations, they can create something out of nothing, but there has to be a synergy between tone, content, pace, and characterization. Play with the language all you want but don't lose sight of your purpose. For a writer, the language should never become more important than the story. When there is time, loosen your grip on those words and let them out, but be ready to knuckle down and get to the point so that the story flows to its conclusion naturally, rather than in meandering starts and stops.

Give Me A Break!
The Need for Literary Pauses

(Originally published in the Writer's Toolbox, Allegory Magazine.)

Have you ever listened to someone tell a story and you can't tell that they've taken a breath? They go on and on, and there is no break for you to interject a comment or to even digest what they've already told you. Besides making the teller seem like a bore, this also makes it difficult for the listener to appreciate the story being told.

Breaks take place for several reasons: To allow you to breathe, to allow someone else to speak, for effect, and to allow what has been said to be absorbed. The same goes for writing.

Taking A Breath

Have you ever found yourself writing, and things just seem to go on forever? What you are writing is relevant to the plot and needs to be there, but things just seem to drag. That's when you need to take a literary breath. Review your scene, looking for natural breaks in the actions or thoughts. It can really help your pacing if you feed the reader details in smaller bits.

Let me show you what I mean with the following literary tools:

Dialogue – depending on your usage, this allows you to break up long sections of exposition, show the interaction between characters, and share information from multiple sources. Dialogue takes you out of a single point of view and introduces the potential for conflict or cooperation. It is also a way to introduce an active component to an otherwise (potentially) static scene.

Example:

Kyle didn't know what he was going to do. Yesterday everything had been perfect: he was days away from graduation, his girlfriend Shelly had received her acceptance letter from the same college he was going to, and Dad had agreed to loan them his Mustang for the big graduation bash... Today? Armageddon.

Overnight the comfortable routine that was his reality disintegrated, casting him and everyone he knew adrift. No jobs, no school, no safe little communities. The cities were in ruin, and the countryside had dangers lurking everywhere: thieves, invaders, wild creatures no one could identify. Kyle had no idea where Shelly was or his mother. His dad was downstairs with Mr. Jenkins from next door, packing all the supplies they could readily carry.

Kyle's hands shook as he shoved climbing gear and his most rugged clothes into one backpack, and first aid supplies and other necessities from the upstairs bathroom into another. He tried not to think too hard about those who were missing, but he wasn't very successful. Where could they be? He wanted to get out there and look for them, but Dad said the first thing they needed to do was to get somewhere safe, where they could defend themselves before they tried to rescue anyone else.

"Son! Move, now!" his father called from the landing. "Mathson spotted shock troops heading this way!"

Shoving supplies in any which way, Kyle hurried to the stairs, taking them two at a time until he stood beside his father. Kyle swallowed hard and tried not to look as frightened as he felt. "Where will we go?"

"We're gathering everyone we can find out at the old mine," Dad answered. "With all those tunnels, they'll have a hard time finding us, and even if they do, there are more than enough ways out so we won't be trapped. Once we get everyone hidden away, we can concentrate on finding those who are missing."

Okay... so it's not a *great* example, but hey... I wrote it on the fly! In either case, basically, it serves its purpose. We have three paragraphs of just being in Kyle's head. Yes, he's doing stuff, and yes, he's thinking thoughts that give us important information, but it's all in isolation, and any threat is distant because he is, after all, just thinking about stuff. However, when his father interjects, all of a sudden, there is an active threat, character interaction, shared information, and a plan. Finally, something is *happening*. From a story mechanics standpoint, all of this serves to advance the plot, inform the reader, and increase the tension.

Underline for Emphasis – Okay... not literally, but let me explain what I mean. When you underline something, you set it off from the text around it. That tells the reader it is important. When you are writing fiction — or heck, even non-fiction — you can do the same thing with ideas. If there is a line or concept you want to impact the reader, you can give it a little punch by setting it off as its own paragraph.

Example:

Kyle didn't know what he was going to do. Yesterday everything had been perfect: he was days away from graduation, his girlfriend Shelly had received her acceptance letter from the same college he was going to, and Dad had agreed to loan them his Mustang for the big graduation bash...

Today? Armageddon.

Overnight the comfortable routine that was his reality disintegrated, casting him and everyone he knew adrift. No jobs, no school, no safe little communities. The cities were in ruins, and the countryside had dangers lurking everywhere: thieves, invaders, wild creatures no one could identify. Kyle had no idea where Shelly was or his mother. His dad was downstairs with Mr. Jenkins from next door, packing all the supplies they could readily carry into backpacks.

It is a small change but think of it as a dramatic pause. The way the original selection was written, all the same information was there, but it blended together, thought leading into thought. By setting off just those two words, they stand out and grip the reader. You don't want to do it too often, but there are definitely places where one-liners like this will have more impact when you let them stand on their own. It also helps to break up a pace that might be plodding along.

Scene (Section) Breaks

Sometimes, it is hard to know when to end a scene. After all, when you are writing in a linear fashion, things progress in a certain way, one idea leading to another. Life isn't a line, though. It's a tapestry. (I know, I know... I use that comparison an awful lot, but you know, if something applies...). With a tapestry, images are formed by bringing one thread to the forefront and then switching to another, repeating as needed until the picture is complete. As writers, it is our job to know when to cut away to present the reader with an intricately woven whole, rather than just a string of linked scenes.

There are several natural breaks writers can make use of:

Cliffhangers – something is about to happen, but the reader is left not knowing the ultimate outcome. This ramps up the tension and the interest, planting a need to know what happens next.

Bombshells – something unexpected happens, rattling the characters and changing the reader's expectations of where things are going. Again, this ramps up the tension and piques interest.

Slow fades – you can also think of this as a transition. Each scene should have one primary objective. Once that objective is achieved, it leaves a natural pause where another related scene can be interjected. In some instances, the next objective will be stated, in which case the scene break represents the passage of time as the characters position themselves for the next step. In other instances, the characters — and the reader — might be in the dark about what happens next, so the scene break represents the revealing of other factors that will impact their eventual actions.

Example:

> "We're gathering everyone we can find out at the old mine," Dad answered. "With all those tunnels, they'll have a hard time finding us, and even if they do, there are more than enough ways out, so we won't be trapped. Once we get everyone hidden away, we can concentrate on finding those who are missing."
>
> The room spun, and Kyle found himself breathing too fast. The mines. He'd always avoided the mines; they were dangerous. Dark and unstable, where an unseen gas could kill you in a few breaths, or rocks could fall from nowhere on the unsuspecting. Kyle's best friend had disappeared there long ago. What were the chances they would find what was left of him?
>
> ***
>
> Beneath the school, there were catacombs, a massive version of the old bomb shelters from the fifties and sixties, where the threat of nuclear attack was the monster in everyone's closet. Most of the town actually had them, in their yards, beneath their businesses. Probably a lot of people had forgotten about them; heck, there were probably quite a few who didn't even know they were there.
>
> Shelly wasn't one of those people.
>
> See, for over twenty-four years, her father had been the custodian of the high school. Her mother had died giving birth to her, and Papa couldn't afford a sitter, so Shelly had grown up with the school as her playground. When the invasion happened, she had been in the choir room practicing a song she was to sing during the graduation ceremony. There had been explosions and screams, and every light in the building went out. In the chaos that ensued, Shelly had gathered everyone she could find and led them into the catacombs.

This is more of an example of the first two types of breaks, but you get the idea (don't you?). This scene break accomplishes several things: it builds the tension by ending the first scene on a traumatic memory, it allows the reader to take a "breath," and the new scene both introduces a primary character mentioned previously and gives the reader information Kyle didn't have about what happened to her. That helps to progress the plot as different variables are brought into play and, hopefully, draws the reader into the story as they come to know the characters and become interested in what happens to them.

Chapter Breaks

These are pretty much like mega scene breaks, which means all of the above applies. The real difference is in the transition. Mostly, there are two primary types of chapter breaks:

Perspective - This is where the same scene continues in the next chapter, but generally with a different focus character. The switch in point of view allows you to have a different slant on what is happening and lets you explore events from inside a different character's head. Sometimes this is just to have a fresh perspective… a change of mental scenery, as it were. Other times, there is information the reader needs to know that can only be gained by switching focus. Example:

> The room spun, and Kyle found himself breathing too fast. The mines. He'd always avoided the mines; they were dangerous. Dark and unstable, where an unseen gas could kill you in a breath, or rocks could fall from nowhere on the unsuspecting. Kyle's best friend had disappeared there long ago. What were the chances they would find what was left of him?
>
> ***
>
> Chapter 2
> Not bothering to hide his concern, James watched his son closely. He knew what he was asking would be difficult for the boy, but what other option did they have?

There was nowhere safe for them, nowhere else to hide, that he could think of. Reaching out, he clasped Kyle's shoulder, trying to reassure him. He was a good kid, but could he handle what they were about to face? When his son took a deep breath and nodded in silent acceptance, James let his pride in the boy seep into his gaze a moment, then he grabbed three of the five packs on the table and led the way to the back door.

The power was out, and the sky was overcast, so there was no light to betray them, but as he scanned the darkness for any sign of movement, he had to wonder if that mattered. After all, what did they know of these shock troops and what they were capable of?

The action continues in a mostly continuous line, but the change in perspective gives the reader a different insight into the situation and the characters involved.

Break-Away – This is when the writer breaks away to a completely unrelated scene. It is a way to further weave together the plots and subplots of longer fiction by alternating scenes only loosely related in the overall plot, touching on characters or events that will eventually converge, but not yet.Example:

The room spun, and Kyle found himself breathing too fast. The mines. He'd always avoided the mines; they were dangerous. Dark and unstable, where an unseen gas could kill you in a breath, or rocks could fall from nowhere on the unsuspecting. Kyle's best friend had disappeared there long ago. What were the chances they would find what was left of him?

***

Chapter 2

The air was thin and harsh, the colors of the landscape soothing one instant, brash and jarring the next. General Aoki curled back his jowls in distaste as he glowered at his surroundings, looking for a hint of movement that would betray the pathetic vermin infesting this place. They were proving surprisingly difficult to suppress, despite their inferior physical capabilities. One had to search vigilantly to find them.

There. There was a flicker at the extreme corner of his vision. Without turning, Aoki motioned his subaltern forward.

"Sir?" the soldier responded, his eyes lowered in deference.

"The structure behind us at your shield side," the general answered, "have a squad clear the vermin from the upper level."

The subaltern dropped to one knee, his head bowed, before straightening and moving off to carry out his orders.

The action following the chapter break is only in the broad sense related to the characters in the previous scene, so it calls for more of a hard division between the two. This type of break fills in details needed later to weave the story more tightly together.

Summing Up

So as you can see, there are nearly as many ways to pause a storyline as there are reasons to do so. The examples and instances I have shared with you here are by no means complete, but I hope they are sufficient to illustrate my point and get you thinking about natural breaks, both how to recognize them and when to implement them. Life is full of them… commercials, halftime shows, choruses. No matter the venue or the form of entertainment, our appreciation is often amplified by a pause of some sort. Learn to use those pauses to your advantage; after all… no one likes a bore, so give the reader a break and take a breath once in a while ;)

Don't Forget the Rule Book: Authors

You can fool yourself all you want, but if there is one thing in life that never changes, it's that there is *always* a rulebook, both for you and your characters. Now, I'm not saying all of you will follow it—you should, but I'm not that naïve.

Let me explain to you why fiction requires rules both in the writing and in the story. I'm not talking grammar and stuff like that. (If you haven't learned why we need that in storytelling, I doubt I am the one to drive the lesson home.) No, this article is about the necessary boundaries in your literary universe. Because let's face it, that is all that rules are. They tell us how far we can go before there are—or should be—consequences.

(Believe me… I know consequences.)

Rules for the Author

Identify Your Characters. If the reader is to care about the characters in your story, they have to know them. Their name, their history, what they look like. How much detail you go into will depend on how important the character is. You don't have to reveal everything at once, but don't delay too long, either. There will be times when you have a legitimate reason for withholding detail, but if it is a primary character and you aren't writing a mystery or suspense, the only good reason for not giving at least the name of your character right off the bat is because your character doesn't *know* who they are—or doesn't want anyone *else* to know who they are. You should make some effort to establish the basics early on because if you don't, the reader will form their own impression, and it might not synch up with what you reveal later on. Basics: Name, gender, age, hair, eyes, and skin tone.

Maintain a Timeline. The more complex your storyline, the more important this rule is. You have to keep track of the details so that things happen in the proper order. If a character needs a particular item to achieve the story's main objective, make sure you provide a scene of them finding or claiming that item, or establish that is something they already have. It is not unheard of to stagger threads in a story so that you are taking two steps forward in one scene and one step back to an earlier time with a different character for the next scene, but if you do this, you have to make it clear or else you jog the reader out of the story as they try and follow the progression.

Pre-Establish Resources. Again, to recycle an example, if certain things will be needed to ensure your character's success — even if they aren't aware of it yet — you need to make the reader aware of the item or ability or whatever it is in some manner. That the character has it in their possession, knows its existence, or learns about it in advance of actually needing it. Unless, of course, part of the goal is to find that item, then you could build suspense by having them attempt their goal, not succeed, and then learn why, thus sending them off on another adventure before the tale is done. Whatever you do, you do not want to arrive at the challenge, reveal that something is needed, and have the character either conveniently have it or suddenly find it right there…

Keep Things Straight. You have to keep the details you've already written consistent throughout the story. Don't contradict yourself, don't make your character's eyes brown, then ten pages later tell us they are as blue as the noonday sun. If you confuse the details, you confuse your readers, and then they won't enjoy the story, and maybe not even finish it if you are sloppy too often. The same goes for the order of events, emotional reactions, etc. Remember what you wrote, or you could contradict yourself later, and your story will no longer make sense, to one degree or another. Even small details can throw things off, and believe me, the readers will notice. Can't tell you the number of times I've flipped back to the beginning of the book to make sure I wasn't reading wrong... and oops, there goes the story; I'm not in it anymore, I'm hunting down particulars.

Don't Push Plausibility. Yes, it is fiction, yes something particular has to happen, but it is your job as the author to make things make sense. That means building in the steps that lead to your ultimate end so that the reader can follow where you were going with things and say "yes, that could happen," even if the story is fantastical, because you have done the footwork. Some things to avoid: Making things too easy for your characters, leading them through the story in a straight line, disregarding time and space in relation to what is happening, etc.

Establish Your Own Rules. Unless you are writing in a universe you've played in many times before, you are likely to figure out your current world as you go along, which means you have to figure out the rules. What social, environmental, or other obstacles does your character have to face? Maybe you have a world where women are forbidden to touch the ground in public, so rich women are carried everywhere on litters, and poor women have to ride on their husband's backs, or maybe gravity works in reverse, or all blue-eyed beings are insane... except for the alien who just arrived from Earth... only no one knows. Give structure to your world that will both define it and challenge your characters because all stories need conflict... something to overcome.

Summing Up

Have you read something and thought, 'Oh! Come on! Like that would happen,' or 'Please, the character is being so stupid! Give them a backbone!'? Or have you found yourself confused about who is doing what, when, in a story? Authors have a lot more to keep in mind than personality and plot points. Logic and physics and temporal continuity are not just the things of science fiction movies. When you are writing fiction, you are building worlds. Even if it looks unsurprisingly similar to the one we walk around in every day, you still have to do a good job putting that world together so that the reader can get lost in it for a while. The more effort you put into your world's foundation, the more the reader will enjoy themselves because there will be a complex backdrop complementing the story you are telling. Don't get sloppy because you think the background details aren't as important as the primary action. Think about it... it's the difference between a multi-million dollar Hollywood set and the painted backdrop from your fifth-grade play. Which would you prefer to have your characters parade in front of?

Don't Forget the Rule Book: Characters

For good or ill, everyone needs rules… if nothing else, so they have something to break.

But seriously now, we really do need them. That goes for your characters just as much as it goes for you and I. (I can hear the whine right now: but *Whhhyyy*?)

Good fiction is propelled by two things: Goals and Conflict. Both basically boil down to "something the main character needs to achieve or overcome." For your character's journey to be interesting, they need barriers to pit themselves against, proving their skill and worth, as it were.

Let's face it, if it's too easy, it's almost always dissatisfying.

Now, since this article is all about the rules, let's take a look at the various kinds you can throw at your hero to plop him in the middle of interesting times.

The Rules of Nature

In many instances, most of us choose to fall back on what we know: birds fly, things fall down, etc. Nice, simple, familiar to both the author and the reader. No one has to think much about it. But if you are writing genre fiction, you get to change those rules by putting your characters in settings that would never occur on our quaint little mudball. When that happens, you have to consider what makes *there* different from *here* and what impact that will have on your characters.

Predators. Let's face it, if you have invented a predator, it is for two reasons: 1) your character is going to encounter it, or 2) your character has to avoid it. Predators can take the form of animals or sentient beings—I know… state the obvious, why don't I—as well as mundane or supernatural.

Things to consider when creating predators:

- What threat do they pose?

- What are their habits?

- What is their territory/natural environment?

- How do they attack?

- What is their weakness?

- What is their goal?

- What defenses are there against them?

Environment. You might be asking, how is environment a rule?

(Oh, don't pretend… I know that's what you're thinking. Don't worry, I have an answer to that.)

In more complex stories, particularly genre fiction, the setting is a character in and of itself. It is the writer's job to figure out how the environment will interact with the hero to either help or hinder the journey. Where a character may go and how difficult the journey is dictated by the environment. For example:

- There may be dangerous storms in one area, treacherous terrain in another.

- The air near the mountains might be unbreathable due to gases escaping from deep within the planet (just saying…).

- The path to the ultimate goal of the story might run right across an enemy border.

- Quests might require a difficult, dangerous, or arduous journey that must be followed religiously to achieve success.

There are many written and unwritten rules related to geography that influence a character's path, each with its own level of risk. The writer must determine the risks and provide viable reasons why the characters avoid or confront those risks.

Now, I'm not saying to create pitfalls just to have pitfalls. Any obstacle the characters encounter should serve more of a purpose than just getting in their way. Generally, this takes the shape of some geological feature or location that is dangerous for various reasons and just happens to be smack dab in the middle of where the main character and their friends need to go. Your task as the writer is to make these features challenging and threatening without making them seem hopeless. There must be some potential for escape, no matter how slim.

Personality. Each person has internal rules of behavior, their own gauge for determining what is and is not acceptable. One of the greatest methods of creating conflict in a story is to force a character to act outside those rules. The lesser of two evils, as it were. Crisis of conscience is a common method of building tension into a story; work it with a gentle hand and balance it carefully with the impression you want to give the reader of the character. Let's face it… if you want the reader to be sympathetic to the character, it is harder to fudge these types of rules. Once you establish what a character does or does not consider acceptable behavior, you have to maintain that personality if you want to hold the reader.

The Rules of Society

So, above, we dealt with rules that just are; now we move on to imposed or implied rules. Any group where individuals live in close proximity — either animal or sentient — has its idea of what is and is not acceptable. Some are guided by instinct, others by experience, yet others by a desire for power and control. No matter how dumb a rule might seem, it originated from some specific situation that someone determined was unacceptable, thus leading to the regulation and enforcement of the desired behaviors. Here… let me break it down further:

Social. You've heard the phrase, "It's just not done," yes? Well, these are the unofficial rules. That means they are not legally binding but carry consequences determined by the community or social grouping a person belongs to or interacts with. There is generally — but not always — a logical reason for the development of these rules. For example, a century or two ago, it was expected a man would always walk on the outside when walking with a lady down the street, a social convention that developed from the fact that people used to dump their chamber pots out the window into the gutter. With the man on the outside (street side), he protects the woman from being doused with waste. Other conventions develop more out of social class than an actual desire to protect individuals (such as one man slapping another man in the face with a glove over some slight (perceived or actual) requiring both men to duel). And finally, a need for self-defense accounts for other unspoken rules, such as the reason we drive on the right side of the road... originally, it was horse-drawn wagons in the Old West, and the pioneers kept to the right when passing opposing traffic so they could have a clear shot with their guns to defend themselves if needed.

Some things to consider when devising social rules for your world or culture:

• Are there classes or castes?

• Are there distinctions between what is acceptable determined by gender, class, or some other defining factor?

• What are the living conditions that would lead to the rule in question?

• What are the consequences of violating these social mores?

Generally, these are rules with less serious repercussions in the bigger scope of things. Perhaps they result in a bad reputation, social shunning, a fight with the offended party, or even exclusion from the community in some manner or degree. They might make life uncomfortable, but not usually very harsh and not anything extreme. Offenses that carry a higher consequence generally transition into law, which leads us, naturally, to legal rules...

Legal. Legal rules can have two objectives: Protect or Control. In theory, and in an ideal society, most laws are instituted to protect people and property from others' inappropriate acts. Examples would be:

- Livestock must be penned to prevent them from trampling people or damaging property.

- People must have insurance when they drive to ensure they can pay for damages or injury should they cause an accident.

- Sidewalks must be kept in good repair to prevent pedestrians from tripping and hurting themselves.

Of course, who lives in an ideal society? There are plenty of rules that come out of a desire to control. Mostly these are zoning laws, at least in the modern-day, but they give you the idea:

- Cars may not be parked on the grass.

- Two-hour parking limit only.

- No liquor to be sold on Sundays (or before noon, or whatever variants there are.)

Religious. Faith-based rules may or may not overlap with Legal or Social, depending on the society you are developing or using as a foundation for your made-up world. In theory, these rules develop out of religious texts passed down by clergy communing with the worshiped deity. In reality, human drives often influence the dictates of religion as much as theology does. (There is a — *ahem* — fine tradition of religion being used as a power base rather than a true calling.) Examples of religious rules:

- Don't eat meat on Fridays.

- Don't drink of the fruit or the grain (alcohol).

- A woman does not show her hair/face/etc. in public.

The level of consequence for violating such religious rules is determined by the amount of power held by the given religious institution and what role they play in the government.

Historically, punishments ranged from being denied food, briefly incarcerated, or even put to death.

Overcoming the Rules

Since it is bad form to have a conflict that your characters have no hope of overcoming, you have to consider how that can plausibly be achieved. Simple enough to do. Here are a few examples:

- Give your character a super-skill, some ability that makes them particularly suited to circumvent the rule in question or that makes it not apply.

- Have an object or talisman that can be obtained that will help the hero achieve what needs to be done.

- Give the character a hand... or several, by writing in support characters that have a skill that will help overcome the conflict(s) faced through combined effort and cooperation.

- Develop a benefactor who can smooth the way if the infraction is discovered.

- If the obstacle (rule) is environmental in nature, write in some other natural feature that would allow the character to overcome the obstacle if they are ingenious enough to recognize its usefulness.

Living with the Consequences

Sometimes there will be no way to circumvent the rules. Hey... it happens, in both real life and in fiction. And each time it does, everyone has a choice whether to respect the rules or break them. That means there are going to be times your characters chose wrong. Maybe it is because of a moment of weakness or ignorance, or maybe it is because the consequences of *not* breaking the rule are worse. Don't be afraid for your characters to take a fall now and then... temporary or otherwise.

Summing Up

I'm sure I haven't covered everything here, but you get the idea. Basically, when it comes down to it, rules in fiction exist so the author can find a way around them, adding tension, excitement, and action to a tale to propel the plot forward (and entertain the reader). In other words… as writers, we need to make our characters work for it, whatever "it" is. After all, readers don't want a walk through the park… they want a Navy SEALs obstacle course, something tough enough that it seems it might almost be too much for the hero. Almost. Very important to remember the "almost."

Cut the Bull – Energy Boosters for Writing

You know, sometimes we just don't know when to stop. No. It's true, even I'm guilty (I know. *Shocker*.) We get so caught up in the language and discovery of these worlds in our heads that we just pile on the detail. We get so caught up in the creativity that we have to build the universe right down to the thumbtacks on the wall, or we're worried about not being clear or missing something important until we end up with a literal checklist of all the steps that took our characters from A to B… for each scene.

Okay, so perhaps I exaggerate, but not completely. There are times in fiction that call for expansive detail, and others where too much clutter kills the action. It is important to know how and when to hold back. Ask yourself a few questions while you're writing:

Have we been here before? If this is the first time your character is in this setting, the reader needs to know something about the surroundings. It helps shape their mental image of where they are. If you don't give them detail, they start to imagine things on their own, and that can screw you up later when you *are* specific about a character or setting.

Now it is tempting to just give a paragraph with all the details and then go on to the character, but in most instances, that gives a choppy, disjointed feel to a scene, kind of like the difference between beads on a string as opposed to a smooth braid where things are neatly woven together. I like braids. It is better to feed the reader details in relation to the character and their actions. As the character notices or experiences aspects of the space, that is when you introduce them. It keeps things fluid, connected, and gives a sense of discovery, rather than of being told something.

If the character has been in a particular setting before, you want to focus on what is relevant to the character, the action, or a future point in the plot at that very moment, and not a lot of extraneous detail that will distract the reader from what is important in the scene.

What is the point of the scene? The answer to that determines how much detail is appropriate. Sometimes you want to feed things in piecemeal. Other times you HAVE to go in-depth.

- *Is this a destination or a transition?* If the answer is a destination, we need to know stuff. What does the place look like, who and what are where? If this is just a transition to someplace more important, any details you give should be important.

- *Is it taking too long to get where you're going?* Are you trying to build tension or move from one part of the plot to another? If so, and you, as the writer, start to feel it is taking forever, take a look at the details you have included. Some things are important for plot or character, but extraneous stuff should be kept to a minimum until you hit a more relaxed portion of the story or book.

- *Is this relevant later?* Sometimes you have to include detail, no matter what the scene. There are always points that you have to reveal the bits and pieces that come together later so that everything makes sense, like mentioning a belt dagger if the character uses it three chapters later to save himself, or noticing a peculiar tattoo on a passerby that seems irrelevant but in the end betrays the villain.

- *What actions propel the plot?* When it comes to the things the characters do, some steps are unavoidable, but others you can skip over. We don't need to know that Jim opened the drawer, took out a pair of socks, closed the drawer, sat on the bed, and then put on the socks. Suffice it to say, Jim took socks from his dresser and put them on. On the other hand, if Jim is fighting an olfactory-sensitive monster and the only thing that can save him is the month-old dirty socks under his bed, making him work to retrieve them in excruciating detail serves a purpose.

When it comes down to it, we must all judge each piece we write by how much the detail adds to the story or how much the detail sucks the life out of it. If you aren't sure, read the work aloud, feel the pacing of it. If a snail could move faster, trim things down. If you reach the end and you have no clear picture of where you are or how you got there, slow down a bit and explore the world you're creating because that is how the reader comes to care, when you make the world and those that populate it real for them.

Structural Assists to Pacing

I know most of this article has had to do with content, but I wanted to mention several ways to use your writing structure to impact the scene's pace. These are the conscious choices you can make to inspire subconscious responses in your readers. Wonderful tools when used properly.

Chop it Up. A great way to increase the tension and pacing of a scene is to use short sentences or even sentence fragments (sparingly, please.) to give a sense of urgency and action. A key place to use this is a fight scene where what is happening is most important. Such as:

Jim dove left. Claws raked his feet but didn't take hold. Thud. His body hit the floor. Air left his lungs. Spots formed before his eyes. Yet instinct sent him rolling out of the way. A massive paw slammed down where he'd been. He rolled again. Scrambled for the safety of beneath the bed. The creature snarled. Its nose wrinkled and twitched.

Violently. Jim spied last month's socks just out of reach and knew what to do.

You get the idea...

Punch the Line. No... don't pick a fight with it. The words would win. Okay, let me explain. Sometimes a point you make in a story is like a sucker punch. Unexpected or profound enough to really grab the reader, but somewhat lost among the other copy. Now, this is another thing you don't want to overuse, but you can get a lot of mileage out of taking that perfect line and letting it stand on its own. Here's an example from my novel, *Today's Promise* (eSpec Books, 2020):

> Looking around the room, she noticed another bed, that one holding a young woman deathly pale and covered in dust. Another woman Agnieszka didn't recognize was tenderly cleaning her up.
>
> The sight left Agnieszka feeling empty and alone. She had had enough. Confirming her own person was free of dust and rebraiding her hair, she felt marginally closer to civilized.
>
> TIME TO REJOIN THE HUMAN RACE.
>
> And she stepped out of the room. There were a number of people waiting there, half of them looking like they'd just come from battle. Again with the dust, and a bit more blood. She swept the group with her gaze. She knew two of them. Agnieszka turned to the young man who she'd first encountered at her own cottage. Back before her life went catawampus. She didn't even know his name, but of the two faces she recognized, he was the one she mistrusted the least.
>
> "Take me home, now."

No, the line isn't printed all in caps in the book. Just high-lighting my example. That line could have easily been run into the paragraph preceding it, but popping it out has much more impact.

Summing Up

Writing is one choice after another. What to say and how to say it, heck, even when. Consider your options to achieve the best effect, keeping the reader interested and moving forward to the next page at the proper pace for what's going on. Use every trick you have to increase your work's (positive) impact, but always remember to include the lulls, the relaxed moments, the times when it is natural to stop and smell… anything. And when it's time to get tense… let the world fade into the background, so all the reader's attention is riveted where it belongs.

Getting to the Root of the Matter

You know, history is important. History is a connection, a foundation, roots. Yeah, cliché, but true.

I've had my own personal encounter with history recently. I can't tell you how exciting it was to discover another branch of my family, to know there was more there than I knew. I'd always been curious but in an incidental, back-of-the-mind kind of way. The more and more I learn, the more I realize how important it is to know where I come from. This is why I feel moved to write on this topic right now because I have had a quite real experience with the importance of knowing where people — yourself in particular — come from. See, growing up, I didn't know much family history. We weren't close geographically, much of the family documentation was lost through several rounds of fires, and many of my family's elders had passed well before I understood the concept of family history. I think I am not alone in this.

Maybe that is the cause of the social disconnect many of us experience today. Family just doesn't seem to mean as much as it used to. We are unrooted, and so we drift and wander and lose our place in the structure.

Now you might be wondering what that has to do with writing, am I correct? Let me tell you.

We might be a society with loose roots, but that doesn't mean that we don't want them! We want to feel connected, anchored, as if we have a place. Consequently, that means we want the same for those we care about, and if you've done your job as a writer, you and your readers care about your characters.

There is satisfaction in knowing the history exists, even if you don't know all the details. Characters with a history are rooted in their world, an integral part of it. To put it simply, they matter. We want the characters to matter. When you have a character that just sort of drifts through their reality without impact beyond the immediate events, in the back of your mind, you wonder what was the point? (Oh! Come on... yes, you do! We all do.)

The Social Footprint

Have you ever pulled up a plant? Not talking a weed or a blade of grass, or the mums once they've died and turned into a hollow, papery brown stalk. Pull up an iris or a lily, or any number of perennial plants, and you'll notice that what appears to be a completely separate plant shares roots with those next to it, or even feet away! People are like that, which means your characters should be like that too.

There has been a lot of talk in recent years about carbon footprints, humanity's impact on the ecological world. I've come to realize that people also have a social footprint. It's measured in memories and documents and other assorted data. Videotapes and audio recordings. All of the little captured details of our lives are our roots because each one is a lasting documentation of our impact on the world in whatever degree... large, small, personal, sensational. It's how those that follow know we've been here, who we're connected with, and what we've done.

(Yeah, yeah... I know, not always a good thing!)

Now I'm not saying to put the informational equivalent of cement shoes on your characters, forcing them to drag their way through the story you are trying to tell. Some background detail is good, but too much kills a story. The reader doesn't have to know *everything* about *every* character, only what pertains to the story, except for maybe a little extra on your primary characters to flesh them out and make them real. After all, you are building a world, and worlds are cluttered.

You, however, are not the reader. You need a better understanding of those whose story you are telling.

Think about your characters, what has made them the way they are. Here are some questions you can kick around:

Who is my character related to? Maybe relevant, maybe not for your particular story, but the presence of parents and siblings and extended family impacts the way we develop. How we get along with those people has even more of an impact.

Where does my character come from? Family history and status is one of the biggest influences on our lives. It can determine how we perceive ourselves and how society perceives us (or how we think society perceives us, which can be even more relevant), what resources we have to draw upon and what skills we are likely to know just as a result of growing up, rather than specialized training.

What has happened to my character in the past? We learn from experience. (I know… I know… state the obvious, why don't I?) There is no way we are not impacted in some way by the events of our past. It colors how we respond and react to everything that comes after in some way. We are the sum of our experiences, and so should our characters be.

What does my character want to achieve? Our goals are very important in defining who we are and what we do. Whether it is directly related to the story's plot or not, the same goes for our characters.

It is up to you how much effort and time you put into figuring out a history for your characters, but there are several ways this helps you:

Continuity – By figuring out as many details as you can in advance and updating them as you go along, it gives you a reference you can check as you are writing to keep things straight and avoid conflicting information as you go. This is helpful for single book projects, but vital — in my opinion — for multi-book projects, take it from me. By book three, you're pulling your hair out trying to remember things.

Connectivity – No… we're not talking electricity or internet access. We're talking about those roots I mentioned earlier… the ones on the lilies and irises that connect plant to plant. Well, the more you know about your characters and the ways they are connected to each other, the more you can make use of that as you are writing to both tighten the story and employ your characters and their interactions with one another to reveal important details in a manner that feels natural.

Familiarity – The more you know about your characters, the better you understand their place in the reality you are building. The more you understand from the start, the less you have to puzzle out as you go along. I'm not saying things won't change, but it gives you a place to start from.

Depth – Whether you put the character details you figure out in the story or not, they help flesh out the character in your mind. If you know why they are doing things and how they are likely to respond for various reasons, it solidifies their personality. Eventually, you might use that background, and maybe you won't, but that doesn't mean it doesn't influence the story by giving you a greater understanding of the characters you are dealing with.

Summing Up

Don't take me wrong here; I'm not saying this is the way you must do things. I know better than that. Everyone's process is different, and what works for one person can completely bollox up the next. What I am saying, though, is whatever manner you choose, it is important to give some thought to your characters and how they relate to their surroundings. Understanding them gives you a clearer sense of where your story is going.

Profiling for Writers

(Originally published in the Writer's Toolbox column, Allegory Magazine.)

No! Not that kind of profiling! Character profiling. After all, when you write fiction, you aren't just conveying the details of a series of events. No. You are introducing the reader to your characters… your babies. Don't you think you should know who they are first?

When I give a workshop, I recommend writers create character sheets when they get started, mostly — but not exclusively — for their primary characters. Gamers do this all the time; it is how they keep track of what their characters look like, some history, and what they can do. It allows them to follow the game (story) the game master is running without being bogged down with trying to remember everything about their character. It also allows them to modify the details as the character grows and learns, acquires possessions, or gets injured. It also makes it easier for them to maintain continuity from game campaign to game campaign, no matter how much time has passed in between. Face it, a character sheet is a condensed version of a life.

As writers, we can adapt that process. Heck, I actually have friends that literally roll up their characters using gaming manuals as guides. The basic details, anyway, particularly for secondary characters. Not saying you have to go that far, but the tracking aspect of the process is something we could all benefit from. Things you might want to consider in advance:

Name – give your characters a full name, first, middle, last, and nickname. You might not use all of them throughout the story, but it gives the character shape and personality. And it starts those threads of connection. Besides, who knows when the information might be useful!

Physical Description – readers like characters they can picture in their minds. To do that, they need things like hair and eye color, flesh tone, height, and weight. The more attention you pay to details, the more real that image is going to be. It also fixes the character in your own mind, so you understand what the character is capable of physically or what type of self-image they might have. Don't get me wrong, though. I'm not saying to lay several paragraphs on the reader at once going into excruciating detail about what each character looks like, but you can weave in threads of description as things are happening without slowing down the pace too much.

Intangibles – If you are familiar with role-playing games—of the D&D variety! Come on, keep it clean… well, unless you're writing erotica, then I guess you kind of can't—anyway, as I was saying, in RPGs, some characteristics are not visible, though the effects are. Things like dexterity, charisma, luck… establishing such details, even if it is only for your own clarification, will help enliven your character as you find places to bring these characteristics into evidence. A stumble here, a giggling starry-eyed girl there, happening upon just the thing needed to propel the story forward (without it seeming as if it happened by the Hand of Author) that will develop more fluidly as you write if you have an understanding of your character, to begin with.

Relationships – Unless you are writing a sequel or in an established universe with existing characters, you might not know in advance all the particulars of each character, or even your main characters, particularly if you are, like me, a pantser, but the nice thing about creating a character sheet is that you can go back later and fill in the gaps. If you know family details or the history between individual characters, make a brief note about the particulars on the relevant character sheets. It helps you keep things straight and also is a resource for figuring out who you can recruit for various tasks later on as the story develops.

Skills – It isn't enough to know what someone looks like. You need to know what abilities they have. Can they ride a bike? Do they know how to use a gun? Did their mother make them take ballroom dancing classes for ten years? You never know what will develop in a story; if your character starts out with certain skills, write them down; if skills surface while you are writing or the character learns something on the fly, write it down. And just as important, note if there are skills they are particularly bad at as well. These come in handy for two things... comic relief and building tension.

The How-To's

There are many methods for tracking characters, from paper to Microsoft Word files to computer programs such as Scriveners (http://www.literatureandlatte.com/scrivener.php) that allow a writer to organize every aspect of a writing project.

In the beginning, I mentioned character sheets, like you would use for a role-playing game. If you want to adapt a gaming character sheet for your purposes, you can likely find examples online, or there are usually blank sheets in the back of gaming manuals. If you don't want to go through the bother of hunting one down, you can just use sheets of paper, index cards, or an electronic file on your computer.

Layout - Think of the information sheet you fill out when you go to the doctor or apply for a job. Name and vital statistics are at the top, followed by more explicit details and history below. For story-specific events (those that develop as you write), start a timeline or a bullet list on the back.

Detail – you can go into as little or as much detail as you like, but keep in mind that you already wrote down what happened as the story developed. What you want here are the cliff notes on the key events and characteristics. For example, if they met someone on the train once, you probably don't have to record that, but if the person they met on the train was the villain that killed their father, then yeah, good idea to make a note of when they first met.

Photographs/Drawings – Not saying you have to do this, but I've known both gamers and writers alike who either draw a representation of their character or find an image online or in a magazine that is a rough approximation of how they envision the character to look. For them, it makes the character more "real," and they are better able to describe physical attributes as they are writing with that example before them.

Summing Up

I've said it before, and I'll no doubt will say it again; I'm not writing this to say that this is the way you should go about creating and tracking your characters, merely presenting a possible method, explaining the reasoning, and giving you some idea of how to go about it. The important thing here is not how you establish the particulars about your characters but the fact that you should.

Think about it, if someone tells you a story about someone one you know, it's both easier for you to follow and more likely you will be interested; if they tell you a story about a stranger, the less you can identify with the subject of the story the less you care.

Writers need the reader to care about their characters. However you do it, it's your job to make sure they do.

Jerking Tears and Tugging Heartstrings
Baiting the Emotional Hook

(Originally printed in The Writer's Toolbox: Allegory Magazine)

So what?
What's the big deal?
Why should I care?

You think you're the only one asking those questions? Think again. Every time a reader picks up a book, that's what's in the back of their minds. As the writer, it is your job to make sure the answers are on the page because that keeps them turning.

Think of it like this: if you're at a party and someone starts to tell you a story you don't care anything about, what do you do? Yeah... you either make an excuse to walk away, or you tune them out, making meaningless sounds of acknowledgment from time to time to make it seem like you're actually listening. Readers are the same way. If they don't care, they don't keep reading (unless it is schoolwork... then they get the *Cliff Notes* and read those).

Face it, you need the reader to *care*, and since we relate to the world through our emotions, that means there needs to be some emotional connection made between the reader and what is happening on the page.

Sometimes excitement will do that on its own, but not for long. You can't really maintain constant action in a story without losing... well... the story, and the reader for that point.

So, how do you inspire an emotional connection without giving a running commentary on how each character feels? Glad you asked...

Visible Physical Cues

Yeah... you've heard it before: "Show, don't tell." It is the easiest, least obtrusive way to inspire a response in your reader because it draws on their own experiences to provide the content that connects with the physical effects of emotion... the shudder, the clench, the frown, etc. For example:

> Tammy was angry.

Simple enough. Definitely clear. But lacking something. To what degree was she angry? How did she respond to the feeling? How did she express it?

> Tammy's lips pursed, and her forehead tightened in a scowl. She glanced away, not meeting his eye as a muscle in her cheek twitched.

See, the first example gives us information, but it's flat. There is no dimension to it. Whereas the second example resonates; it calls up memories of how the reader might have felt faced with a like situation, when they may have reacted in ways similar to the character. There is an intensity to such memories that transcends a mere statement of fact.

Most people reveal emotions by what they do before they even say a word. In fact, often, the physical cues are more honest and informative than anything they tell you. Not because everyone is dishonest, but because we typically grow up with two understandings: emotions are vulnerability, and emotional displays are impolite. Because of this, we don't always let our emotions loose. (Yes, I know, this doesn't go for everybody. Some people thrive on emotional displays. But it's true enough.) Because of this, we have learned to put more faith in the physical signs of feeling, those unconscious, sometimes uncontrollable indicators. In gambling, they call it a "tell." Sometimes they are obvious, sometimes subtle.

Because this is how we interact with our world and gauge our encounters with others, employing that in our writing establishes a connection between the reader and the characters.

Internal Reactions

Emotions are messy.

(Yeah… tell you something you didn't know, right?)

Because of that, for various reasons, we internalize a lot of how we feel. Repression has become quite acceptable when applied to emotions. With that in mind, you can set the tone for your reader by addressing the emotional and related physiological responses a character may have to a situation in the narrative or the inner monologue, writing in such a way that it is clear the character is aware of the reaction, but those they are sharing the scene with are not. For example:

> Carl smiled. "You'll do it. You have no choice."
> Tammy stared at him a moment. "No, I don't think so."
> Without another word, she turned and walked away.

There really aren't any emotions in this exchange. A smile is an action that could have many different emotional motivators. This is a statement of facts and actions with no clues about what the characters are feeling or how the reader should feel about them. Let's give it another go:

> Carl smirked. "You'll do it. You have no choice."
> Tammy felt a sharp jab deep in her gut, brutal and cold. Swallowing a gasp, she locked down her expression, refusing to let her features betray her as he just had. "No, I don't think so," she answered, her tone deceptively calm. Despite the cold tinges running the length of her body, threatening to grow into uncontrollable shudders, she silently turned and walked away, holding her heartache deep inside until she reached the privacy of her room.

Thanks to Tammy's internalized responses, we know how to react to the scene, and we also know that Carl is not aware of the emotion he has inspired in her. Maybe he suspects, or maybe he assumes, but he doesn't know, which sets the tone for the encounter and the relationship between these two characters.

Can't you just hear the reader asking, *What's the deal? Where is this going?* People respond to emotion. True… in their own way, colored by their own experiences, so you can't really predict what reaction the reader will have absolutely, but there are some universals that you can be reasonably sure will resonate with the reader, particularly the physiological responses to emotion, if not what inspires said emotions.

Don't be afraid to get into the character's head — and heart — and give the reader a peek.

Unconscious Signifiers

In fiction, characters are not the only ones with emotions. Sometimes writers need to set a scene. They need to build a tone that will culminate somewhere down the line. Because of this, we need to be aware of the emotional impact of words and descriptions that motivate responses, rather than just describing them. Mostly this deals with building some sort of tension or mood in a scene that puts the reader in the right mindset or emotional state for the pending action.

For example, a character moving from one place to another can be a simple statement of fact, an action completed, and nothing more, such as:

> Chrissy stood in the doorway. Anthony moved across the room.

Or an act can be a part of the emotional climate:

> Chrissy stood in the doorway, her face pale and her dress torn. Frowning, Anthony hurried across the room.

This is a simple adjustment that layers the detail and implies the emotion, rather than putting it right out there. The reader — drawing on their own inherent responses — has to interpret the actions and events based on the cues you provide and the context surrounding them. Not only does that draw the reader in and help provide them with the "why" behind the "what," but it also further immerses them into the story, connecting them to it almost without them realizing it.

The Roles of Emotions

Emotions are a powerful tool in the writer's toolbox, adding depth and impact to any prose, particularly if properly utilized. Keep in mind that there are subtly different roles that feelings can play in a story.

Communicate – emotions and how characters react to them tell the reader and other characters about their personality, character, and motivation.

Relate – emotions provide — with hope — common ground and a basis for understanding.

Affect – emotions draw a response from others, sometimes predictable, sometimes not, often changing the course of actions.

Manipulate – emotions, in the wrong hands, can be tools or weapons, putting pressure on characters to change their stance or act against their nature.

Summing Up

As both readers and individuals, we are often left wondering. That's frustrating in life. In fiction, it is extremely dissatisfying. Let's assume we don't have much choice about life; the book, however, we can put down and forget it ever existed.

You need to remember that the reader isn't the one the character is trying to hide from, so keep that in mind as you are writing. Share with the reader, give them a glimpse of what's going on inside. They will love (or hate) your characters for it even more. But most important of all, they will *care*.

If you leave too much for the reader to infer or figure out on their own, you relinquish way too much control over your story. Tug here, jerk there… guide them through the world you have created and inspire them to see it from your perspective, through your emotional filters, or you never know what they will get out of the story… if they even finish it.

You Got Your Anachronism in My Period Piece!

Words are funny things. You think you know what they mean… and then bam! A colloquialism sneaks up and bites you… well, you get the idea.

Language is like a secret code. The same word can mean ten different things to ten different people. And you want to know what makes it worse? They change. Language is not static; it is fluid. Tell a man from the eighteenth century that he looks gay, and he might smile and nod in agreement. Tell a man that today and watch out. He's likely to punch you. And it isn't just time that changes words. They can have different connotations from region to region and across social classes.

For instance, take the word "fag;" did you know it has three different meanings?

- It is a derogatory term for a homosexual or an insult to any male.

- In England and most of the British Commonwealth, it is a slang term for a cigarette.

- It is a verb meaning 'to tire.'

Can you see how using this word in any of its contexts could confuse some portion of the world population?

If you can master the trick of this linguistic metamorphosis, you can write anything from homage to Shakespeare to a riff on Tennessee Williams just by choosing your words wisely.

It isn't easy, and you might think it doesn't really matter — say if you write fantasy, or mainstream, rather than historical or period fiction. But you know, no matter what you write, if you use the wrong word or phrase or use the right one in the wrong context, you are going to yank that reader right out of your story quicker than you can blink.

Your job as a writer is to be aware of how your words might be taken, of the tone they are setting. For example, I'm currently writing a Victorian steampunk tale, and I've chosen very formal language to convey that era:

> The gentleman stared at her with shock and affront clearly visible in his gaze, if not his expression, but he did not argue and went to do as she bid. Clara allowed him a slight, encouraging smile before he looked away. That smile quite disappeared as she turned to the inventor upon whom she bestowed her patronage.

Words like affront, bid, bestowed, and patronage are not commonly used today, at least not in everyday conversation, but you can see how they have set a formal tone to this piece. Now, look at the same passage with more modern language:

> The man stared at her with shock and outrage heating his gaze, though his expression was blank. Yet he didn't argue as he went to do as she asked. Clara allowed him a slight, encouraging smile before he looked away. That smile disappeared as she turned to the inventor she sponsored.

From the second paragraph, you would never know that this is a period piece though it conveys the same information.

Of course, most words are just words with no particular tie to a timeframe, but once in a while, something will slip in without you even realizing it, such as calling a pretty girl a babe or mentioning penicillin when your story is set before 1928. Some of that can be combated with research. As for language, try reading a sampling of things actually written in the time period you want to replicate or visit the region where you are setting your work if it is a modern piece. This will let you pick up on phrases and slang peculiar to that area.

Now, most of us are not going to pull out the dictionary every time we type a word to make sure it was in usage at the proper time or that it doesn't have some embarrassing alter-meaning that can't be distinguished from the one intended by context, but in most cases, it should be evident if you read your work aloud if something among the wording sounds off. You can also enlist a friend or two to read through and point out anything that made them stumble while reading.

And remember, watch your language… after all, you might not be saying what you meant to.

Building with Allusion

If there is one defining characteristic of the human race, it is the overwhelming need to know *why*. *Why does the sun rise each day? What makes a rainbow appear? What causes the thunder in the heavens?*

Let's face it, as a race, we have much in common with a two-year-old.

And much like that self-same two-year-old, we have a history of making up a reason to soothe our soul if one is not readily understandable. Just look at the parallels throughout the civilizations of the world. In each of them, there is a myth or legend dealing with those questions above, as well as all the other at-one-time unfathomable occurrences both in nature and human experience.

This is the second defining characteristic of the human race: creativity. Now, imagine the two paired together…

As writers, particularly of speculative fiction, old answers—myths and legends—can add depth and meaning to our writing as we present our readers with new questions. Whether it is a key part of the plot or a hidden significance in the details, literary allusion is like the spice in a good sauce, not always obvious, but definitely enriching. No matter what myth cycle or legend you borrow from, chances are at least a percentage of your readership will be familiar with the original.

I believe very much in borrowing such references, not only because it keeps them alive, but because they make for great fiction. Let's take a look at how…

Names

Borrowing names — or even whole characters — from mythology serves several purposes for you, the writer. First, it makes the reader feel good when they recognize the reference, like they got the in-joke. Second, it helps both you and the reader define the characteristics at play. For instance, if you name a character Lucifer, that name comes with some automatic connotations based on the biblical reference. This tells the reader right away what they should expect, or gives you as the writer a foil to work against if your purpose is to overturn those preconceived notions. And third, it can be used to foreshadow events to come. For instance, in my science fiction story "Building Blocks" (*Barbarians at the Jumpgate*, Padwolf Publishing; 2010), I named a ship the *Cortez*. It was an exploratory vessel that unknowingly caused harm to a life form the crew was not even aware of until it started to fight back. In another story, "Carbon Copy" (*Space Pirates*, Flying Pen Press; 2007), I named a state-of-the-art warship the *Rommel*. In these cases, both historical references, but still relevant.

Ultimately, my point is mythology (or history) is full of names: heroes, villains, creatures, all of them can help build a character, defining for the writer — if no one else — what that character should be like, or provide a focal point from which your story can grow.

Plots

There is a popular opinion that there are no new stories, only new tellings. That doesn't have to be a bad thing. By using an established legend or myth as the foundation of your story, you have a better understanding of the steps that need to take place, and that gives you the freedom to play along the way, rather than having to figure out where you're going next. For example, my first novel, *Yesterday's Dreams*, takes aspects of Celtic mythology and actually weaves them into the plot. This is how it happened: I named my antagonist Olcas — which is Gaelic for evil — and while researching Irish mythology, I discovered there actually *was* an Olcas in legend. He and his family terrorized ancient Ireland until they were brought down and destroyed by the Sidhe (Irish elves). By incorporating these details into my novel, I now had a concrete goal for my bad guy (other than just being the bad guy). He wanted revenge, he wanted to triumph over those that had destroyed his family, and he wanted power like he had had before. And what was more… he had two brothers who wanted the same thing, which meant I had much more story to tell and more factions to play with than those I had when I started out. Two other books worth, in fact!

Another plot use for myths and legends is as a template, not using the actual details of the myth but using the familiar landmarks to tell a different story. In fact, mimicking existing myths with legends of your own is a great way to ease a reader into a universe of your own creation.

Characters

Both legends and myths have archetypes or tropes that most of us recognize… the white knight, the wicked witch, the damsel in distress, and the learned wizard, to mention some of the most familiar. Now, you can call them whatever you want, but the reader will still recognize them for what they are and anticipate what is to come, and understand what their role will be in the story.

Again, not necessarily a bad thing.

Whether it is a primary character (like the above-mentioned Olcas) or a background character, drawing from mythology awakens an echo in the reader's subconscious or even outright recognition. That makes the writer's job easier and frees up your mental muscle for those things you do have to figure out on your own. It also gives you room to play. For instance, my novel *The Halfing's Court* is about biker faeries. Most people don't realize that the first biker gangs were started by retired Air Force personnel. In the Air Force, if something went wrong with the plane, it was gremlins; when they became bikers, that translated. Anything that went wrong with the bike was blamed on *road* gremlins. I was able to incorporate and expand on that myth. Now, most people have some vague understanding of what a gremlin is, and probably some concept of what they look like, but where I got to play was in describing one tailored to the road. Mythology is full of descriptions of legendary beings that mimic their surroundings... I capitalized on that... and had a lot of fun! Here is my description of a road gremlin:

> "As the biker rode away down the center of the road, the puddle bubbled and seethed. Up from its shallow depth popped an odd, tiny creature, clutching at its ears. "Smear doesn't like the faerie-man. Not at all. Or his bloody little shrill bell. Smear wants to grind his face, crush the bell." Crouched upon the road, he slammed his thick, meaty fists against the asphalt. Microfissures formed: the conception of a pothole.
>
> He was joined by another, and then another, crawling up through the fissures, expanding them, until the puddle was gone. Standing in its place was a troupe of inch-high gremlins, identical in every way: Skin as grey as asphalt, with an oily, rainbow shimmer. Hair long and thick and spiny, like a porcupine mated with a box of nails. A thick white line ran down the center of their faces, like war paint, and along their arms were thick black squiggles. Like tats or tribal markings, only with the dull gleam of tar snakes. Each finger was like a spike, reminiscent of those found at toll booths and security gates, only jointed. The minuscule troupe rumbled and grumbled as they watched the bike speed away."

As you can see, I used physical characteristics of the road, combined with the slang bikers use, to take the concept of a road gremlin and not only make it my own but did so in a way that the reader can identify with and appreciate.

Summing Up

Literary allusion—be it mythology, history, or current events—is an invaluable tool for enriching your fiction, and not just that of the speculative type. Mythology and legend are a fundamental part of who we are… use that, stir up echoes in the mind that make the reader wonder, that put them in awe, draw them into your telling of a timeless story. This is a tool of such diversity. Grab it with both hands, and have some fun!

Doing Battle with The Anti-Muse

Writer's Block is a myth, right? Sad to say, it is not.

Sometimes things go beyond Writer's Block.

I went through a period in my life where I could not write. I knew what I needed to write. Basically, what needed to happen. They were all established characters. And yet, the story refused to be told.

It was very demoralizing. In trying to push my way past, I aggravated the situation by failing time and again.

Yes… I've done this. I literally owed fans a novella. Just a novella! Not even a full book. It took me five years to complete it. Part of the problem was that the novella was a spin-off from a trilogy. Another part of the problem was the novella was the start of a new series. The scope of the project boggled me.

How much does the reader need to know? What don't they? Whatever that ends up being, how do I convey the back story without bogging down the tale in infodumps?

It wasn't an easy prospect, this novella. And yet, I was committed. Not that the fans hadn't given up hope after a certain point. There are only so many times they can hear, 'Life happens, but I'm over it. I've got this now… '

Five times I had false starts. How do you get past that?

Here are some tips.

Know Your Material

If you are writing based on existing material, review that material first. Reread everything relevant and note those elements that could potentially relate to the new content you are writing. This is both for continuity, and so you know what to include, not just for those familiar with the universe, but for those who are encountering it for the first time. You don't want to retell the existing books, but if the storyline is related, a certain amount of back story will need to be included in some way for your current story to make sense.

Decide What You Need To Write

Sounds obvious, right? Not so easy, not so straightforward. For one thing, not everyone works with an outline. For another, if you knew what you needed to write, you'd just do it... right? Oh, if only!

I am a 'pantser.' This means I write without an outline. I get an idea and run with it until I get another idea. Kind of like a scavenger hunt where my prize is the story. Or maybe a hedge maze! I do a LOT of wandering around. It works for me. But I still need an idea of the story I want or need to tell.

In the case of *Eternal Wanderings* (the novella I owed everyone), I knew precisely the tale I was going to tell. I'd even written a good piece of it. But it was dry and boring and angsty. My character, Kara O'Keefe, had moved well past angsty at this point. With each of my many false starts, I got a better idea of what needed to be on the page and what did not. I read and reread what I managed to get down and identified where the gaps were and what I was missing. Everything took place within the confines of a Romani caravan, so I ended up with a lot of repetition, a lot of the same feel. That needed to be switched up.

I also ended up with many tense scenes, all with the same emotional tone and dwelling too much on past events. Some of that was needed, but not only does a good story require contrasting tones, but I also needed to keep in mind character growth. Without that, you don't have much of a story. Static is not interesting.

So, whether you outline or not, think about the story you want to tell and consider how to make it well-rounded. Know the points you don't want to leave out and consider which ones you do.

Research Until You Drop

When you write, you are creating a world. Sometimes it is completely made up. Sometimes it is a mirror of the world we live in. In either case, it should be clearly drawn and explored for the reader. Not necessarily every extraneous detail, but elements relevant to the character's experience and the story you are telling. For me, that meant I needed to learn what a Romani caravan looks like, how the people dress, something of their outlook on life. What is acceptable. What is *not*. For me, the internet provided pretty much all I needed to fill in those details.

Not writing a real-world analog? That just means you need to explore your world in detail, so you reveal that world to your reader. Understand the how and the why of things, research how things work, and what different types of environments or cultures are like and what they produce so your made-up world can follow guidelines that will make sense to the reader.

Try Something Else

Is it everything, or just one thing that you cannot write? Has your current project become an albatross? Take a break. Try writing something just for the heck of it. Something that doesn't matter nearly so much as the one hanging over your head. And if that doesn't work…

Be At Peace

If you can't write, you can't write. Accept that.

Now, I'm not saying that you shouldn't try. Sit down, give it a go. But don't follow your doubts down a rabbit hole if today isn't that day. When I was supposed to be writing *Eternal Wanderings,* I second-guessed everything I had on the page and just could not see which direction I should go. I was convinced everything I wrote was crap, and I was no longer a storyteller. My mind no longer generated random ideas, and my thumb drive was full of isolated files where I pulled stuff out of the manuscript and just couldn't throw it away.

Then… one day… five years later! I woke up with my mind buzzing and a new direction to go in. I wrote or rewrote a third of the story on that day. Within two weeks, I was done. It was nothing I could predict. The stresses of life hadn't gone away. New things kept happening. There were still life problems I had (and need) to sort out. But I had stopped second-guessing myself. I had relaxed into 'when it's time.'

Sometimes it is the anxiety of needing to write that makes it impossible. Give yourself a break because agonizing over it is counterproductive.

Don't give up, but don't try to force it either.

Writing Exercises

This section is meant to complement the articles you've just read. They are exercises I have used in writers seminars over the year and have found useful. I hope you do as well. There is one exercise to a page so that you may photocopy them if you wish to complete the exercise on the page with the instructions for reference. Feel free to do so for the purpose of honing your craft.

Writing Exercise – Nonverbal Cues: All of us have been told over and over, "Show, don't Tell." Easy to say, but how do you do it? Particularly with feelings, it is easy to fall into telling. How do you show how someone feels? I'd say to pay attention to your own reactions, but most of the time, we don't even notice. So what are you to do? Just look at those around you! All of us have subconscious or conscious reactions to emotion. While everyone does react differently, there are some typical physical acts that correspond to recognizable feelings. Unfortunately, that makes them not only cliché but also potentially repetitive in fiction. In this exercise, describe three different physical cues for the listed emotions.

Example: Anger – (Her fists clenched. His temple pulsed. She ground her teeth. He punched the wall.)

Embarrassment

Excitement

Frustration

Hatred

Despair

Confusion

Fear

Hurt

Writing Exercise – Nonverbal Cues: People and emotions are both complex. Sometimes we feel more than one thing at once. Sometimes certain reactions represent different feelings for each person. We can get an idea of which is appropriate by context, but knowing what is potentially conveyed is important, so you know when you need to make it clearer. For this exercise, write down all the different feelings you can think of that could apply to the different physical cues (For this, I am counting anything that would complete the sentence "I feel," which could be an emotional or physical feeling).

Example: Bright eyes. Sorrow, Excitement, Pain, Joy

Clenched jaw/hands

A twitch/tic

Taut muscles

A scream

Looking away

Tears

A smile

A head toss

A clap

Writing Exercise – Description: as writers, we need to be observant. Capturing a person, object, or scene with just a few lines of description can be difficult, but we are called on to do it all the time, introducing a reader to a world or character in small glimpses at a time. In teams, go to a public location and select a person to observe for about five or ten minutes. You should both select the same subject. If it is a person, do not stare or otherwise make them uncomfortable, be discreet. When you are done observing, leave the area and go somewhere you can write. It doesn't matter where, as long as you leave the vicinity of your subject. You and your partner both write down a description of what you observed. When done, compare to see the differences of what you picked up on. Be sure to note physical characteristics, actions, and expressions, where applicable. This can be done individually as well, but doing it as a team exercise allows you to see the differences in perspective and how people can see the same thing at the same time but see it differently.)

Writing Exercise – Character Building. When writing a story or a novel, it is important to know your characters. What they look like, what drives them, and what experiences in their past impact how they act now. Some characters will only be seen in passing; others will be the foundation of your story. Waiting to discover who they are as you write can lead to pitfalls and inconsistencies later… or extra work re-writing as you have to go back and clean up the details. Using the description you came up with in the previous exercise, develop a character filling in the points provided.

Name:
Hair color:
Eye color:
Build:

Goal:

Strength:

Flaw:

Unique identifying feature:

Defining personal history:

Getting Down to Business

Putting On Your Virtual Game Face

(Originally published in Infinite Horizons Issue 1, by Avalon Games)

The internet is amazing! Absolutely amazing! In the last twenty-five years (give or take), it has totally transformed most of our lives, including how we do business. It has simplified the way we communicate, the way we pay bills and buy goods—not to mention the astounding plethora of ways in which we can now be taken advantage of—and, as writers, it has in many cases completely revamped how we submit our work for publication.

Like I said… Amazing!

And as easy as it has become to submit our work; it has become correspondingly easy for that work to be rejected.

So, why have I felt compelled to write about this? Well, as some of you might know, I am also an editor.

You know what that means?

I see up close and personal many of the mistakes individuals make when submitting electronically.

I also happen to know that most editors and publishers receive so many submissions on a daily basis that they *look* for reasons to reject them. Heck, they look for reasons to not even read them, or to stop reading them if they have indeed started.

Don't get bent out of shape about that. It's the only way they can get through the piles of submissions in anything resembling a timely manner, and if you have not put forth your best face in the cover letter or the first few paragraphs of your work, they are going to presume you haven't in the rest of it either, automatically relegating you to the dreck pile whether that descriptive applies or not.

So, that brings me to the problem with email. It fosters a sense of informality. That's fine when you are chatting up your new internet love or sending a letter to your mom, but when you are doing business, it's important to remember that while the medium has changed, the proper conventions have not. Sadly, this does not seem to be as common knowledge as I would expect.

(Time to get out the *Miss Manners* books, folks.)

If you haven't gathered yet, this is something of a pet peeve with me. Nothing bothers me more than someone sending me a query or submission that is informal to a fault or downright unprofessional. It is even worse when it is someone I know or have worked with previously. Frankly, it shows a lack of respect, and if I as an editor am to do my job, it is vital that there be an exchange of respect.

First Contact

In most cases, the first time you interact with an editor will be via a letter, be it print or electronic. That makes it that much more important to make the right impression. With that in mind, let's take a look at the proper elements of a formal letter and see how they need to be adapted for the electronic medium:

Date – Here is our first difference; in written letters, the date comes first at the top of the page, and that must be added. With email, the date is part of an automatic timestamp, so this is a no brainer... you couldn't get it wrong if you tried... well... unless you happen to be submitting before a submission period has opened or after it has closed, but that is a topic for yet another article, isn't it? Anyway...

Address – well, that one is likewise simple enough, whether print or electronic, mail must include information on where it is to be delivered. If this information is not correct, your communication will not reach the individual it is intended for. With that in mind, always confirm you have the address correct. With print mail, sometimes a simple error in the address will not matter as the post office goes to some extreme effort to make sure mail gets where it is intended to go, practicing some amount of detective work when an address is clearly incorrect or in part illegible, or returning the mail to the sender if delivery is not possible. With electronic mail, errors are of much more concern. There are three possible outcomes:

- You will get an error message that says your mail cannot be sent.

- You will get a Mailer Daemon message saying your mail cannot be delivered.

- Your mail will be delivered, but to an individual other than the one it was intended for. If you are very lucky, they will be kind enough to email you to inform you of your mistake; if you are just a little lucky, all they will do is delete it, but you will never know it has not gone where it is supposed to; if the luck gods completely frown upon you, this unknown individual will use your content for their own gain.

So… be sure to confirm the address to ensure it is both typed correctly and the proper address to send your material to.

Subject – Unlike a personal or informal letter, business letters sometimes contain a subject line, making them much like emails today. In the case of submissions, it would likely be something like the following:

- RE: Story Submission – <Insert Title>, or

- RE: Story Proposal – <Insert Title>, or

- RE: Query – Story Submission – <Insert Title>

You get the idea. Again, this is yet another parallel between print and electronic mail. It is also one of those areas where professionalism often breaks down. When you are just connecting with friends or family, the subject line and its formatting doesn't really matter. In fact, there are times when many of us haven't even bothered to include one. Not a big deal, right?

Mostly, unless we are talking about business.

When communicating by email, always... *always* include a subject line. Make sure it is professional, clear, and spelled correctly. Do not get clever. Do not be sloppy. Do not be informal. Depending on the content of your communication, something similar to the above examples would be appropriate, unless, of course, the venue you are mailing to has provided specific guidelines regarding what the subject line should be. Always check to confirm, as this is a common practice among the major magazines and publishers that accept online submissions. Ultimately, your subject line should be relevant, brief, and pro-fessional when dealing with business matters. (In case I have somehow been unclear in this, that includes all initial communi-cations between prospective authors and any publishers, agents, or editors you may contact regarding your work; the only time you should be informal is if the professional you are contacting has initiated and/or encouraged that tone themselves.)

Greeting – It is important to acknowledge who you are email-ing. It shows you have manners, and it also confirms the email went where it was intended to go. In some cases, you will know who that is by name, sometimes you will not. Here are some ways to deal with the matter:

- **To Whom It May Concern** – This is perhaps a bit dated but acceptable to use when you do not have the name of the individual that will be receiving your submission.

- **Dear Sir or Madam** – again, this may be considered dated, but a reasonable greeting for situations where you don't have a specific name, or for situations where you have a name but the gender of the individual is not readily identifiable.

- **Dear Mr. or Ms. <Insert Last Name>** – In an initial contact where you have a person's name, and that name is gender-specific, it is best to opt for a more formal approach unless and until that individual indicates otherwise. In the case of women's names, always preface with the suffix Ms., unless you know their marital status. You want to be formal initially because you want to establish your professionalism and because it is a sign of respect.

- **Dear <Insert First Name>** – This form of address is recommended in only three instances: when you have a previous relationship with the individual; when the individual makes it clear you may be familiar by closing an email with their first name only; when the individual specifically requests that you use their first name. Again, this comes down to professionalism and respect.

- **Name Only** – Some feel the use of "Dear" as a greeting is dated and somewhat uncomfortably personal, resulting in its omission in many communications. Each person will have their own feeling on the matter, but apart from using the word "Dear," the two previous bullet points should come into play in this regard.

- **Omitting the Greeting** – as I mentioned earlier, the internet fosters a sense of informality. Thus, the trend has developed of omitting a greeting altogether, with the assumption that email addresses are so specific to an individual that a greeting is not needed. It is assumed that the mail is clearly for that individual. That is your call, but keep in mind that your level of professionalism will sometimes be the deciding factor in the outcome of a query. In those instances, the recipient's view on the matter will be the deciding factor, not your own. My advice is to always err on the side of being more formal; it is much less likely to reflect poorly upon you as a professional. This, of course, applies to initial communications only, as you should be able to use your own judgment after that point to determine what is appropriate based on the other individual's responses.

Content – in publishing—as with most businesses—people generally have more work than they do time. With that in mind, the body of your email should be brief, clear, and professional. Before you email a query or a submission, always be sure to check the publisher, agent, or editor's website for any specific guidelines that might apply to your situation. They will often list exactly what they want in a cover letter (if they want one at all), what additional information they might need, and how they would like to receive it. And for goodness sake, make sure you spelled everything correctly and used good grammar! They aren't going to have much confidence in your submission if you can't show them you can write a basic letter properly.

To give you an idea of what they look for:

- **Information on your story (or proposed story):** title, word count or anticipated word count, genre, and if it is part of a planned series.

- **Information on you:** your name, contact information, the highlights of any pertinent publishing history, and any major awards you may have received.

- **Proposals/Synopses:** Some publishers don't want to receive a full manuscript. They ask for the first three chapters, or sometimes just a proposal and a marketing plan (that's a whole other article's worth of information, so don't even ask… yet). When a proposal is requested, they want basically a book report on exactly what happens, not every single detail—because, you know, that would be, like, sending them the whole book—but the key events. This is not the time to be coy and mysterious; they want to know what makes your book interesting and unique, they do not want hints and implications. Check the internet and you will find plenty of resources telling you how to write an effective proposal.

Conclusion – This is your choice, but I always like to end on a gracious note. Thank them for giving them your attention before you sign off.

Closing – Yet again, another convention that may seem out-dated, but traditionally all letters included a polite sign-off before the name of the person writing the letter. This is still a good practice. Some of the more common and applicable ones are: Sincerely, Best regards, and Thank you. Don't get fancy, don't be quirky. It is more likely to reflect poorly on you than anything else. The cover letter should inform, not distract.

Signature – Or, in the case of the internet, eSignature. This should be your full name, first and last. There are several reasons for this. First off, it is both polite and professional; second, in all likelihood, the person receiving this does not know you personally; and lastly, particularly with submissions, there is a very good chance that your cover letter may become disassociated with your actual manuscript. All of that makes it important that someone looking at one or the other can identify that they are related, and you can't bank on your title being unique and distinctive.

A second note on this, you should use your legal name on a cover letter, rather than a pen name, as that is what the publisher will use for contracts or checks, should you be fortunate enough to reach that stage. If you write under a pen name, however, mention that in your cover letter. (If nothing else, it will help them verify which letter goes with which manuscript when things get invariably jumbled.)

> Example: Submission Letter
> To: editor@publisher.com
> RE: Submission – Yesterday's Dreams
>
> Dear Sir or Madam,
> Attached, please find my novel, Yesterday's Dreams, an urban fantasy based on Irish Mythology. The manuscript is approximately 119,000 words long.
> While this is my first novel, my short stories have appeared in Tales of the Talisman Magazine and the award-winning Defending the Future anthology series. I am also the senior editor of the award-winning Bad-Ass

Faeries anthology series. To find out more about my work, please visit www.sidhenadaire.com.

Thank you in advance for your time and consideration; I look forward to hearing back from you.

Best Regards,

Danielle McPhail (writing as Danielle Ackley-McPhail)

Example: Query Letter
To: agent@getmebucks.com
RE: Query – Yesterday's Dreams

Dear Sir,

My name is Danielle Ackley-McPhail, and I am looking for representation for my novel, Yesterday's Dreams, an urban fantasy based on Irish Mythology. This is the first in a proposed three-book series.

In the novel, Kara O'Keefe, a first-generation Irish-American with elven blood, must pawn her cherished heirloom violin to save her family from eviction. To that end, she takes it to the pawnshop, Yesterday's Dreams, where the pawnbroker, Maggie McCormick, is actually one of the Celtic Sidhe sworn to protect the O'Keefe clan. This chain of events brings Kara and her magical potential to the attention of Olcas, an ancient and evil foe of the Sidhe. Unwittingly caught between the two forces, Kara struggles with the changing boundaries of her world while fighting to remain free.

The novel is complete, at approximately 119,000 words. May I send it to you for your consideration?

Thank you and best regards,

Danielle Ackley-McPhail
www.sidhenadaire.com

Following Up

It is very tempting, particularly with the ease of internet communications, to pester someone you have sent your work to for consideration. Resist. Hard. Editors are overworked, short on time, and often short on patience. If you make a nuisance of yourself, there is a good chance it will have the opposite of the desired effect. Most publishers' websites give you an idea of the response time you can expect. Look for that, mark it on your calendar, create a reminder in Outlook or whatever calendar program you have on your computer, and whatever you do, do not email the editor about your submission until after that date. It is okay to follow up, but not to pester.

When you send a submission directly to an individual, they will send you an acknowledgment email. Respond to that with your thanks, and then forget about the whole thing for a while until sufficient time has passed to make a follow-up reasonable.

Example: Follow-Up Letter

> To: editor@hurryupandwaitpub.com
> RE: Submission – Yesterday's Dreams
>
> July 6, 2011
>
> Dear Editor,
>
> I submitted the above novel to you for consideration on January 6, 2011. It has been six months, and per your website, I am following up to ask if you have had a chance to review the manuscript.
>
> I await your decision.
>
> My best,
>
> Danielle Ackley-McPhail

Dealing With Rejection

I guarantee you that you will receive a rejection in response to a query or submission at some point. In fact, there is an excellent chance you will receive many; more, in fact, than you will receive acceptances or contracts, if you are like most of us. (Let's face it, if it were otherwise, you wouldn't be reading this book!) It is very important for your potential career that you never, *ever* respond to a rejection letter, unless it is to thank them for their time and the opportunity to submit.

- Do not rail at them for not seeing the brilliance of your work.

- Do not threaten them.

- Do not plead or pester.

- Do not demand to know why.

All of the above will serve but one purpose: to lock you into the publisher/agent/editor's memory as, at best, a difficult person to work with and not worth the hassle; at worst, a crackpot worthy of a restraining order. I cannot tell you how many stories I have heard about hopeful authors that have damaged their chances by such unprofessional behavior.

However, if you do choose to respond to the rejection politely and professionally, you will likely stand out in the editor's memory, which may serve you well in the future, should you submit other stories to the same venue.

Example: Rejection Acknowledgement Letter

To: thatdamnededitor@publisher.com
RE: RE: Your Submission

Dear Editor,

Thank you for informing me of your decision. I am sorry the story did not meet your needs, but I appreciate your feedback and look forward to future opportunities to submit.

My best,

Danielle Ackley-McPhail

Summing Up

There is a lot of competition in the publishing industry. A lot of those people don't know what they are doing. Not saying that to be mean. It's just a fact. Heck, there have certainly been times when I've been out of my element, so I definitely know of which I speak, as they say. Your job, should you choose to acknowledge it, is to distinguish yourself from those who haven't got a clue. Clearly, you have already displayed initiative in that regard.

Think of it this way: letters—even by email—are a time-delayed conversation. You aren't there to clarify. You aren't there to respond to questions. That means you have to be clear the first time. And wait... it gets better...

When dealing with editors, it's more like speed-dating... with someone whose calendar is already booked. That means you have to do all the above in sixty seconds or less. You want to make a good impression, you want to hook their interest, you want to be asked out on a date, in a manner of speaking. That means you get to be on your best behavior, or you find some other goal to pursue.

So... *be* polite... *be* professional... and eventually, there's a better chance you will *be* an author.

The Importance of Respect

This should seem obvious. Professionals doing business show respect. This is from both sides of the table. So many times, I see evidence of disrespect. Sometimes overt, sometimes subtle and unrealized.

If you wish to be taken seriously as an author or publishing professional, always remain respectful.

Guidelines Exist for a Reason

One of the biggest ways I feel disrespected as a professional is when I receive an unprofessional manuscript. This can take many forms, from non-standard formatting to missing information. Take the time to check a publisher's website for submission guidelines. How they want things sent, which information they want included, and how they would like it to appear on the page. There are reasons for all of these. You may not know or understand, but respect that they serve a purpose.

What? You say there were no guidelines? Fair enough, but standard guidelines do exist. Look for them. It shows that you care enough to be professional.

Something I see quite often, which is my personal pet peeve, is when an author sends in a manuscript without the basic information at the top of the page. Maybe they have left off their address, maybe they have left off their name, maybe all of that. There have been times when they have even left off the title of the work. There are several problems with this. First, even if you have provided the missing information in your communication, the person receiving the file may not have access to the original file. What does that mean for you? Unless they are extremely forgiving, it means you have blown your chance. Most publishing professionals don't have the time or inclination to track down missing information, and if they don't know who to send a contract to or where to send it, you're never getting to the stage where they don't know where to send the check.

For me, every manuscript I send out has the basic information, even when I am sending it to someone I know. Heck, even manuscripts I am writing for *myself* include the basic information. Not only is it a matter of professionalism and not forming bad habits, but who is to say the story won't be sent to someone else at a future date? Including legal name, address, email, story title, and penname on your manuscripts shows you respect the person receiving it and do not want to make their life more difficult by forcing them to request or track down the missing information… or too easy, should they simply decide to reject the piece without reading it.

What You Say and How You Say It

Communication is an important part of respect. Both in your choice of words and the effort you take to use them. Even more so is knowing when not to say a thing. Of highest importance, however, is tone. As an author, editor, and publisher, I know from experience how difficult it can be to show restraint and how important it is.

As authors, you should always be aware of your words and the impact they have. Whether you are sending in a query or responding to feedback, your comments reflect on you more than they reflect on the other person in the conversation.

Queries – be confident, but not arrogant. Always thank the person you are submitting to for their time and express that you are open to feedback. These tell the person receiving the query that you are professional.

Feedback – If the feedback is private, such as editorial, be respectful. Do not challenge, even if you do not agree. This does not mean you are obligated to accept the feedback, but discuss the elements in question and explain your disagreement. This is a matter where tone is of utmost importance. Editors invest hours of time and effort to help authors polish their work. You may not agree with everything said but find a way to address the issues pointed out to you, rather than question their need, to begin with. Most editors are open to discussion and will not push a point unless it is major. You always have the option to withdraw, but it is not wise to be arrogant or combative if you wish to work in the industry. At the least, you will have blacklisted yourself with that editor or publishing house; at the worst, you will have blacklisted yourself with anyone that editor knows, should they share their experience.

If the feedback is public, such as a negative review or blog, be silent. You can say little to nothing in response to such things that will not reflect more poorly on yourself as a public figure than the original feedback by itself. Responding to such things can easily escalate and become even more visible than if you left it alone.

Public forums – Whether online or in person, you may have occasion to interact with your fan base or potential fan base. Never forget that you are a public figure, a celebrity to those who aspire to what you have achieved. Fans and potential fans deserve respect from you just as much as editors and publishing professionals do. They are the ones to lift you to whatever level of success you achieve. Connect with your fans, and you have loyalty beyond imagine; disrespect them, and they will let the world know.

Respect Yourself

When you are a public figure of any kind, there is no such thing as private. What you say or do in your downtime has the potential to affect your public persona. Does this mean your life is no longer your own? Not really. But it is possible that your private life will become a matter for public discussion. Whether an indiscretion or a harsh altercation, a political view or a crazy-ass stunt. Public opinion can be harsh, even about things that are none of their business… what am I saying, especially about things that are none of their business. Not only can this impact you with your fans, but it can also impact you with publishers who may not wish to be associated with some aspect of your past. Such things make them question what you might potentially do or say in the future.

Give 'Em What They Want!
Why Formatting Is Important

(Originally published in The Writer's Toolbox, Allegory Magazine)

Telling a great story is not enough.

Having the best grammar is not enough.

Hitting the perfect market trend is not enough.

Nothing is enough if the editor in question is not willing to read your manuscript.

The Truth about Submissions

Psst! I have a secret for you… well, not really a secret, unless you are *really* new at this, but anyway… here it goes:

Editors *look* for reasons NOT to read your manuscript.

(ooh… I can just hear a lot of minions going, "Wha?!")

Sorry, it's true; I'm not making it up.

See, the reality is thousands and thousands of people want to be authors. Even though only a small portion of those following the dream ever reach the stage of actually submitting something, that still means that editors of all sorts have piles and piles of things they need to go through. And frankly, most of it is dreck. Editors just don't have the time or inclination to put in extra effort puzzling through a manuscript that only might be acceptable and then cleaning it up afterward. Think about it. The longer the production process takes, the longer money bleeds out instead of — with hope — flooding in.

Besides, they want to know you can follow directions, and there are very few publishers out there — book or short fiction — that do not have submission guidelines available somewhere.

Look for them. And if you don't find them, ask! You want to stand out because of the quality of your writing, not because your manuscript is an annoyance filled with stylistic errors. The best thing you can do is show that you will make extra effort to meet their requirements.

Of course, even if you don't have the publisher's submission guidelines, there are plenty of things that are standard. Let's take a look.

The Basics

Contact information. No matter who you are sending your work to or how many times you have sent them work before, you always—let me repeat that—ALWAYS include your full contact information in the upper left hand of the page. (The editor could be your brother, and you should still follow this rule, if nothing else but because it is common courtesy and shows you respect the relationship between hopeful author and potential publisher.) For me, I make sure to do this even when I am writing something I intend to publish myself. Why? Because one, who is to say I won't at some point send that story to someone else for consideration; and two, it is all too possible I could do it the wrong way when it *does* matter if I let bad habits form by not being consistent in how I set up my files.

If you aren't sure what is considered full contact information, here it goes: legal name, mailing address, email address, and optionally, phone number. I can't tell you how many times I have received manuscripts without this information. Usually from an author I've worked with before, but not always. See, we fall into a trap of informality thanks to the internet. With so many manuscripts being submitted electronically, we don't always consider that the email might become disassociated from the manuscript file, thus leaving the publisher no way to contact the author. Bad enough when what is forthcoming is a rejection. An absolute tragedy when they want to send you an acceptance. Face it... they have to know where to send the contract... or the check!

Identifiers. To simplify, I'm grouping several things under this heading, so bear with me.

Title – you would be amazed how many people neglect to put titles on their manuscripts (coincidentally enough, more than a few of them are the ones who forgot contact information as well).

Name – your pen name or your legal name, whichever one you write under. Editors like to know whose work they are reading and what should appear on a published work (should you be fortunate enough to make a sale.) The problem is that if the contact information is missing *and* there is no title or author name, the publisher has absolutely no way of cross-referencing to try and determine what story goes with which submission email (assuming they will even try).

Page Numbers – now you might be thinking, "But manuscripts are electronic. How can the pages get out of order?" Well, first, you can't assume that whoever receives the manuscript won't prefer to review a hardcopy. Second, even if they are reviewing something electronically, it is easier for them to make notes or track back if there are page numbers to reference.

Running Headers – This is the space at the top of the page (starting with page 2) where you put the story/book title, the page number, and your legal last name. This is so no pages go missing, and the editor knows what they are reading.

Author Bio – Optional, but a good thing to include, particularly if you have a few sales under your belt, but only if they are professional sales of note, not a piece of flash fiction you sold to a fanzine. What this tells the editor is that you are already established.

Besides the more practical reasons for not omitting any of the above information, consider that it is just plain sloppy and unprofessional. This isn't a matter of wanting to impress the editor. It is showing them that you are not an amateur without a clue. Professionalism will do much to smooth over any other short fallings you have in the editor's eye.

Format

Some things are just industry standard. If you are serious about becoming an author, you should learn what those are. If you are submitting somewhere that for one reason or another does not have submission guidelines, always assume they want the following formatting:

Font – Courier or Times New Roman, 12 point. These fonts are clear and easy to read, and 12 point is generally a comfortable size for most people.

Spacing (Print) – paragraphs should be first-line indented and double-spaced, with no line break between paragraphs. Some programs have an automatic indent feature. These can cause problems in the typesetting process, so, personally, I feel it is better to use a tab for your first line indent. Not sure if any publishers or editors (besides myself) express a preference on that. In either case, whichever you chose, use it consistently.
It also used to be the convention to double space after a period. This hails from the days when manuscripts had to be manually typeset. It is no longer necessary in the age of computers and digital typesetting, though many still do so simply because it was how they were originally taught.

Spacing (Online) – paragraphs should be flush left (no indent) and single-spaced, with a line break between paragraphs.

Section Breaks – when a scene changes, it is very important the transition is clearly marked. Some authors simply use a line space between the scenes. Others use either a number sign (#) or three asterisks (***), making it clear the break is intentional. It is better to use an actual character; otherwise, a scene break might not be evident if a scene break happens across a page break.

The End – Generally a good idea to close your manuscript with these words, so it is clear to the person reviewing it that nothing is missing.

Special characters/formatting – originally, when manuscripts were all submitted in hardcopy, it was not possible to implement certain formatting or characters on a typewriter. Because of this, certain conventions were developed to represent the formatting desired. As technology progressed, this changed, thanks to the advent of electronic typewriters and word processors, which had features for special formatting. This formatting issue was rendered altogether moot once computers were on the scene. However, even once we could represent format true to form, manuscripts still had to be physically typeset to create the plates used on a printing press as recently as the mid to late 20th century, and publishers held to the traditional conventions because special formatting was often easy to miss, causing errors in the typeset manuscript. Even now that most books are digitally typeset, some publishers still require these methods to mark the format. Here they are, for your writerly edification:

Bold – represented by asterisks bracketing the text to be set in bold.

Italic – represented by underlining text to be set in italics.

Underline – I am afraid I could not find a reference to how this was represented originally (before the age of computers), particularly given that underlining was used to indicate italics. I can only presume that is because it was and/or is exceedingly rare for underlined text to appear in books. (That, or I'm just not hitting the right search phrase that would give me the information I'm looking for.)

Emdash – represented as two hyphens. In this time of computers, most programs automatically convert the double hyphen to an emdash. Depending on the publisher's preferred style, they will have a space before and after the emdash " — " or " — " in the finished book.

Ellipsis – depending on the publisher's preferred style, these can be represented in multiple ways:

- Three periods in a row with no spaces before, after, or in between. "… "
- Three periods in a row with a space before and after. " … "

- Three periods with one character space between each period and a space before and after. " . . . "

Quotation marks and Apostrophes – many word processing programs have a feature for smart quotes or straight quotes. (For those who don't know what I mean by smart quotes, those are the curly ones.) I have never encountered a publisher who has expressed a preference either way, but I can tell you that as an editor and a typesetter, one of my biggest pet peeves is straight quotes. And let me tell you why… Even though it is possible for me to do a simple "Find and Replace" to convert straight quotes into smart quotes, it causes several formatting problems. First off, quotation marks sometimes end up facing the wrong direction when they follow punctuation that is not a period, requiring that I go in and manually turn them around. Second, in the case of apostrophes — as opposed to single quotes — when those occur at the beginning of a word, as in the case of dialect ('em, 'twere, 'twas, etc.), the program does not recognize the convention and flips it around as if it was intended as a single quote, again requiring the typesetter to go through the entire manuscript manually correcting. These aren't so difficult to correct, but they are definitely easy to miss, thus making them a headache of the highest order when they introduce errors into an already edited manuscript.

Now, as I mentioned, even though virtually every word processing or layout program has toolbars, options, or auto-formatting features that facilitate all of the above, some publishers still request that these conventions be employed when formatting your manuscript. This is one reason why it is very important to find those submission guidelines or find out which style guide the publisher employs because that will tell you how to set things up.

Don't lose heart if you can't find this information or, for some bizarre reason, can't find someone to tell you. Most editors are more forgiving when it comes to things like italics and all that as long as you are consistent in your usage. So… if you pick a style (even if it's not the one preferred) and stick with it, you will lose fewer points than if you switch back and forth.

Matters of Style

No matter what I type here, there will be plenty of examples of publishers that do things differently from what I've covered. Sometimes that is just a product of their experience or how they were taught. Sometimes it has to do with style guides. You may or may not have heard of these; the most familiar are the *AP Style Guide, the Chicago Manual of Style,* and *Strunk and Whites*. Many of these have their roots in print journalism and are meant to unify style for consistency. Basically, they are journalists' grammar and style bibles. But their use is no longer limited to newspapers or magazines. Not only do they guide a writer in matters of style, but they also cover grammar issues that are often confused or lost in depths of time-fogged memory.

Keep it Simple!

Before the time of electronic submissions, not listening to this advice was one of the biggest mistakes beginners made. You would laugh your butts off if you had heard some of the stories I have about how some hopeful authors have submitted their manuscripts. We are talking complete bells and whistles here of the type you would expect from the ad campaign of a major corporation. Everything from fancy, scented paper to puzzle-box packaging, all of it intended to catch the eye and stand out like a psychedelic dream. Unfortunately, all that does is relegate your manuscript to the list of over-drinks stories editors tell.

Things might have changed now that most submissions are handled electronically, but it is still important for you to know that a story should be noticed for the quality of the writing, not the inventiveness or style of its presentation. If you are submitting by conventional mail, use plain white or cream bond paper and observe the formatting guidelines I reviewed above; if you are submitting electronically, don't use fancy type or try to set your manuscript as if it is a finished book; don't use colored text or insert photographs (unless they are a key point of what you are submitting, such as an academic text or how-to); and don't add any other bells and whistles you might be considering. Let me be clear: The manuscript should stand on its own merit. If the writing isn't any good, none of the flash is going to make a difference. What it *will* do is distract the editor from your work and likely cause them to reject it outright as being unprofessional.

Summing Up

You might think this article was about the technical aspects of formatting, but you would only be partially correct. What this article is truly about is respect. If you want to succeed at this dedicated hobby you've chosen to pursue (believe me, you don't want to think of it as a career… it only leads to masses of frustration), then you need to get your head in the correct mindset. You are not alone in your desire. Countless individuals want to be authors. There are considerably fewer individuals who are in a position to make that possible. Editors have to look through hundreds, even thousands of manuscripts every year. I don't think I have to tell you that they can't accept them all. You know what that means? It is your job to make *their* job as easy for them as possible. You can do that in two ways:

- Ignore what I've shared with you here and start deciding which room you are going to wallpaper with rejections first, or

- Do everything you can to make your manuscript clean and formatted to the publisher's preference so that technical issues don't distract the editor from your work's creative aspects.

Now I'm not saying if you follow all the submission guidelines your work is guaranteed to be accepted, but I am saying you stand a heck of a better chance of getting noticed.

Convention(al) Opportunities

One of the most valuable lessons a beginning author can learn about conventions is that they are as much about seeing as about being seen. Yes, you want to get yourself and your books in the public eye. Yes, you want to distinguish yourself and get started making that pen name a household name (oh... come on... just try and tell me that's not what we're all after...) But what opportunities are you overlooking in your efforts to be noticed?

Don't let yourself be blinded by your own "celebrity." Pay attention... let your creativity stew on the occasional thought not centered on your fiction. There are many opportunities out there for cross-promotional efforts if you have the vision to recognize them. You never know when you might have an untapped resource that dovetails with someone else's need.

I've had several different instances of this crop up recently that I want to share with you as examples of the potential in all things.

You've no doubt noticed that I go on about networking. What you might not have picked up on is that networking goes both ways. At a recent convention local to me, Philcon, I had this brought home to me. First, I connected with an editor who had purchased a magazine where I had a submission under consideration. Unfortunately, my story was lost in the shuffle of transition between the old guard and the new. By introducing myself to the editor in question, I made a connection that bagged me two sales in one weekend. The editor did not want me to fear I was lost in the cracks and so instructed me to send him my story directly. I was fortunate that he enjoyed it and another story I sent along with it very much, and he took both of them.

The next day at the same convention, I was approached by one of the musical guests, Jonah Knight, purveyor of modern paranormal folk. He had seen me around the conventions and noted my visibility and success in the dealer's room, as well as having been on a rather successful panel with me earlier that day and was interested in discussing the possibility of my carrying some of his CDs at events. I was cautious about this because when you are a personality rather than just a vendor, selling others' works can be difficult if you are not directly associated with the project. That brought Jonah to his second point... he was interested in compiling a soundtrack based on my novels. We pooled our resources: connections to assemble a group of musicians and artists to participate in the project, as well as enlisting the aid of various conventions in spreading the word and arranging promotional parties.

Now, not only did I get some fantastic promotions out of the arrangement, but so did everyone involved, from the conventions down to the individual performers, the publishers, and anyone else participating. And all of it started with a handful of connections made at various events over the years.

Conventions are not just places to connect with fans. They are your best opportunity to network with other professionals. Connect, support, be open. Helping others can often prove to be the best way to help yourself and your career, not because you want to get ahead, but because the friendships you make along the way expand potential in so many unexpected ways.

Now, I know not all of you have the opportunity, desire, or resources to go from convention to convention throughout the year. If you can, great; if not, don't feel like you are doomed to be left on the outside. A lot of what I have written here can also be applied to online groups and professional organizations with an online presence.

However you reach out and try to connect, remember this: don't plot, don't scheme, don't weigh everyone and everything for prospective value to you, but never shrink away from putting yourself in the path of opportunity. It can be both fun and profitable. And oy! The people you'll meet along the way!

Building Credibility

Who do you think you are?

Yeah... confrontational, maybe, but we've been over this before. There are a LOT of would-be authors out there. That means a lot of people brandishing their first-ever book expecting the world to take notice. I'm sorry, but one book does not instantly make you a success. Not saying that to belittle anyone or scoff at anyone's accomplishments (And finishing a book is a major accomplishment). Not even saying it to discourage anyone, just trying to prepare the beginners out there for the harsh reality that blindsided me.

See, I work in publishing. That means you would expect I might have had a bit more insight than everyone else going into this wacked-out industry cold. Nope... I was a total noob.

I won't go into all the ugly details, at least not in this article. But one cold, glaring point in all of my ignoble beginning actually is relevant to what I'm writing about. As mentioned, I work in publishing, and at the time my first novel came out, I was employed by one of the "Big" publishing houses. The reason this is relevant? My first book (and every other book after that one) was not with a "Big" publisher. I am very solidly a small-press author — or independent, as they now say to put a prettier face on it. Anyway, as I was going through the initial production process, needless to say, I was very excited and would share the details with my co-workers, or those that would listen, anyway.

No big deal, right?

One day my boss's boss pulled me aside to tell me he didn't want me to talk about my book. He cited it as a conflict of interest. He really meant he thought I had self-published the book and considered it an embarrassment that reflected badly on our parent company.

(Very ironic, that, considering... but I those tales aren't mine to tell.)

At that moment, I realized that I had learned about credibility and the fact that in many eyes, I didn't have any yet. I had one book with a publisher most people had never heard of before, so yeah, I got a lot of "Who do you think you are?" Here's my point: No one knew my name. Having it printed nice and big on a couple of hundred copies of my book did not instantaneously make it common knowledge (heck, having it on several thousand hasn't either... just to put it in perspective.)

Now, if your only goal is to have your name on the front cover of a published book, credibility isn't a big deal. However, if your goal is to share your writing with the world, in as many variations as your fertile mind can come up with, it's going to take a lot of work building that credibility.

How? Well... funny, you should ask...

Making A Name

One mistake that many authors — beginning or otherwise — make is promoting books.

No, you didn't read that wrong. See, by promoting *books*, the focus is directed away from the author. What you want to do is promote yourself foremost and individual titles secondary. It's called branding.

(No, it doesn't involve superheated iron.)

Visibility – Have you ever seen playbills and promotional posters plastered over a city? I encountered this a lot in New York, boarded-up buildings or construction site fences completely covered by posters, sometimes all the same one. Now, I'm not telling you that is what you should do... precisely, but it is close. I'm actually talking about doing this virtually. Go on the internet and look for interview opportunities or author databases. Make sure you are posted on every one you can find. Use that social media for something more than bitching about the weather or groaning over your relationship drama. Create a page or user id that is just for author-related posts, and every time you have some news, share it with the world. If you can increase awareness of yourself as a good author, attention to your books (existing and upcoming) will follow. That doesn't mean make everything about you alone, but when you promote something book-related, it should be (for example) "Danielle Ackley-McPhail's new book, *Eternal Wanderings*," not "*Eternal Wanderings*, by Danielle Ackley-McPhail." I'm not talking literally. This isn't about form. The book should be as important as the next great thing from *you*. If they can remember your name, they can find everything else on their own, so whatever opportunity you have to promote, always filter it through your Brand (which is you).

Have a website where you are the focus, and the books are mentioned in relation to you. Have a printable reading list so people can more easily find your work. Do author events at conventions, schools, libraries, and bookstores.

Whether virtually or in the real world, you want the readers to associate the book title with a name and the name with a face so that you become an icon, a presence, instead of just type on a front cover.

Productivity – In most cases, it isn't enough to write one book and expect to get somewhere. It's been known to happen, but it is rare. Most authors have to build up their publishing credits. It's sad, but a lot of people are cynical. Get published once and they think it could be a fluke, you could be a one-hit-wonder, or worse, you signed with a publisher who doesn't know good fiction. That doesn't mean they are right, but it does mean you have to prove them wrong. Novels take a very long time to write and publish, but if you are one of the fortunate individuals who can write both long and short fiction, you have a branding goldmine. The more credits you have to your name, the more people will take notice of you, even if they've never read your work before. What you're showing is that your writing is good enough that someone bought it. Each sale adds to your credibility because it shows that you can stick with it and people are interested in what you write. It shows dedication and reinforces the quality of your work in their minds.

Consistency – speaking of quality of work, make it the best you can produce, grammatically, literally, accurately. Don't depend on the publisher to clean things up. There is, in theory, an editor assigned to your book who is supposed to help with that, but you can't depend on their knowledge and thoroughness. Sadly, I have learned that from experience. Produce high-quality fiction – over and over again – and then sell it to reputable, established publishers, and you will build the recognition you are looking for.

Association – There are a couple of ways this applies. First off: the publishers, since I've already mentioned them. It's not enough to get published by just anyone. You need a venue known in the industry for producing your chosen genre with quality production values, good writing, and good business practices. Face it, having a story printed in a magazine that is photocopied pages folded and stapled in the middle is not the way to come across as professional.

Speaking of professional... professional organizations. Not only are these great opportunities for networking, mentoring, and inside knowledge about the market, but they also tell the world you are serious about being a writer and elevate your visibility through the company you keep and the opportunities the organization offers.

Summing Up

Want a more positive approach? Here's a better question for you... who do you want to *be*?

(Sorry, Faith Hunter and Steven King are already taken).

If you want to be a successful author (whatever success means to you), it takes effort and the ability to put yourself out there. Engage your audience directly and indirectly. Most people like to feel touched by celebrity, and authors fall into that category, no matter the level of your success. Sell them on yourself as a brand and the books will move; sell a book with your name on it, and you have to hope the reader remembers who wrote it—and that they enjoyed it—by the next time one of your books comes out.

A Genre Primer

Are you one of those that are confused by the term genre? In truth, all fiction and media can be broken down into one genre or another; it has to… that's how the bookstore knows what section to put each book in…

(Okay… maybe that wasn't the best example…)

Mostly when people classify something as "genre fiction," they are generally talking about science fiction, fantasy, horror, mystery, or romance, and if they are old enough to know about them, they'll throw pulp or western into the pile as well. Basically, genre fiction has, to most people, come to mean anything besides mainstream (drama) fiction. Another term for this is speculative fiction.

Still confused? Well… let's look at what some of these genres are:

Fantasy – this can primarily be described as any fiction that does not adhere to reality as we experience it, where magic or supernatural creatures are a significant part of the plot, theme, and setting, and things you would consider impossible are possible. The setting is generally a world other than our own, either drawn from mythology or the writer's imagination. Well-known authors in the genre are Patricia Briggs, Mercedes Lackey, Faith Hunter, J.R.R. Tolkien, and C.S. Lewis.

Science Fiction – broken down into near future, far-future, and epic, these stories often involve projections of technology, either existing or of the author's creation, as a primary part of the plot, theme, and setting. There are often themes of military conflict (where the military aspect is secondary), colonization, and exploration. Well-known authors in the genre are Isaac Asimov, Harlan Ellison, Robert Heinlein, and Arthur C. Clark.

Horror – distinguished by the macabre or frightening, this genre is often blended with elements from fantasy or science fiction, but those elements are secondary to the primary objective of scaring the shit out of the reader. Monsters, demons, psychopaths with chainsaws… that's what we're talking about here. Expect graphic violence, depravity, and extremely dark plots, themes, and settings. Well-known authors in the genre are Stephen King, Joe Hill, Jonathan Maberry, and Bram Stoker.

Romance – Happy endings, simple, sweet romances, and lately, a bit of spice, but not too much, or this rolls over into erotica. The happy endings are the key to this genre, though… without them, it's called drama. Those who read romance know that the damsel (or dude) gets the hero by the last page. There is usually inner turmoil, perhaps nefarious deeds by a rival or other calamity, but Romeo comes to the rescue, and all conflict is resolved by the time the two of them hook up at the end. Well-known authors in the genre are Danielle Steel, Nora Roberts, and Suzanne Brockmann.

Western – historic fiction that features cowboys, robbers, steam locomotives, Indians, and some dealing with gold, for the most part. Pulp adventure for those that were loathed to put up their popguns. There may or may not be a romantic interest, but it's all about the white hat against the black, whether it's set in a bygone era or more urban in nature. Well-known authors in the genre are Louis L'Amour, Zane Grey, Willa Cather, and Larry McMurtry.

Mystery – Your basic *whodunit?* where the reader is presented with… well… a mystery, suspects, and clues throughout, and all comes clear at the end (one hopes). Sometimes the mysteries are themed, such as those involving cooking or pets, and those are usually called cozy mysteries. Well-known authors in the genre are Sir Arthur Conan Doyle, Agatha Christie, and John Grisham.

Pulp/Noir – These adventure novels featured mostly gumshoe detectives and vigilante justice, but they really touched any genre. They all had the same gritty, daring-do, cheap paper, and stylized art covers. The genre is full of icons like Tarzan, The Spider, the Domino Lady, Kolchak, and Jack Hagee. Adventure, danger, guns and violence, mobsters and dames, and rogue avengers. The good guys always get beat up, but in the end, rarely get beat. Well-known authors in this genre are Ray Bradbury, Robert E. Howard, Alfred Bester, and Arthur Conan Doyle.

Subgenres

Dark fantasy – when elements of horror play a central part in the story, but not to the extreme that would classify it as horror. Well-known authors in the genre are Neil Gaiman, Karen Marie Moning, and Scott Nicholson.

Science fantasy – when there is a scientific element to the fantasy realm (or a fantasy element to the scientific world). Well-known authors in the genre are David Sherman, Larry Niven, and Piers Anthony.

Urban fantasy – Urban fantasy has the stipulation that the story, though using the same fantasy tropes, is at least in part is set in the real world, generally in a city or the suburbs of a city, rather than a country setting, though those are seen as well. Well-known authors in the genre are Charles DeLint, Holly Black, and J. K. Rowling.

Steampunk – I classify this as a subgenre because it is really, often, a blending of both fantasy and science fiction, though, in popularity, it is a force of its own. The setting is historic, most of the Victorian era. Basically, it is technology with the rules of science thrown out the window. A good example of the subgenre that everyone should be familiar with is the works of Jules Verne. It's all about the mods and gadgets. Stereotypically there are goggles, airships, detectives a la Sherlock Holmes, and steam... lots of steam. Well-known authors in the genre are Cherie Priest, Jeff VanderMeer, and Jules Verne.

Inspirational romance – The relationships are pg-13, and the story includes a religious theme or overtones. Well-known authors in the genre are Keira Knightley, Janette Oke, and Karen Kingsbury.

Historical romance – Also called regency romance as most of them are set in that era but can be in any time period though generally not current day. (Some authors do mingle now with then, but those books generally fall more under the venue of paranormal romance.) Well-known authors in the genre are Catherine Coulter, L.M. Montgomery, and Eloisa James.

Paranormal romance – At least one, if not more, of the romantic interests are a "monster," mythological creature, or ghost. The rest of the story can travel any route. Well-known authors in the genre are Sherrilyn Kenyon, Charlaine Harris, Patricia Briggs, and Jeri Smith-Ready.

Military science fiction – In this genre, the military conflict, structure, and mindset are predominant; otherwise, it is just science fiction with military elements. Well-known authors in the genre are David Weber, Jack Campbell, C. J. Cherryh, David Sherman, and John Ringo.

Thriller – I like to describe this as psychological horror, mostly about the depravity of madmen and psychopaths, and the hero saving themselves just in time. Edge-of-your-seat nail-biters, rather than behind-the-seat. Well-known authors in the genre are Lisa Gardner, Heather Graham, and James Patterson.

Erotica – Romance that is edgy and explicit. More about exploring sensuality, with "socially acceptable" boundaries pushed to the limit and beyond. Plot is generally a secondary concern. Well-known authors in the genre are Laurell K. Hamilton, Stephanie Burke, Alessia Brio, and Desiree Holt.

Media Tie-in/Shared Universe – Fiction based on popular movies, television shows, games, and occasionally comics or cartoons, or non-media-based shared world contributed to by multiple authors. There is an established universe and a "bible" that authors must adhere to when writing these types of books. Well-known authors in the genre are Keith R. A. DeCandido, Greg Cox, Will McDermott, and Alan Dean Foster.

I could keep going, you know, only I think you get the idea. But more to the point, do you understand why genre is important?

(Other than knowing where to put the book on the shelf...)

So that the reader has some idea of what is in store for them when they pick up a book. And also, to allow them to seek out other similar books to those they have enjoyed in the past... and as an excuse for fanboys and girls around the world to start up conventions so they can meet their favorite authors.

Okay... maybe not so much on that last one...

Stepping Back

Don't panic... this isn't a Dear John (or Jane) letter.

What I want to talk about now is becoming overwhelmed.

It is such an easy thing to happen to a writer or any other creative person. All of us experience it at one point or another. There are deadlines and promoting and new ideas every time you turn around... and that's just the writing stuff! We won't even talk about the family, home, and work also bidding for our times (yet.)

I know... you're nodding your head, looking a little mystified that I understand exactly what you're going through.

(Oh, come on, you know you are.)

Believe me, this dilemma is exponentially increased for those of us writers who work on the flip side of publishing, as well. Smacks of masochism, really; what, one low-paying, thankless job isn't enough?

Anyway, back to the program...

Remember to Breathe

Sounds simple, right? One of the most basic precepts of life, but have you ever been in that place where you are so overwhelmed you have to remind yourself to breathe? No? Just wait... it will happen. One of the dangers of having too many options (or obligations) is that you freeze up from time to time; you don't know what to do first, so you do nothing. The thing about nothing, though, is it fosters entropy. When you do nothing, it only exacerbates your problem.

Don't get me wrong, I'm not talking about the occasional blowing off steam or taking time for yourself or other non-writing concerns. I'm talking about the benumbed, shaking-your-head kind of nothing, you know, where your eyes glaze over, and you want to find a bed to hide under.

No? Well then, you're more fortunate than I.

Two things to do when you do reach this state:

- Take one step back and turn around. (No! Not literally!) Pick up something for fun and clear your thoughts a moment. Read a book, play a game with your family, watch a TV show. A short one! No Bingeing.

- Make a list of all the things you need to do and prioritize them. If there are deadlines, those obligations go to the top of the list, closest date first. Follow those with things that have been waiting the longest or those closest to being done. This should include all immediate concerns, whether they are writing-related or not. I'm not talking about stuff that takes five minutes, like taking out the garbage or brushing your teeth; this list is for time-consuming tasks. Not that the little stuff doesn't add up, but it is also generally stuff that can be sandwiched between other tasks.

Once you have your list, you have a better idea of tasks that need managing. Now, this list's purpose isn't to go from top to bottom—unless, of course, there is a rather urgent deadline. Mostly this list serves three purposes: to help you remember your goals and responsibilities, to put things into perspective, and to give you the satisfaction of having something to cross off as you accomplish it.

Now… take a deep breath.

Enforcing Order

The list is only the first step. Next, there are several different things you can do. If you are the type that works better with a schedule, make a schedule based on the prioritized list. If this isn't for you, though, you can set goals. Here is a list. Either borrow from it or use it to get your own ideas:

- I will complete one thing on my list a day

- If I finish a story, I can read a book for fun (or insert some other guilty pleasure)

- If I meet my deadline, my honey and I are going to dinner

- I will write XXX words today

- Between 5pm and 6pm (or whatever time best fits your schedule), I will do nothing but write

- I want to be published by the end of the year

- I will submit one story a month to a major publication

- I will sit down to write once a day

By structuring things in some way, you can exert control and keep things manageable. This doesn't mean if you can't keep that schedule or meet those goals, you do nothing; these are just things to aim for to keep you focused. Often, we feel overwhelmed because we can't get a clear picture of what needs to be done or what is most important or time-sensitive.

Discipline

When you have the time set aside to write, make sure you are writing. Don't fuss with email or chat on the phone or even think of starting up that computer game. Your time is, most likely, limited. If not, you are much more fortunate than the majority of the writers out there. Assuming you are in the limited camp, you have to put your best effort into the writing time you do have. If you aren't inspired, edit; if there is nothing to edit, research; if there is nothing to research, plan. Deviate from this too often, and you will find you have squandered the time you might have been writing. The occasional defection is to be expected; desertion is not.

Saying NO

There are times when no amount of organization or schedules or goals will do you a bit of good. Why, you ask? Because we are overachievers. We take on too much. We bury ourselves in tasks and obligations because they interest us, or because we feel (or are) obligated, or because we just don't know how to say no.

Learn. *Now.*

You can't do justice to yourself or your writing if you take on too much responsibility. This doesn't mean you have to avoid everything or that you should shirk things you truly ought to do (feeding the dog is mandatory), but you can regulate when you add new projects to your list, either of your own creation or someone else's request. For example, I am, first and foremost, a writer. However, particularly in recent years, I have also delved into being an anthology editor, a promotions manager, and a freelance typesetter. (Yeah… that masochism I mentioned earlier.) I'm sure you can imagine exactly how often those responsibilities conflict with one another. Needless to say, I have not been getting as much writing done as I might have. Clearly, I need to remember how to say No to myself. Fortunately, I can choose the projects I work on, and none of them have hard deadlines, other than the actual writing.

- If you want to be published in a major magazine, stop submitting your work to semi-pro publications,

- If you want to publish a novel, stop writing short stories for a while,

- If you have a book with a deadline, shelve the other ideas you get until you are done.

- Don't let others pressure you into taking on more projects

Letting Go

No. You can't do it all. Yes, you read me right. Sometimes you have to let projects go, at least temporarily, if not for all time. See, when you are a writer, you tend to find ideas in everything:

conversations, encounters on the street, things you see in life. I repeat: You can't do them all. There just isn't enough time. Write passing ideas down but limit yourself in how many you develop at one time. Yes, it means you might lose the thread of inspiration you first saw in it, but you are more likely to get more work completed on established projects, which means more finished projects in the end. Don't let your focus become divided. This is important because if you are going at this with an eye on a dedicated hobby (or career if you prefer), you will have to weigh what is likely to aid you to that end and attribute importance accordingly.

Summing Up

I know what it is like to want to do everything at once, and I have been in that place where I can't bring myself to do one single thing. Temper your enthusiasm, or you will burn yourself out or leave more loose threads trailing behind you than you do finished works. Do not neglect your non-writing obligations because those are the things of life, but make time for your craft because that is the essence of the soul. It is important to find a balance. Perhaps what I have written here will help you toward that end — I certainly hope so, anyway — or perhaps it will inspire you to ideas of your own. Do something, though, because this should be a joy, not a chore or a strain or a looming black cloud.

The Literary Handyman

Build-a-Book Workshop

Dedicated to you,
the brave soul forging your own path
in the publishing world.

Contents

From the Author...

The publishing industry has come through a lot of changes in the last ten or twenty years. So many changes that you could almost say it has returned to its beginnings. You see, when Guttenberg developed his marvelous press and books for the masses became a thing, pretty much every book was self-published. There was no other way. The publishing industry as we recognize it did not take hold until about the 19th century, with vanity presses quick to follow.

Little wonder a stigma developed in the 20th century against self-published works. Most authors had little understanding of how to construct a well-built book, or how to recognize the signs of one poorly done. Vanity presses—a self-published author's only option in the age of sheet-fed or offset printing—are all about quantity over quality. They don't care what your book looks like or if it's any good. They want to produce as many titles as possible as quickly as possible, charging the authors for every step of the process. I say *are* because they've never gone away, they've just changed their tactics and terminology. Be wary of any publisher using the term subsidy press or one who *guarantees* they will get your book into bookstores.

Predatory presses are no longer the only option for authors going the non-traditional route. A lot has changed since those days.

Welcome to the digital age. The 21st century. The DIY era, the era of doing it yourself.

Sadly, many authors still have little understanding of how to construct a well-built book.

Don't be one of them.

We have the knowledge, and the tools are out there. You just need to do a little homework. That's where I come in. I have worked in publishing for nearly thirty years. In that time I have worked at virtually every task there is in the industry. I have also typeset nearly two hundred books at the time I am writing this. This book is my effort to provide you with a blueprint to better design a book. As such, you won't find a lot of actual illustrations as the print book itself employs the elements I describe to you.

Primarily, it is written with fiction books in mind, but I have addressed many design aspects specific to nonfiction as well, so this should be of basic use no matter what you intend to publish.

I hope you enjoy, but most of all, I hope you find this useful!

Danielle Ackley-McPhail
The Literary Handyman*

---

*Because "Handywoman" just doesn't have the same ring.

Preface - The Basics

For simplicity's sake I am going to assume that if you are reading this book you intend — or at least hope — to do the work yourself. If I'm wrong…well, it won't be the first time. Either way, you should still come away knowing how to tell if the job is well done, whether you're doing the work yourself or paying to have it done.

The following are things you may need if you are going to self-publish, start your own press, or freelance as a designer. Not all of them will apply, depending on which aspects you decide to undertake yourself:

- An art program, such as Adobe Photoshop, Corel Photopaint, or a similar program – this is what you will use to create your cover. It allows you to layer text over images and apply special effects features to make your cover pop. It should be able to save or export a file as a PDF, JPEG, or a TIFF, the standard formats you will need. These programs can be expensive and many of them have transitioned to a subscription model. I use Affinity, a program that simulates and in some cases vastly improves on features similar to what you will find in Adobe Photoshop, but for a one-time nominal fee.

- 3D modeling software, such as Daz3d or Poser (optional) – this is so you can pose and light characters for cover art, then take that file into an art program and apply filters and finishing touches to create a final image. Daz is a free program, but it costs to buy the models and accessories you will use in the program. Poser is a program you have to purchase, but it comes with at least a basic library of models.

- Desktop publishing software, such as QuarkXpress or Adobe InDesign – this is to create the interior of the book itself. Programs such as these are a costly investment but are worth it in the long run if you plan to publish books on an ongoing basis. Any word processing program can also be used to generate a book design, but not always with same ease or end result as a program with specialized tools.

- A PDF program, such as Adobe Acrobat or FoxIt – this will let you convert a file to a PDF or allow you to modify a PDF file created by another program. You might need this to process your production files or to create a PDF ebook.

- An ebook conversion program, such as Calibre – newer versions of desktop publishing software can generate an ebook file but can be more complicated to use. Free programs like Calibre convert and manage ebook files from an RTF file and are designed to be easy to use.

- An account with a self-publishing platform, such as Kindle Direct Publishing or Ingram Spark – Once you create your book, you need a way to produce and distribute it. There are quite a few options for this. The two listed are the most commonly used. All of them have pros and cons. Be sure to consider the pros and the cons before you chose one to print with.

- An account with Bowker – This firm manages and supplies ISBNs (International Standard Book Number). Each version of you book is required to have its own unique ISBN. They can be expensive if purchased individually, but do go down in cost when you buy in bulk. Bowker will also offer you other services, such as creating bar codes. These are not needed as places like KDP and Ingram supply you with a bar code when you request a cover template. (More on that later.) Note, many publishing services will provide you with an ISBN for a nominal fee when you use their service, but it is an ISBN they own so they show up as the publisher of your book.

I mention all of this now because they will come up later. Forgive me if some of the information ends up repeated.

Now let's get started!

Part One – The Cover

Cover Lexicon

Rather than have you flip back and forth from where you are reading to the back of the book, at the front of each section you will find a list of terms relevant to that chapter. Not everything will be there, just industry terms that relate to the subject that I may not explain as fully in the chapter itself. A full glossary will also be included at the back.

Bar Code – A graphic representation of the ISBN (see below). It is made up of bars of varying widths that represent the individual numbers that make up the ISBN. It is traditionally printed on the back cover.

Bleed – This is extra space that you add to your cover design where the image or background color extends past the boundary of your final trim size. The bleed is there to provide a safety zone when the cover is trimmed down to size by the printer. This ensures that you do not end up with a white border along the edge of your cover if the trim is a little off.

Blurb – The text that appears on the back cover (or jacket flaps, in the case of a hardcover) that describes the book, enticing the reader to want to know more. Also called Cover Copy, Cover Blurb, Book Blurb, or Jacket Copy.

CMYK – This is a color profile, or mode, that stands for Cyan, Magenta, Yellow, and Black. That means that every color on your cover is made up of different values of some combination of those four colors.

Cover Template – A file provided by the printer showing the exact dimension of your book cover, including guidelines indicating where the cover will be folded and trimmed. Templates also include your basic book data, the bar code matching your ISBN, and markings indicating the minimum safe zones for where you can place your text and important elements of your artwork. Templates are provided electronically as PDFs or InDesign files.

DPI – Stands for Dots Per Inch. The clarity of all images is measured in DPI. The more dots per inch, the clearer an image is. The less dots per inch, the more jaggy an image is. The higher the DPI, the bigger the file will be.

ISBN – International Standard Book Number. A unique identifier assigned by the publisher. Each version of a book requires its own ISBN, which is tied to basic data about the book, such as but not limited to publisher, title, author, format, page count, and price. The ISBN is used by booksellers and librarians to order your book and manage their inventory. All ISBNs are purchased via a service called Bowker. If you purchase from Bowker, the ISBN will show you as the publisher. ISBNs are expensive purchased individually through this service, but the price goes down when you buy in bulk. Standard options are one, ten, and one-hundred ISBNs, with the cost per number going down the more you order at once. If you obtain an ISBN through a publishing service, such as Kindle Direct or Ingram Spark, they are less expensive, or even free, but those numbers indicate that the company you received them from is the publisher of that book, which will also imply to those in the industry that it is self-published, whether it is or not.

Logo – A graphic element representing your brand or imprint. The icon or design should be unique to you. Keep it simple so that it can be scaled up or down as needed and still be legible. It should also be distinct so that it can be readily identified as representing your company. You will want both a black-and-white version, for use in the interior, and a color version, for use on the cover. You will also want to use this logo for advertising purposes.

POD – Print on Demand. This is a digital printing method that allows you to print as few or as many copies as you need. Rather than a printing press, this method makes use of a more advanced copier-type printer where a book prints on standard paper sheets, which are trimmed down to the desired size.

Price-Specific Bar Code – A graphic representation of the ISBN. It is made up of bars of varying widths that represent the individual numbers that make up the ISBN. It also includes additional bars that represent the retail price you have set. You can find free software online that will generate any type of bar code you need. Your printer should also be provided one by your printer if you request a cover template file. There is no need to purchase a bar code, it is an unnecessary expense.

RGB – A color profile, or mode, that stands for Red, Green, and Blue. That means that all the colors on your cover are made up of different values of some combination of these three colors.

Stock Art – Photographs, illustrations, or works of art that have been posted by an artist on a Stock Art website where individuals can purchase a non-exclusive license to use the art for use as interior illustrations or cover art. The cost of the license depends on which rights you wish to purchase and the cost will differ from site to site. There are subscriptions you can sign up for that reduce the overall cost. It is not unusual for artists to create portfolios on multiple sites and there is no limit to how many individuals may license that image. Once you secure the rights to use an image you are able to modify it or combine it with other art to suit your needs but must credit the original artist or artists on the copyright page of your book.

Text Treatment – The words that appear on your cover and any special effects you may employ to embellish them via an art program or internet site.

Trim Size – The final dimensions of your printed book. A standard trim size for a Trade Paperback is six inches by nine inches (or 6 x 9). These dimensions are set, though the actual measurements of the book might vary slightly depending on how precisely the book is trimmed on the production line. The spine width of your book is determined by the weight of your paper and the number of pages in the finished book.

Chapter 1
Putting a Pretty Face on It

It's all well and good to say "don't judge a book by its cover" but you know we all do it, even you (come on, admit it!). That's what it's there for! That is its job! To lure you in and convince you that you might like what's inside. The never-ending question is: Will you be bitterly disappointed, pleasantly surprised, or get what you expect? It's a different story every time, isn't it? No pun intended. Really.

A cover is the first step on a reader's journey. It is their invitation to explore a new world. To this end, it is meant to lure in potential readers. Your cover is your bait. A good cover design will make the reader want to know more. Intrigue them, make them curious. Make them pick up the book. How do you achieve that? How do you stand out—in a good way—from the thousands of books that come out every month? Heck…every day!

I'm going to say this a lot…by doing your homework!

With the sheer volume of books being published each year you have plenty of clear examples of what or what not to do. Just go to your library or your local bookstore or anywhere there is a variety of physical books and browse through the shelves in your chosen genre section. Take a close look. See what draws your eye, what looks good and what doesn't. Does one cover appear more professional compared to another? Learn to recognize what a pretty face is in the publishing world. Books have their own version of symmetry and style. It's constantly changing, but there are certain key points that will always remain the same. I'm going to go through the basic elements of a front cover for you here, just keep in mind that stylistically trends change so it is always a good idea to get a feel for the current market any time you're about to start a project.

For most books there are three basic elements to the front cover: the title, the author's name, and the art. Other things that might appear are a subtitle, series name, a review blurb, or an award the author or book has won...of course, we might be getting ahead of ourselves here. Let's get through your first book.

How to Pick Art

Cover art is often the first thing that gives away a self-published or small-press book. This applies to both the image and the design. We're going to address the art first.

Your challenge is to stay within your budget—whatever that is—without looking like you had one. It doesn't do you any good to save money on art if what you have isn't going to sell books to anyone except friends and family and a few kind-hearted souls who don't want to hurt your feelings.

There are several different ways you can approach cover art:

Stylistic. You can try to capture a style or feel representative of the content, such as making a printed book appear like embossed leather for a steampunk or historic esthetic, or using a tooled metal look for a science fiction book. This avoids the need for actual art and can be accomplished digitally in an art program or by using stock art backgrounds or texture effects. (*Illus. 1.*)

Iconic. If there is a significant symbol (such as a squad icon, heraldry symbol, or tribal marking) in the book, try recreating the image by traditional or digital means, then using an art program to enhance the symbol with etching, embossing, or glow features. This has the added benefits of branding the book with something unique to the story without trying to capture a scene, and saving you money. Just be sure that the finished product looks polished and professional. (*Illus. 2.*)

Illustration 1 - Stylistic cover.

Using Photoshop effects and a layered file, this cover mimics the look of an embossed leather cover embellished with gold foil in an effort to capture the feel of a 19th century faerie tale book.

For the same reason, the design choice was made to leave the editors names off the cover.

Illustration 2 - Iconic cover.

Through texture and design, this cover gives a futuristic military feel and makes use of an established 'squad' icon relevant to the book to brand this and other titles in the series.

In addition, by maintaining this design, then adapting the icon for each project, each title is distinct while still identifiably part of the series.

Illustration 3 - Key Elements cover.

While not representative of a particular scene that takes place in the book, this cover draws on key elements of the story to capture the essential themes of music and magic and the unknown.

Illustration 4 - Montage cover.

For this short story collection, an artist was hired to create a rendition of the author, plus one element from each story in the book, to give an overall feel of the content, without focusing on any individual story.

Key elements. You (or an artist of your choosing) can either create a piece of art representing a scene, or compose a scene that captures the feel of the story without actually depicting something that happened in the book. This can be done through traditional art mediums, digitally in an art program, using a 3D posing program like Daz3d or Poser, or a combination of all three. (*Illus. 3.*)

Montage. That is where you take a few individual images that have relevance to the book and arrange them in an artistic manner. Think of it as a mini story-board you're using to sell the book. (*Illus. 4.*)

In the end, however you approach the cover it should make sense, be clear, clean, engaging, and capture the essence of your book. Above all, it should be eye-catching.

Where to Get Art

Let's face it, most of us don't have any kind of budget for art, let alone a graphics department dedicated to making our books look pretty. You have three options:

Do it yourself. Not a bad option if you have some artistic talent. Super-bad idea if your efforts look like your five-year-old niece was finger-painting. Always consider your skill level before opting to create the cover art yourself. Good for you isn't good *enough*. Bad cover art isn't going to inspire confidence in potential readers. You have to balance the need to save money against the likelihood of selling books.

Pay someone else to do it. If you have a budget, this is always a possibility, particularly if you know a decent artist that will give you a break, or someone with skill trying to build their portfolio. Everyone deserves to be paid for their efforts, but often artists just starting out set crazy-reasonable rates just to get the experience and art credit. This doesn't mean you shouldn't pay them, but it does mean you might be able to afford them. If you find an artist with graphic design training you could negotiate a finished cover, text and all, at a reasonable rate.

If you are hiring an artist, make sure the specifics of the project are spelled out in the contract, including what rights you are purchasing, the details of what you are looking for, what you are allowed to do with the art, and what is and is not included in the artist's fee. Also make sure to request several concept sketches to choose from, to make sure both you and the artist are working toward the same vision. If you are not happy with the results and will not be using the artist's work you can always pay a kill fee (generally half of the agreed-upon price) and look for a new artist.

If you attend fan conventions in your genre, the art show or Artist Alley is a great place to make connections when you are looking for artwork.

Stock art. Don't know any artists? There are so many sites out there that license art and the rates can be quite reasonable. Shutterstock, Adobe, and Fotolia are just a few that I have used. The quality can vary greatly, but if you are patient you can find what you need. Shop around, look for the best deal. Often you can get a subscription, a set number of downloads for low, fixed price. The site I use gives me five images for $50 on a revolving subscription (I use them up, and they charge me $50 for the next batch.)

Is there a lot of dreck out there? Heck yeah! Does it take time and effort to find something that is both good and applicable? You bet! Is it worth it? In a heartbeat! I can't tell you how many book covers we have created with stock art. Sometimes without needing to alter anything. It could take a few hours of search-ing to find a worthwhile image, but there isn't a project we have done where we couldn't find something that worked as-is or with just the right application of filters. We have even composited several images to achieve the right look for a hard-to-match title. Searches on the stock art platform turn up a lot of image that are low quality or don't apply, but if you look long enough you can find something. I have even found traditional art and images that have already been put through filters to simulate an art feel. And new content is being uploaded all the time.

Learn from Others' Mistakes

While I am sure all presses have a gallery of shame when it comes to bad cover designs, there are some practices that seem endemic of small press. Avoid doing the following if you want to raise the bar in small press or independent publishing cover design:

Using a 3D posing image as final art. 3D modeling software is meant to create the foundation for finished art, not be used as the end product. This goes hand in hand with using a bad 3D posing image as art. If you are going to use this tool, use it right. Make the poses natural, not too stiff, rigid, or awkward, and always take the image into an art program and use filters and effects to finish that image and give it life. Raw 3D posing images inherently look fake, flat, and untextured. A lot of small presses and self-published authors make this mistake. Don't be one of them. Avoiding just this one mistake will elevate you above most of the independent books out there.

Using unaltered photographs. Most personal photographs just don't have a finished feel. If you are going this route, you really want to clean up the image and enhance it with effects to enhance the final product, perhaps even compositing the image with other photographs or digital elements to create a more cohesive and relevant feel for the cover, otherwise it can come across like you did the project on your home computer. No matter how accurate that may be, you don't want it to appear that way.

Using stock art that has been used as cover art by others. This is a bit harder to avoid, but try. If you are considering using a stock image search the image in your web browser to see if any other covers come up. You can do this by dragging the image file up to the search field. Another approach to avoid this issue is to composite the image with other stock art to create something new or crop the original image so that you are onlyusing a piece of it.

Getting the details wrong. If you are basing your cover art on characters, details, or events in your book, make sure they match. Little things like hair and eye color or skin tone matter. Readers assume the character on the front of the book matches the one inside. They get annoyed when they don't match up. Details like this are very easily altered in most art programs so there really is no reason not to get it right. Remember, yes, it has to look good, but it also has to make sense!

Lack of contrast. All the elements of a cover should work together, if the art image and/or the text doesn't have enough contrast you end up with a 'muddy' or flat cover. That's where it is hard to figure out what is going on or difficult to read the text because it is fighting or blending in with a portion of the image behind it.

Using confusing art. This is usually caused by two possible things. First, using a cover image that doesn't visually make sense or can't readily be identified for what it is. Second, art with a style, tone, or composition that conflicts with the content or genre of the book so that the potential reader doesn't know what to make of it. When they are left confused the book is generally left on the shelf. Or, if it isn't, you could lose their future business if the cover gave them one expectation and the book delivers another.

Chapter 2
The Fine Details of Composition

Once you have your art, it is time to consider your design. By this, I mean what is going on your cover and where. As I mentioned earlier, the text treatment will be the title and the author's name. Where those appear on the book depends on the composition of the art. You want the text to flow harmoniously with the artwork, rather than fighting against it. Your best bet — if you are doing the design yourself — is to open the image in your art program and play with it (always on a copy, never on the master file.)

Look first for natural negative space, the open areas around the image itself. This is always the first option when placing text. One, you aren't covering anything up, and two you are filling an empty space in the art in a way that allows the text to work with the image. Just don't fill up too much space. You don't want your cover to look cluttered. It's all about balance.

Another option is to place the text over an unimportant part of the image, one where it's not going to cover up too much of the central detail. An example would be across the top, where there is sky or trees or whatever makes up your background, or across the bottom where there is floor or some other element of the image people don't really need to see.

A third option is to have the text interact with the image in some way. This is where your art program comes in handy. By creating layers, you can duplicate parts of the image to overlap the text or you can use the effects tools to give the text a similar treatment to an aspect of the art. With tricks like this you integrate the text so that it becomes one with the image.

Design is as much a creative process as a technical one, you don't have to limit yourself. As long as the final design works to create a cohesive professional-looking cover with good flow, there are no real rules, just standard conventions. This is where you want to look at examples of what other people have done. Not just to get ideas, but to also know what to avoid.

Readability

Is your text easy to read? Back in the day when typesetting meant literally setting metal blocks of type, the guideline for designing a title treatment was, can you read it from six feet away? Basically, from across a bookstore aisle, would you know what book you are looking at? While bookstores aren't as much of a concern these days, the premise still applies, only we aren't concerned about six feet away. Now the question is can you still read the title clearly in a thumbnail? Because face it, for many people, buying books these days is done from a computer screen… or heck, from their phone. Thumbnails are generally one inch by one and a half inches in dimension or smaller. A good cover will be recognizable at that size, if not legible.

How do you achieve that? First you pick a font that is clean and easy to read. One without superfine detail that will disappear against the background or when reduced. A font that will complement the content of your book and pair well with the artwork. Most computers come with a wide range of fonts already installed, but if you are downloading one online make sure that it is either free for commercial use or that you are paying for a license that allows for commercial use. Once you've chosen your font you can play with the many features in an art program to accent the title, such as embossing, drop shadow, glow, etc. Sometimes, depending on what art is in the background, even the cleanest font will need embellishing to stand out. A simple outline can make the words more crisp and readable, or you might need to create a frame because the background image is too busy.

Another aspect of readability is contrast. Do the elements on the cover stand out individually? You don't want the title or author's name to get lost against a busy background, but you also don't want them to distract from the art image. Just remember, the elements of the cover should work together, not compete.

The final consideration is flow. Is there a natural path that your eye travels when looking at the cover? Do the elements focus you toward a specific point, or do they individually compete for your attention? Every cover should have a focal point. That single element that grabs the eye and makes the reader want to look closer. All aspects of your design should work together toward that one end.

The Spine

Much like the human backbone, the spine of the book is what holds everything together and makes it work. If you are producing electronic books only, skip this section. It is not relevant to you.

If you are producing print books, the spine is where the book is bound together. Originally, books were literally bound... or sewn together. Now they are glued to keep all the pages in place. As far as cover design is concerned, a basic spine includes only three things: the title, the author's full or last name (depending on available space), and the publisher's imprint (generally in the form of an icon). In the case of thick mass-market paperbacks, the publisher might include a thumbnail of the cover art. One other optional element, if space allows and it is applicable, would be to include a volume number if the book is part of a series. If the title is particularly long you might consider leaving off the author's first name on the spine, rather than cram things too close together.

Readability is the most important aspect here. The spine is what most people will see when the book is on a bookshelf. You want to make sure the text is clear, easy to read, and doesn't come too close to the edge of the spine, otherwise the words could partially fold over to the front or back of the book if the binder is not precise when they place and trim the cover. Sadly, this is more common with print-on-demand printing.

Chapter 3
No Junk in the Trunk

If step one in a reader's journey is picking up the book, step two is turning it over. The front cover is the bait. The back cover is the hook. This is the first place the potential reader goes for more information. Not just how much the book costs or who publishes it, but to find out what the book is about.

That text on the back is called a cover blurb or jacket copy. It is important to understand what job that text is supposed to do. This is not a full description of the book. You are not telling the reader what happens. This is your teaser, a playful little dance to entice them, to make them want to know more. To follow the fishing metaphor, the cover blurb is your lure. Needless to say, cover blurbs aren't easy to write. How much do you tell? How much do you imply? Where do you stop? There is a fine art to writing cover copy. It's not a book report. It's more like a movie trailer.

You want to introduce the main character, their objective, and the threat to that goal, but in a jazzy way that sounds exciting without giving any deeper details. I generally start with a banner for visual interest and to break up the copy so it isn't just a solid block, then I feed out some teasers with a little flare, using more lyrical language rather than straight prose, and I finish with a question. In truth, if I have done my job right, all the reader has is questions…and a desire to know more! Here, let me give you an example:

Mortal. Immortal. Musician. Mage.

On a journey from the boroughs of New York to the heart of Tir na nÓg, from innocence to the deepest darkest crevices of her soul, Kara O'Keefe found power and strength in the discovery of self. But with that peace came a hard truth. As a bridge connecting many worlds, none of them held a place for her.

She must find her own way, forge her own path.

To honor a vow to Granddame Rose, a matriarch of the Kalderaš Clan, Kara joins the Romani caravan, only to find herself even more of an outsider than before. While she strives for acceptance, and to honor her vow, little does she know she has once more become a lure to an ancient and deadly enemy, drawing danger into the midst of her unsuspecting hosts.

Once savior of the world, Kara must now save herself and the innocents around her.

She has come into her legacy, but where will destiny take her?

(Back cover text for *Eternal Wanderings*
by Danielle Ackley-McPhail, Paper Phoenix Press)

Now, this might not suit your style, or the tone of your writing, but the basic construction would work for any book. Banner, brief introduction, setup, conflict, question. Again, the end goal is to leave them wanting more. If the front cover is meant to make them pick up the book, the back is meant to make them open it. To do that you can't give too much away. You want brief and punchy. I usually aim for between 100 and 150 words, give or take.

There are two reasons for this, one, you don't want to give too much away; and two, you want to leave room for everything else that needs to go back there without things being too cluttered. So…shall we get into the technical bits?

Back Cover Design Elements

Please note: I am only touching on basics here because an entire book could be written just about cover design... and I'm sure someone already has. That having been said, there are certain details you want to include on the back cover:

Artwork. (Optional.) The back cover can be a solid color, an artistic treatment, or art that wraps around from or mirrors the front cover. This is the designer's choice. If there is artwork behind the text, make sure it is subtle and does not make the text difficult to read, or use something like a screen or shadow technique between the text and the art to make the text stand out.

A Banner. (Optional.) A tag line or banner at the top can catch the eye and draw the reader in. It can also help frame the text and give it visual interest and style.

The Cover Blurb. We've already talked about this, basically it is your sales pitch. The text should be clean, easy to read, and not compete with the background. Don't make the font too small or too large. It can be justified text or centered or freeform to run around a graphic element on the back. It doesn't really matter as long as the design is clear and makes sense, with the text and any graphic elements working together to create an appropriate feel.

Author Biog. (Optional) If you have too much blank space on the back of your book, you could put a brief author bio after the cover blurb. If you do, make it concise and professional, not your full bio, but the highlights. Awards, bestsellers, things that may impress a potential reader. That means you don't include that your book was a Reader Choice selection on an obscure web site, but you do include that it was a Recommended Read in an industry magazine that carries weight in your chosen genre. Same goes for awards. If you won a local writing contest...or one in school, I wouldn't mention that, but if you won a national or international award, by all means! Don't let the bio take over the back cover, though. These days most publishers put them in the backmatter of the book, that is where your extended biography should go.

Your Imprint. Whether you are setting up your own press or just self-publishing your work, you need an imprint. This is the brand you will publish work under. All traditional publishers have what are called imprints, that is a name and a logo representing that company or brand. In fact, larger publishers have multiple imprints, each one known for a different type or genre of book, so potential readers know they can look for that imprint and find the kind of thing they like to read. Most potential readers will look for this information to see if the publisher is one they recognize and perhaps already trust. The absence of an imprint is a red flag that a book is less than "professional". This could lead some to make unfounded assumptions about the quality of your book.

ISBN and Bar Code. All books sold commercially are required to have an ISBN (International Standard Book Number), a unique identifier that allows bookstores and libraries to quickly access information about your book, including author, title, and publisher. This is the number they need to order the book. The bar code is a graphic representation of that number that can be scanned with the proper equipment and read by a computer. It appears on the back of your book, generally in the lower right-hand corner or the bottom middle of the cover. Commercial retailers have very specific requirements. For them to order the book, the bar code must be what is called 'price-specific'. That means that in addition to your author, title, and publisher information, the bar code has an extra portion that includes the price. As most places use scanners to scan the bar code for both sales and inventory purposes they generally will not order books that do not have price-specific bar codes because they cannot easily input it in their system or track their sales.

Non-Distribution SKU – a Stock Keeping Unit is a number similar to an ISBN that is used to track information for a book that will not be distributed commercially. In other words, the number is for internal purposes and will not be used by an outside party to look up or order your book. Most online printers will generate one of these numbers for you if you do not provide an ISBN but only you will be able to order stock. You would use this to produce special stock you intend to sell directly.

Price. Even though, with hope, you have included a price-specific bar code, it is a good idea to also include the actual price on the cover of your book for the potential reader who may not know how to identify the price in the bar code.

Genre. (Optional) Most potential readers should be able to tell genre based on your cover art and back cover copy, but some publishers like to include a genre designation on the back cover. In most cases genre is more for bookstores and libraries anyway, so they know where to shelve the book, but it is nice to clarify for the reader, just in case they are getting a different impression from the cover.

Website. (Optional) Is it required? No. Is it a good idea? It can be. It depends on how professional your site is and how serious you are about publishing. It could be specific to the book/series, you as an author, or you as a publisher. If you are going to include it on the cover of the book it should be a dedicated custom domain, not a social media site or page on an unrelated site. Those would appear unprofessional. You also want to ensure that you are only providing links to sites that have a professional appearance, without errors, missing images, or broken links.

Artist credit. (Optional.) This doesn't have to go on the back cover, as long as it appears on the copyright page, but it is a nice gesture to the artist and fosters good will.

Award Citation. If your book has been a finalist or winner of a reputable award that is definitely information you want to include on your cover. Same thing goes for bestseller status, but only for something big. If you make a bestseller list in a mainstream or applicable industry publication (such as *The New York Times, USA Today,* or *Locus Magazine,* for example) that you want to include. If you made your hometown's bestseller list, best to leave it off. It's not going to win you any brownie points with potential readers or industry professionals.

Review Blurbs. (Optional.) Tread carefully here. You don't want to clutter your book, but if you receive a favorable review from a respected source like an A-list author or an industry magazine like *Publishers Weekly* or an applicable genre magazine like *Analog*, that is something you want to include. Be wary, though. There are some professional review sites that require payment for a review. That may or may not be in your best interest. I always recommend pursuing free review options first as the pay sites can be quite hefty and may not give you a positive return on your investment.

Now that you know what to include, let's talk about how it should appear. (*Illus. 5.*) In the end, you want to keep it clean and simple, including details that will increase your chances of selling that book, without cramming on so much that that the back looks cluttered. Always aim for a professional look.

Illustration 5 - cover design. This example labels the basic elements of the front, spine, and back cover and gives you some idea of how they would be arranged. To make room for elements such as award citations or review blurbs, the existing copy would be resized or truncated.

A. Cover Blurb
B. Banner
C. Spine Title
D. Front Title
E. Price
F. Website
G. Art Credits

H. Imprint/Logo
I. Genre
J. Price-Specific Bar Code
K. Spine Logo
L. Spine Author Name
M. Front Author Name
N. Art

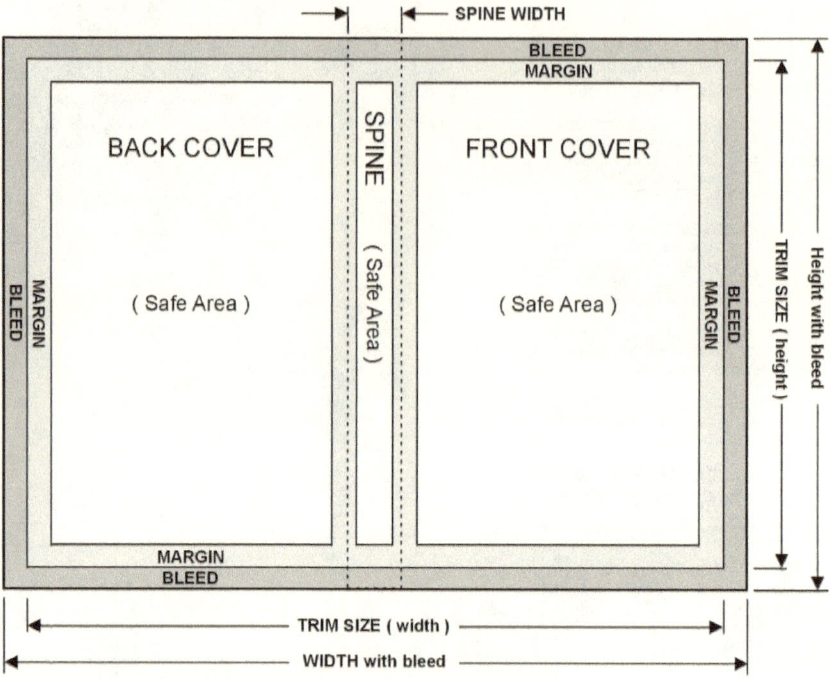

Illustration 6 - cover template. This is a generic example of the template a printer may provide. It is created to the specific dimensions of your book based on the page count and the paper you selected when you set up your title. Your finished design is layered over top of the template so that when the cover is printed the workers on the binding line know where to cut and fold the cover so it fits on the finished book.

Chapter 4
Putting it All Together

When you are preparing your files for production, standard practice is to request a cover template from the printer you are working with. (*Illus. 6.*) They generate this based on the page count, trim size, and weight of the paper you have selected for your project. This gives them the final dimensions of the printed book.

The template they provide uses those dimensions to give you a diagram of where the different elements of your cover need to be placed. There are crop marks showing you where the final edge — or the trim — of your cover is, where the fold points for the spine are, and where your bleed is (all industry-specific terms I use appear in the lexicon at the beginning of each section, as well as in the glossary at the end of the book). It shows you the safe areas where all of your text and critical image elements need to fall within. That having been said, that does not mean you should run your text right up to that line. If you do, your book will definitely look unprofessional. Always leave a quarter- to a half-inch margin all around the text on the front and back covers. Also on the template is the ISBN/Bar code for your book. You can reposition this by saving just the bar code and importing it as a separate layer on your final cover file. Do this stage last as the bar code needs to be unaltered to work. Most places will want you to save the cover file as a PDF.

If you need ideas on how a book cover should be designed, look at a variety of books in your genre. That truly is the best way to get an idea of what is done short of taking an actual design class. Use your critical eye. Look at a wide selection of covers and take note of things like text treatment, art, and placement of the individual elements. Get an idea of what works and what doesn't. The best way to do that is with actual examples of things that have already been published. Don't look just at one publisher, seek out different imprints. Look for names you don't recognize so you are sure to get a wide range of examples that run the gambit from successful to unsuccessful.

Preparing Final Files

First and foremost, whatever print service you are using, they should have guidelines that tell you how they want to receive the final files to produce your book. Find those guidelines and read them. It will make the process that much smoother.

These guidelines will specify everything from file format to DPI to minimum margins, etc. Generally, they want you to provide the print cover files in PDF or TIFF format, in CMYK mode, 300 DPI. For ebooks they request JPEG format, in RGB mode.

If you aren't sure what you are supposed to do, read the guidelines and then call tech support to make sure you are doing it correctly.

Cover Checklist

Front Cover

- Is the text treatment easy to read?
- Is the text too close to the edges of the book?
- Is the artwork engaging?
- Is the artwork applicable to the book?
- Can you identify what the image is?
- Does the text treatment detract from the art or complement it?
- Can you read the physical cover from six feet away?
- Can you read the digital cover as a thumbnail?

Back Cover

- Is the text treatment easy to read?
- Is the text too close to the edges of the book?
- Do you have a hook or noteworthy review blurb?
- Is the back cover copy enough to catch the reader's attention without telling too much?
- Have you included an icon representing your company or brand?
- Have you included a price-specific bar code?

- Have you included the book price?
- Have you included your website?

Spine

- Is the title readable from six feet away?
- Is the author legible?
- Have you included an icon representing your company or brand?

Part Two – The Text Block

Text Lexicon

Acknowledgements – This generally goes at the front of the book, though some publishers choose to put it at the back. It is a list or written section where you acknowledge those who helped make the book possible, helped work on it, or supported you while you wrote it.

Appendixes – This is additional or expanded information presented at the end of the book. It is a way for the author to share research, theories, or back story without interrupting the flow of the story or text when the additional information might not be immediately relevant, just of interest.

Back matter – The extra content located at the back of your book, such as but not limited to the author's biography, Appendixes, Glossary, or Index. Content that is separate from your story or nonfiction, but complements it.

Chapter/Story Title – The identifying text that appears on the first page of your chapter, story, or article, depending on if you are producing a novel, collection/anthology, or nonfiction work.

Contents Page – Also called the Table of Contents. The list of sections that appear in your book, including titles and page numbers. If the book involves contributions by multiple individuals, the author's name would appear following the title of their work. This only includes materials that come after the contents page.

Copyright Page – The page following the title page, including the relevant details and disclaimers required in publishing, such as, but not limited to, the publisher's contact information, the copyright notice, the relevant ISBNs, Library of Congress Control Number, and legal disclaimers, also included are the credits for the cover art, any illustrations, the editor, and the designer(s).

Drop Cap – When the first letter of the first word on a page is larger and inset into the first paragraph by two or more lines. Often the font is different and more ornate than that used for the base text. Take care which font you choose as some have florishes that will obsure the surrounding text. The font should be easy to read and complement the feel of the book.

Facing Pages – These are pages that will be visible side by side when you open the book. In other words, you can see them at the same time without turning the page. You can think of it this way, if you close the book they are facing each other. Well…more than facing, but what happens behind closed covers…

Folio – The technical term for the page number.

Front Matter – The extra content located at the front of a book, such as but not limited to the title page, Table of Contents, dedication, maps, list of characters, list of terms, or pronunciation guides. This material is generally numbered with lowercase roman numerals when there is a page number on the page. A running head or page number is generally only used if the element (such as the contents page) is longer than one page.

Full-Bleed – When a background or image extends all the way to the edge of the printed page. To allow for this and make sure there is no white space where there shouldn't be, the designer extends the background or image a quarter inch past the desired trim size of the book.

Glossary – A list of terms that generally appears in the back matter giving greater detail regarding terms or concepts depicted in the book.

Gutter Margin – The extra space you should add to your text design on the inside edge of the page where the book will eventually be bound. Typically, you would add a quarter of an inch or more depending on the thickness of the book. This extra space allows the book to be bound without the text disappearing into the binding of the book.

Half-Title Page – The same as the title page, but with only the title of the book printed on it, not the author and the publisher. When there is a half-title page, it is generally the first page in the book, followed by a blank page, a list of other titles by the author, or a quote or image the author wishes to start off the book with. Half-title pages are a legacy from offset or sheet-fed printing, where a book's pagination must be in increments of four-, eight-, or sixteen-page signatures. If there are too many blank pages at the end of the book (which looks bad) a half-title page is included in the front matter to adjust the signatures and reduce the number of blank pages in the back. In digital printing a half-title page might be included if there is some design element the author or publisher wants to include on the page facing the title page.

Imprint – The brand under which the book is being produced. Sometimes this is the publisher's name, but sometimes a publisher will create a separate sub-brand to group books by genre or type.

Index – These are used for nonfiction, textbooks, and cookbooks. It is a list of the relevant terms in the book and where they are discussed so that readers can go directly to the passages that may contain the information they are looking for.

Introduction – Some books will have an introduction. In most cases, these are collections or nonfiction books. The introduction may be written by the author, or by a notable individual, such as a professional in the industry or a well-known author.

Layout – 1. How the elements of your book are arranged on the page. 2. The act of arranging the elements of your book, including placement and style.

Logo – A graphic representation of a publisher or imprint.

Margins – The blank space running around the edge of the text block denoting the edge of the page.

Review Blurbs – Occasionally, a book will include advance reviews or reviews of a previous edition. When these are particularly favorable and from a reputable source, publishers will often include these at the beginning of the book on the first page following the front cover.

Running Foot – When the page numbers appear consecutively at the bottom of the printed page.

Running Head – The text and/or page number that appears at the top of the printed page. For novels, it generally contains the title of the book on one page and the author's name on the facing page, both accompanied by the page number. For collections or anthologies, it generally contains the title of the book on one page with the story or article title and author on the facing page, both accompanied by the page number.

Section Break – A decorative element that appears between two separate sections of text, generally in a work of fiction. It can be a font-generated symbol or an actual art graphic that complements the theme of the book.

Style Guides – In many desktop publishing programs—if not all—there are tools where you can define the formatting for different aspects of your book so that when they reoccur all you need to do is select the correct style and the formatting will be implemented. The style guides also allow you to change the style of an element in one place and have it automatically apply to all instances of that style.

Templates – In many desktop publishing programs—if not all—you can create a standard template, or Master, for a type of page in your book that you can drop into place as needed changing the existing layout to the desired layout.

Title Page – This page includes the basic identifying information of a book. In most cases, the title, series, book number (where applicable), the author or editor's name, the imprint and the publisher's location.

Chapter 5
The Nuts and Bolts

You've opened a book some time in your life. I know you have. You can't deny it. If nothing else, I know you have opened *this* book. If you stop to think about it, we all know what a book should look like. The problem is we've seen so many that the fine details of what goes where blend into the background. Unless they are wrong, then they really stand out.

There are some elements of book design that *should* blend into the background. If they don't, they should at least work with the text to create a cohesive feel, not compete with the text for the reader's attention.

Title/Chapter. Depending on what you are publishing, you will have either a Story or Chapter Opening Page. On the first page, the text starts roughly a third to halfway down the page and the story title, chapter title, or chapter number appears somewhere in the white space above it. Where and how it appears in that white space is a design choice. Titles/Chapters are generally in a more stylized font that matches the tone or genre of the content, but should always be clear and easy to read. If possible, I match this font to what was used on the front cover.

Author Name. If the publication includes works by multiple authors, such as an anthology or textbook, the author name will appear beneath the applicable title. The font will generally be smaller and simpler than the title font, but larger than the text font. Again, placement is a design choice.

Text Block. The main text of your book, consisting of words, sentences, and paragraphs. Yeah, I know…duh! But it had to be said. The text should be justified (the lines align straight down both sides of the page), single-spaced, indented, with no extra line space between paragraphs (that is an online convention.)

Some designers make the choice to leave the first paragraph of a story, chapter, or section without an indent to reinforce that it is the beginning or to accommodate a Drop Cap, where the first letter or word of the first paragraph is larger that the rest and drops down into the lines below. This is a stylistic choice and fits industry standards. As long as you do it consistently, it will not be seen as a design error.

If the text block is too solid, with long paragraphs and little white space to break it up, it can be a strain for the reader, leading to eye fatigue. If this occurs, consider looking at your paragraphs to see if they can be broken up into several shorter paragraphs, or, in the case of fiction, if there is an opportunity to interject some dialogue to break things up.

Finally, keep in mind is that the text blocks on facing pages need to align with one another across the bottom of the pages.

Alignment. There are four type alignments in typesetting. Left, Right, Center, and Justified.

- Left and Right are where the indicated edge lines up (or aligns) and the other edge is ragged (the sentences end when there is no room for the next word on the line.)

- Center is where neither edge aligns but the middle of the sentence lines up with the center of the page.

- Justified is when the spacing between the words adjusts so that both edges of the text block align to create a solid rectangle.

The first three alignments are most typically used for design elements like the Title/Chapter, Author, quotes, lines of verse, or section breaks. When it comes to the text block, it should always be justified.

Font. To meet industry standard, text fonts should be a simple, easy-to-read serif font. That is a font with the little extra bumps and points on it, for those not familiar with the term. Serif fonts are more usually used for print books because they are easier to read over long periods. Sans Serif font (those that are just lines without embellishment) can be hard on the eyes after a while. You also don't want to use a fancy font for your text block. Most of them are not very legible in smaller point sizes and you don't want the reader to become frustrated by difficult to read text.

The next concern is the size of the text. Back in the day, when typesetting was literally putting together little metal blocks to form the words, font (or point) sizes were uniform. Most text was printed in 10 point font with a 12 point leading (the leading was actual lead bars placed between the sentences to space them out.) This presented a uniform and consistent page that was easy to read. In the digital age fonts are no longer consistent. 10 point in one font is a completely different size from 10 point in another. Because of this, text that is digitally set can be anywhere from 10 point to 14 point in size. Whatever point size you use, the leading should be two points higher. In the end, it is all about readability.

Some standard fonts used today are Garamond, Bookman Old Style, and Book Antiqua. Font to avoid are Times New Roman (generally used for journalism), Courier and other "typewriter" fonts, overly ornate or script-type fonts like *Brush Script* or *Freestyle Script* that will distract from the content or make it difficult to read.

Indent. Formatting styles have transformed over the years. Originally, there was just manuscript format and print format. Then people developed their own formatting style for online viewing and it further confused matters. Sometimes they forget (or never knew) that print formatting is different from either manuscript or digital. Do not use manuscript or digital format for a published book. It will stand out as self-published and unprofessional. A print paragraph is typically indented a quarter of an inch.

Spacing. I have addressed this briefly already, so forgive me if I repeat myself as I go into greater detail. Text in a published book should be single-spaced, generally with a leading (extra padding) two points larger than the font size but can be selectively adjusted if the text block is a little too dense, or you need to adjust how the text lands on the page. To correct a typesetting issue — such as a header separated from its text or facing text blocks not ligning up across the bottom of the pages — you can increase or decrease the spacing by up to a point in either direction without it being too noticeable. Double-spaced lines should not be used in a published book.

The other type of technical spacing is kerning, where you adjust the space between individual letters to achieve a more pleasing visual or to correct for other typesetting issues, such as too much hyphenation, bad breaks, and widows and orphans (don't worry, I'll explain later).

Line spacing is another matter, as in having a blank line between design elements. As already mentioned, paragraphs should not be followed by a line space. Here are the exceptions. If you have a quote or other type of insert that breaks up the text block and changes format, a blank line before and after sets off the element and makes it evident the change in formatting is intentional. Examples would be lyrics, a letter or journal entry, a flashback, tables or other illustrations.

Margins. In publishing, for a trade paperback book, the margin on a text page is half an inch on the top, bottom, and outside edge. The inside edge, where the book will be bound, has a three-quarter inch margin. The extra margin is called a gutter margin and is added so that when the book is bound text and images do not disappear into the crease, where the pages curve. This is called bottling. If you make your margins too big, it will appear you are padding the book to make it longer…putting fewer words on a page so that there are more pages. If you don't put enough of a margin, the page will look too dense and your text and images could disappear into the gutter. Both of these instances make your finished product look unprofessional and can lead to an unsatisfactory experience for your reader.

Running Head. This is the information printed at the top of every text page *except* the Title/Chapter Opening Page or blank pages. In a novel, the book title typically appears at the top of the left-hand page and the author's name appears at the top of the right-hand page. In an anthology, collection, or textbook, the book title would be in the same place, and the story or chapter title would be on the facing page, along with the author's name if the book includes multiple authors.

The placement of the running head is below the top margin, about a quarter of an inch above the text block. This information can be centered or appear at the outside edge of the page. You could align it on the inside of the page (where the binding is), but this may prove difficult to read. While you can use a more stylized font, make sure it is legible in a smaller point size. If possible, I usually match this font to the one used on the cover or Title/Chapter Opening Page.

There is some room here for creative design. My best recommendation is to look at other published examples and be guided by what looks good to you. In the end, all elements of the design should work together to create the proper tone and feel for the reader's experience.

For consistency, create templates or style guides in your design program so you are only entering data for each element once.

I generally create two templates for a novel, Chapter Opening Page and Text Page (which is for anything that is not a Chapter Opening.) If there are back matter elements that would have customized running heads, I create templates for those too.

For anthologies, I create a separate Text Page template for each story in the book and any relevant back matter so that I can customize the running heads.

Page Number. These would appear either in the running head, at the outside edge of each page, or in the running foot, centered on the page. If you use a stylized font for the running head, make sure it includes numbers and they are clearly identifiable. If they are not, use a different, simpler font for the page numbers. Most word processing or design and layout programs have a feature that will automatically number your pages if you add the code to the design.

Section Break. In fiction, scene breaks will occasionally happen. As a part of your design, these breaks should be clearly marked in some manner. In many instances, publishers use a simple or decorative graphic element that works with the overall design of the book. This is the method I recommend, otherwise it can be confusing if the reader misses that there has been a break, as can happen if the break occurs at the bottom or top of a page, particularly in the case of an ebook. A graphic element makes it clear there has been a change.

If you chose not to use a graphic element and instead denote section breaks with an extra line space between, I would recommend formatting the first line of the next section in a distinct manner to make it clear it is the start of a new section. Examples would be to have the first line in small capital letters (small caps), italic, or bold, or to use a drop cap on the first letter of the first paragraph of the new section.

Quotes/Lyrics/Poetry/Correspondence. If you are quoting an outside source of one of these types, a line or two is quoted within the text, and three lines or more is offset from the main body of the text, separated from it with a blank line before and after the quote. Often the quote is also indented on both sides to further distinguish it from the body of the text.

- Quotes – These could appear at the beginning of a chapter/story, or within the body of the text. The formatting is stylistic. Some people use italics, others use quotation marks, some use both. Pick a style that suits you (or refer to a style guide), and remain consistent.

- Poetry/Lyrics – When interjected within the text, the formatting for poetry is usually indented and/or centered, in stanzas, with a blank line before the piece, between stanzas, and after the piece.

- Correspondence – This could be any kind of communication: a letter, memo, email, or journal entry. The text is set off from the body of the text with a line space above and below and indented on either side. The font is often in italics or in some other way different from the text body. Some use a script type font, but if you do so, ensure it is simple and easy to read.

Numbered/Bullet Lists.

- The list is set off from the body of the text with a line space above and below and indented on either side.

- The text of the list aligns on the first word of the first line, not the bullet.

- A number, dot, or some other symbol sets off the points of the list.

Footnotes/Endnotes. When you have a note, citation, or reference that applies to a specific point in your text you use a superscript numeral to indicate the text to which the footnote or endnote applies. A footnote would be placed at the bottom of the page as a full-sized number, a period, a space, and then the full citation (if you are referring to an outside source) or the text of your footnote if it is just a note providing additional information. If the same source is referenced throughout the book, the first use of the footnote is a full citation and subsequent footnotes are an abbreviated citation. (What a full or abbreviated citation includes or how it is formated is dependent on the particular style guide you elect to follow, i.e. *Chicago Manual of Style*, etc.)

If you prefer to have the notes appear in a separate section in the back of the book, all of the above still applywith the noted exception of where the note is printed.

Embellishment. (Optional) Many traditional publishers shy away from artistic embellishments in their designs. They are an additional expense that will add to the bottom line, without increasing the monetary value of the end product (ie: you can't charge more for a book just because you've made it pretty.)

However, that having been said, it is done. A graphic embellishment repeated on each title/chapter opening page, done properly, can increase the professional appearance of a book and add to the reader's experience by supporting the tone of the book, when matched properly with the content. Embellishments can be a graphic flourish or icon that comes as a part of a font package or simple line art licensed from a stock art site. It can also be a custom graphic element created by an artist to your specifications based on the content of the book, either line art accent pieces or even page borders (preferably only on the Title/Chapter Opening Page). Some publishers make the design choice to have a different embellishment on each Title/Chapter Opening Page, customized to the text that follows. Your call. If you use an embellishment make sure it is professional, complementary, and well-done. If you use multiple embellishments, make sure they match in style and quality. If not, you are much better off not using them.

Illustrations. (Optional) I have always loved illustrated volumes. To me, they enhance the experience, making it richer. That having been said, I wouldn't sink big money into them. If you include pictures, they should be high resolution, well-executed, with good contrast and line density so that they reproduce well, something that can be a challenge with POD production. If the effort is amateurish, you are better off without them. While illustrations don't add to the value of a book, bad ones can certainly detract from it.

With nonfiction books, things are a little different. Sometimes illustrations exist to clarify, supplement, or demonstrate information being explained in the text. When this is the case, clearly mark all graphic images with a number or letter and include that citation at the relevant text mention. Always cite your source and be sure to secure permission or license to use anything you haven't generated yourself. All images should be clear and in high resolution (300 DPI). If there are multiple illustrations or graphic elements in the book, make them consistent with one another. If you include illustrations of different styles and quality it can make the work look unprofessional.

Graphic images can come in many different forms:

- Photographs – Unless you have taken the photograph yourself, be sure to secure permission or a license to use any photographs included in your work. Also, always cite the source and/or copyright, where applicable.

- Art – Whether an illustration or a graphic of some sort, make sure all lines are sufficiently thick, clean, and crisp to reproduce well and anything not line art has good contrast and clarity.

- Tables – if using tables or charts, be sure to include a key, where applicable, and make sure everything is clearly labeled.

- Timelines/Family Tree – These may be text-based or image-based, but should be consistent throughout.

Summing up

Design is an art, what works for one project may not be appropriate for the next. As long as the end product appears professional when you are done, with all the elements working in concert with one another in a consistent manner, there is no one right way.

The best way to accomplish this is by using the tools in your design program to their fullest potential. Once you establish a format, create templates and style guides locking in those settings, that way when you encounter that element as you work you can use those short cuts to implement the correct design.

Chapter 6
Typesetting Pitfalls

There are a number of design *faux pas* that will instantly give a work away as self-published or small press. Not that the traditional publishers haven't been guilt of them as well, but it is generally less common because they have dedicated staff or freelancers whose job it is to specifically look for such things.

I have already mentioned some of these in the previous chapters, but I am addressing them separately here to go into more detail.

Bad Breaks. This could manifest in a variety of ways, but basically it is when the text cuts to the next page in an unfortunate way. Here are some examples:

- There is not enough room for the section break at the bottom of the page so it migrates to the top of the next page, leaving extra white space at the bottom of the previous page.

- The page ends with a header or section title at the bottom of the page, but the relevant text at the top of the next page.

- The first line of a poem or an insert prints at the bottom of the page and the rest appears on the next page.

- All of the words from a sentence remain on one line, while the punctuation is all alone on the next line.

These are just a few of the ways you can end up with bad breaks, but by no means are they the only ways. You will have to use your judgement and address the issues accordngly. But in the end, any break that is visually unpleasing or awkward should be dealt with.

Bad Hyphenation. Hyphens are a fact of life with justified text. There is no way to avoid them altogether. However, there are cases where you will need to eliminate hyphens. A bad hyphenation is when you break a word in a way that is awkward and confusing. For example:

- Contractions – never hyphenate contractions. It will break before the "n't" portion of the word and you do not want that starting the next line.

- Proper names – this one is not a hard-fast rule, just a suggestion. If possible try not to hyphenate a proper name, such as the name of a key figure or place, particularly the first time it appears.

- Compound words – If you have two words joined by a hyphen to create a compound word, do not introduce a second hyphen into the word or allow the automatic hyphenation to remain. Adjust the spacing until the line breaks on the existing hyphen or the compound word is all on one line.

- Breaking across pages – Hyphens can be disruptive at the best of times, even worse if two parts of the same word are on separate pages. If you can't adjust the hyphen out in the paragraph where it occurs, see if there is another paragraph where you can adjust the spacing to drop the last line to the next page so that the hyphenation is at least occuring on the same page. You can do this by adjusting the tracking (spacing between characters) or the leading (the spacing between lines.)

While not bad or wrong, you also want to avoid having too many lines ending in hyphens on the page. It just looks sloppy. A few will be unavoidable, but I generally try to have no more than three on a page, where possible. However, you won't always be able to adjust the spacing to eliminate a hyphen. Even when it is possible, you could find that eliminating the hyphen causes another problem. You have to decide which is the lesser of two evils, (or, if it is your own work, you could just revise the text to remove the issue.)

Lastly, while not technically wrong, I try to avoid hyphenation in the first or last line of a paragraph. You can't always, but it does feel more glaringly evident to me at those two points.

Hyphen- or Word-Stacking. Related to the above but a different issue, this is when you have more than one sentence in a row that either ends a hyphen or ends in the same word. This creates an uncomfortable visual pattern, and, in the case of the repeated word, can visually confuse the reader into losing their place.

Improper Alignment. The primary body of your text should always be justified (the text running from one side of the page to the other, with both sides aligning in a straight edge.) This creates a clean visual on the page that is easy to read and looks professional. While you may make the design choice to set portions of your text that are not justified (such as poems and letters) this should not be standard throughout.

Improper Spacing. This manifests in a variety of ways, but in general is when some spacing is visually excessive. For example:

- Double-spacing – Manuscript formatting is very different from publication formatting. While a manuscript should always be double-spaced to make it easier for an editor to read and allow them room to mark corrections, a printed book should never be double-spaced. The leading (or space between the printed lines) should be two points higher than the font size. (10 point font, gets a 12 point leading). Some publishers elect to make leading three points higher for a more comfortable read, depending on the font, due to irregularities in characters that extend above or below the line.

- Misaligned pages – This is when facing pages do not line up at the bottom of the page, ie, one page has more white space at the bottom. Text blocks should always be consistent in size when the pages face each other. This does not apply to facing pages where one is the end of a chapter and the other is the start of the next chapter.

- Excessive tracking – Remember on the previous page where I mentioned chosing the lesser of two evils? When you are adjusting your spacing to correct the other pitfalls listed in this section it is possible to over-correct, causing a more unsightly issue than the original problem. You may get rid of the hyphen or the bad break, but it causes too much or too little space between words or characters. You don't want one line to be very loosely spaced and the next one crammed together until you can hardly tell where one word ends and the other begins.

In some cases it is better to leave the original issue, with the understanding that you can't fix everything. An extra hyphen (in most cases) is less obtrusive than irregular text spacing. Always use the minimum of adjustment possible to correct an issue. When a reader looks at your book, it should be a seamless experience.

Improperly Placed Running Heads. Most pages in your book will include a running head, but there are instances where you would omit this, such as the opening page of a section, chapter, or story, and blank pages. This is where your templates come in. Most design programs have a way for you to create a template for each unique type of page you might use. You can also manually delete or change elements as needed.

Inconsistent Formatting. When you set a style for an element in your book, such as how the title will appear, or if the first paragraph of a page starts with a drop cap, it is important to be consistent and implement that formatting throughout your work. Most design programs and even word processing programs include tools that allow you to set style sheets or style guides to make it easier to format consistently. In most cases, it is just a matter of selecting the text element you wish to format and clicking on the style you have established. And the best thing, if you set a style sheet, if you need to change the formatting you can change the style sheet and it will update all instances where that style sheet was used so they all remain consistent.

Widows and Orphans. Most of us have heard of this taboo. How many of us actually know what it means? I am embarrassed to say that until last year my understanding was flawed. I can remember always being told to avoid them, but can't recall anyone explaining the issue in detail. For those who don't know, a widow is when the first line of a paragraph appears on one page and the rest of the paragraph is on the next page. And an orphan is when the last line of a paragraph falls on the next page.

It doesn't matter if it is one word or a full line, you want to avoid this.

For widows or short orphans, adjust the leading in the preceding paragraphs slightly so that one line moves to the next page, dealing with the orphan. To deal with longer orphans, you can adjust the tracking in the paragraph to add a little extra space on select lines to bump a word to the next line until there are two lines on the next page, instead of just one.

Summing Up

Don't get me wrong...this is by no means a comprehensive list of the potential pitfalls out there in the book-design world. I could likely write you an entire book on the fiddly bit things that can go wrong when typesetting—before you say it, I know, we don't actually *typeset* anymore, but since when has that ever stopped an industry from maintaining the lingo?—in any case, I have covered the most common issues encountered.

The key is to be consistent, clean, and professional. If you are adding space, don't add so much it is obvious what you have done. If you have set a style, don't change that style halfway through the book and make sure you use the correct style every time that design element appears.

Basically, check and double check that your book remains true to the blueprint from start to finish, and address unforeseen issues if and when they come up. If you do a proper job of it, the reader will never know there were issues along the way.

Chapter 7
Standard Amenities

Front Matter

There are two types of front matter, the kind that should appear in every book as a part the standard construction (Title, Copyright, and Contents* pages), and those the author chooses to include (Review Blurbs, Other Titles List, Dedication, Acknowledgements, and supplementary materials). The order these appear is pretty standard:

Review Blurbs. If a book has a number of high-profile positive reviews from sources that carry weight in the genre or industry, a page can be added before the title page where these can be included to entice potential readers. This page does not include a running head or page number.

Half-Title Page. A relic from another era, still used by printers who produce their books by offset or sheet-fed presses to prevent too many blank pages at the back of the book. Occasionally used by POD publishers when they have information they want to appear on a page facing the title page. This page does not include a running head or page number. If there is a Review Blurbs page a Half-Title Page would not be needed.

Other Titles List. Typically, this is on a left-hand page facing the title page. It includes other books by the author or anthologies or collections including the author's work. If the book is published through a publishing house, this list tends to include just books by

---

*Only in books where sections are distinctly identified with titles and/or authors.

that publisher. This page does not include a running head or page number.

Title Page. This is generally the first page in the book, but not always. The exceptions are listed above. They are optional and not always used. There will always be a title page and it will always be a right-hand page. There is no page number or running head. All a title page does is list the title, author, and publisher/imprint, and perhaps the series name, if there is one.

Regarding layout and design, one practice is to match the text treatment from the front cover, only in black and white. This can be done easily by extracting the text layer from the cover file in your art program and saving it as a separate file in black and white or grayscale, (depending on the available settings) then importing the title page as an image file. You can also replicated it in your desktop publishing software by retyping the text using the same fonts and styles so that it is an approximation of the cover text without matching it exactly.

Copyright Page. This should be the page directly following the title page, so it prints on the back of it. It should always be a left-hand page and there is no running head or page number. It includes the publisher's contact information, copyright notice, ISBN, Library of Congress Control Number (LCCC), any legal disclaimers, and production/art credits. Occasionally, publishers might include additional information here, such as if a series has a dedicated website, or if the author is available for events. It all depends on the space available.

If the book or part of the book has been published previously elsewhere that information will also be included on the copyright page, though I have seen it also placed on a separate acknowledgements page. Placement is at the publisher's discretion, as long as the information is included. This is a courtesy to the previous publisher, but also a courtesy to the reader so they don't pick up the book thinking it is new content, when they might have read all or part of it before.

Dedication. This is optional, but nice. Most books have one. The dedication can appear on the top of the copyright page, if there is room, or on a separate right-hand page facing the copyright page. If on a separate page, there is no page number or running head. A book can be dedicated to a loved one, in memory of someone lost, to someone you look up to, your hero...whatever you want. I once dedicated a book to "Albatrosses Everywhere" which seemed apropos for a collection titled *Consigned to the Sea*. A dedication should be either of special relevance to you as the author, or of some significance to the theme of the book.

Acknowledgements. This would start on a right-hand page. If it is one page long, there is no running head or page number, if it is longer than one page the subsequent pages do have running heads and page numbers.

Sometimes, an author wants to recognize family, friends, or professionals whose efforts were particularly noteworthy in making the book happen. Those that cheered them on, those who helped polish the manuscript, those who gave the author a chance to achieve their goal, or just someone who inspired them. This is what the Acknowledgements page is for. It is where the author thanks those who played some part in the realization of the dream.

However, it can also be where the publisher/author acknowledges previous publications of the work, particularly if, as in the case of a collection, there are multiple listings and insufficient room to include the information on the copyright page.

Contents Page (or Table of Contents). If the work is a novel and the author has only numbered the chapters and not titled them, there is no need for a contents page, unless the author includes additional content that is noteworthy, such as appendixes, excerpts, bonus stories, or glossaries. In that case, the author may chose to use a contents page so the reader is aware of the other content. With an anthology, collection, or nonfiction book a contents page is used to denote where stories, chapters, or other types of content appear in the book. This should start on a right-hand page. If it is one page long, there is no running head or page number, if it is longer than one page the subsequent pages do have running heads and page numbers.

Introduction. This is a part of the front matter, but would appear after the contents page (if there is one,) and would be included on it, whereas most of the other front matter elements would appear before the contents page and would not be cited. This would start on a right-hand page. If it is one page long, there is no running head or page number, if it is longer than one page the subsequent pages do have running heads and page numbers.

Introductions appear at the front of collections, anthologies, or textbooks and can be written by the editor, a respected professional in a related industry, or by a celebrity of some sort relevant to the content of the book. They could be written by the author themselves, but more often it is an endorsement by someone whose name carries weight. If the author writes it, it is more typically called a Foreword, A Note From the Author, Author's Note, or some other variation.

Supplementary Materials. Primarily with fiction or historic nonfiction, authors may chose to include bonus information at the beginning of the book to assist the reader in keeping details straight. Things like maps, timelines, lists of characters, and pronunciation guides for names and made-up or foreign words. Depending on what the material is and what space is available would determine where this information goes. Maps can go anywhere, but typically are before the title page, or right before the book proper begins. Lists and pronunciation guides appear after the dedication or Acknowledgements. If they are extensive, such information would more likely be included in the back matter, but it really depends on personal choice. This is the type of material that is non-standard to begin with, so there aren't really any rules. It is important to note, though, that if there is too much supplementary material at the beginning of your book, many readers have a habit of skipping it to get to the story.

Maps would have no running head or page number. Other types of supplementary material would start on a right-hand page. If they are one page long, there is no running head or page number, if they are longer than one pag,e the subsequent pages do have running heads and page numbers.

Back Matter

The following are the types of content that appear in the back of books. I have tried to put them roughly in the order I would expect them to appear, but to be truthful, I don't know that there are any hard and fast rules for what order things appear in the back matter.

Afterword. Similar to the Foreword, only it comes at the end of the book. It is where you as the author have a chance to expound on aspects of the book that you wouldn't want to talk about in the beginning before the reader is familiar with the content, either because the reader wouldn't get the references, or because you don't want to start off with spoilers. In the afterword, you can give a bit of insight into what inspired you, how the book came to be, or the challenges you faced in writing it.

Appendixes. Sometimes when you are researching or world-building for a novel you end up with more detail than you can feasibly include in the story without disrupting the flow or slowing down the pacing. This is content that can be included as Appendixes in the back of the book. If there are several different types of content, each one would be a separate Appendix. For example, if you have a scientific theory you researched and then extrapolated from, that would be one Appendix, but a detailed back story lending to the history of the universe would be a separate Appendix. Bonus content is nice, but don't overdo it. The more extra content you have, the longer the book. The longer the book, the more it costs to produce. The more it costs, the harder it might be to sell.

Glossary. If your book includes details or terms your reader may not be familiar with, you might want to include a glossary at the back of the book that provides expanded detail on those items so you aren't bogging your writing down with excessive explanation and the reader has a source to check if they get the details confused or want to know more if they are not familiar with a reference. These are alphabetical definition-style entries, with pronunciation guides (where applicable), definitions and origins of words or terms, and brief biographical entries on key characters. With a glossary, you have the option of going into greater detail than might be appropriate in the book itself.

Index. More applicable to nonfiction books, an index is where you list key terms and people mentioned in the book and what page numbers they appear on so that a reader can quickly locate specific information. Many programs have features that allow you to build indexes as you go along, but be wary of building your index in a word processing program. Often features like this do not import properly into a layout and design program because the coding is different. If your book has an index, this would be the last thing in the book, excepting, perhaps, your bio, depending on where you decide to place it.

Excerpts. With fiction books, it is not uncommon for a publisher (or author) to include excerpts from other works in the back of the book. This accomplishes two things: one, it lets the reader know there is more content out there; two, if the book is a little short an excerpt can help flesh it out to a desired page count. Sometimes they are excerpts of other books in the series, or just other books the author has written. Keep it short, and if it is not a related book, keep it relevant. (i.e. Don't put a hardcore science fiction excerpt in the back of an urban fantasy.) There isn't exactly a rule against it, but the audience for one genre doesn't always overlap with the audience of a different genre. Since excerpts are meant to entice readers to want to read the next thing, best to keep the content similar.

Bibliography/Sources. If you did any amount of research for your book, whether it is fiction or nonfiction, it is a good idea to include a listing of the sources you used in the back of the book, both to show you have factual contexts, and so that the reader can go to those sources for additional information, if they like. Of course, if you are writing nonfiction, you also want to cite your sources so you can't be accused of plagiarism.

About the Author. You put in a lot of work to write, format, and publish that book. Don't forget to tell them who you are and what else you've done. Some authors include personal details, others stick to their professional creds. Others interject humor and tailor their biography to the project at hand. However you approach it, things your bio should always contain are your name (duh), your publishing credits, and any major awards you may have received. Placement of this page varies. Some publishers put it right after the end of the book, and others put it after any back matter, so it is the last thing in the book. I have even seen publishers that put it in the front of the book...though I wouldn't recommend it.

In the case of anthologies, author bios can be handled in one of two ways. First, you could run the bio at the end of the author's story or chapter. Second, you could have a section at the back of the book where all the author bios run back to back either alphabetically or in the order they appear in the book.

Often, bios are also included for the editor or editors, and the artists, where applicable, those would always be at the back of the book.

Summing up

I am sure there are other types of front and back matter I haven't touched on here that are project-specific. There will always be variations, and for those you will have to use your judgment on what would look the most professional and best enhance the reader's experience.

As this book isn't about the technical aspects of writing, I will just say here that there are resources such as the Internet and style guides that can show you the proper way to write an index, glossary entry, or bibliographic reference. Seek those sources out and figure out which one suits your needs. Or, if you are doing design work freelance, confirm with your client if there is a particular style guide you should be following.

Just keep in mind, if you establish a style for something and that instance comes up again, whether in the same book or in a future project, remaining consistent to that style is an important part of establishing professionalism and building credibility. Sometimes, in this industry, that is all you have.

Text Checklist

Front Matter

- Does the title page include the title, author, and imprint or icon representing your company or brand?
- Does the copyright page include your company/brand and contact information, copyright information, standard disclaimer, and art credits?
- Do you have a dedication or acknowledgements page?
- If applicable, do you have a Contents page and do the chapter/story titles/author names match what is listed on the corresponding pages in the book? Are the page numbers correct?

Chapter/Story Opening Page

- Is the running head removed from this page?
- Is there comfortable space at the top of the page, with the title or chapter offset from the text copy?

Running Head/Foot

- Is the page number clear and visible, either at the outer edge of the running head, or centered or on the outer edge in the running foot?
- Is the title and author name clear, legible, but not over-whelming in the running head?

- Is there a comfortable space between the running head and the text block?

Text Block

- Is your font clear and readable?

- Is your text block justified (from margin to margin)?

- Is the spacing between lines comfortable? Not too open or too dense?

- Have you corrected for widows and orphans (one line of a paragraph alone at the top or bottom of a page)?

- Have you avoided having multiple lines ending with a hyphen or the same word stacked together?

- Have you adjusted the spacing to avoid hyphenated contractions or double-hyphenated words?

- Do you have a section break that complements your text without overwhelming it?

Illustrations/Graphic Treatment

- Does your graphic treatment complement the theme of your story?

- Are your illustrations properly placed in relation to the text they are related to?

- If applicable, do your illustrations have a corresponding citation that is noted in the relevant text?

- Are the images clean and clear? Are the lines crisp and solid? Do they complement the text?

- Is the art/image style consistent throughout the book?

Back Matter

- Did you include an up-to-date author biography?

- Have you included an excerpt? Is it genre-appropriate to your book?

- Do you have a glossary, if so have you included all the unique terms/primary characters in your book? Is it properly alphabetized?

- Does your book have an index? Is it properly formatted and does it include all relevant terms and key references?

- Does your book have references? Are they properly/consistently formatted and complete?

Part Three – Bonus Content

Chapter 8
But Wait, There's More...

What? You didn't think that was everything, did you? I covered the basics, things you encounter in any book, for the most part. Publishing, however, is rarely that simple. There are niche markets and specialty publishing and all kinds of books with rules of their own (how else can we break them, right?).

Consider this a bonus chapter touching on some of the most common specialty books with unique formatting to consider.

Epistolary Novels. Have you ever read a book that is nothing but a series of letters or journal entries, with little to no narrative in between? That is an epistolary novel. In most ways they are very much like any other book. They may be segmented into chapters, or they may just run from letter to letter until the end. I don't know that there is a set form since it is not a frequently used format.

The key is consistency. Create set formats for the specific elements and carry those through in every instance. For example, if this is a modern interpretation of an epistolary novel it could be told in an email format:

FROM: joe@mail.com   March 31, 2020, 4:44pm
TO: you@email.com
SUBJECT: The Message I Wrote

Do tell.

On Mar 30, 2020, at 8:45 PM, You Yourself <you@email.com> wrote:

>This is all I have to say.

This goes for letters, texts, memos, or any other type of correspondence (collectively called missives) through which a tale could be told. Use the format conventions associated with that style of communication, but don't go too crazy or it could be difficult to carry out through a full book or for a reader to even read. A simplistic but recognizable representation on the page will more deeply immerse the reader in the story.

If you are intermixing narrative between the letters, format things in such a way that there is a clear distinction between the different elements. Generally, this is done by making the missives italics, but I would not recommend that if most or all of the book is epistolary. It can be taxing on the readers' eyes. Another way to address this is to have the narrative in a conventional font, and the missives in a distinctly different font.

Whatever style you set, always keep in mind it should be consistent, clean, and easy to read.

Poetry Books. The major difference between a book of poetry and a book of prose is in the text block. Pretty much all the other elements are consistent. Here is a list of elements specific to poetry:

- A new poem starts a new page, unless they are very short, such as a haiku, and you chose to put several on one page. If this is the case, make sure it is clear they are separate poems. You should not, however, have a short poem followed by a long poem that runs to another page. It is acceptable to have a short poem follow a long poem, if there is sufficient space for it to appear fully on the page.

- If a poem does not have a title you generally put (untitled) at the top so it is clear it is the start of a new poem and that would be formatted in the style of the title formatting.

- The first page of a poem is generally handled the same as a chapter opening page, with distinctive styles for the title and poet, if applicable, and a simple style for the poem itself.

- If the collection consists of poems all by one poet, the poet's name would appear on the cover, the title page, and in the running head, but not on each poem.

- It is a design choice of how you will handle the running head. I have seen poetry books where the first page of the poem (as with chapters or stories) does not have a running head, but subsequent pages do have one. This is tricky, though, especially if most but not all of the poems are just one page long. Because of this dilemma, some designers put a running head at the top of every page in a poetry book and titles are treated in a simple manner. It is really up to you. As long as you are consistent in your choices and take into account the overall visual esthetic as it applies to your particular book, either choice is acceptable from an industry standard.

- Page numbers are generally centered at the bottom of the page in the running foot, especially if there is no running head or the running head only appears on certain pages.

- Alignment is either flush left, flush right, or centered, not justified. Unless there is a special case where lines or stanzas are specifically arranged as a visual part of the experience, alignment and indent should be consistent from poem to poem.

- While the page has standard margins, poems are generally indented so they are closer to the center of the page even if they are not center-aligned.

- Watch your spacing. If you need to run a poem to the next page and it has short stanzas, break it in between stanzas, not in the middle of them.

- With the exception of the first poetry page of the book, poems can start on a left or right page. Unless the book is divided into sections, there is no need to have a blank page in a volume of poetry.

Cookbooks. Again, as with most of these niche formats, all the basics still apply. A cookbook would have both a contents page and an index. It could potentially have Appendixes depending on the level of detail you want to provide.

Here is where things are different:

- The recipe name serves as the title.

- Ingredients list showing amounts and units of measure in a consistent format throughout, plus any specific preparation instructions (i.e. 1 cup of carrots, diced). This can be the total of each ingredient needed, or you can break it out for how much of the ingredients are needed for each stage of the recipe, in the order they are used. With this method, just as an example, the ingredients list for a dutch apple pie recipe would have butter listed two times, two tablespoons to dot the pie filling, and one stick to make the crumb top.

- Materials list showing what tools will be needed, per the instructions. Not every cookbook does this, but I find it helpful so I always include one.

- How many servings the recipe makes.

- Temperature to pre-heat to if the recipe is oven-based.

- Detailed instructions in the order they need to be executed.

- Helpful hints or recommendations.

- Variations or substitutions.

Cookbooks can be simplistic and text-based, or they can be full-color with photographs and side bars and all the bells and whistles. When you are ready to make your design choices take a field trip to your local bookstore and check out the cookbook section. That is the best way to get a feel for the design choices you can make.

Game Manuals. Now here is where things get interesting...and confusing. This type of book is what I would call a chimera. It is almost always part technical manual and part art book, with production values dependent on available resources and budget (not always the same thing.) It is difficult to tell you what to include where because layout and creative design are so tightly woven together in this format.

Here are the basics of what you usually find:

- Overview/Introduction to Game Mechanics
- The Game Universe
- Character Types
- Basic Skill Sets
- Advanced Skill Sets
- Weaponry
- Equipment/Techology/Magic/ Spells/etc.
- Non-Player Characters/Opponents/Monsters/Aliens/etc.
- Combat Mechanics
- Game Scenarios
- Quick Reference Charts

While there is typically a stylistic design running throughout the book, there may be a number of variations on page templates depending on the information being conveyed. Creating style sheets or templates for each different type of page you need streamlines the process. They can always be adjusted for special situations. As for formatting, much of it is design choice, but here are some standard design elements you should know:

Trim Size. Most game manuals take their format from a technical manual. As much data as possible is put on one page to facilitate ease of use and access to information during game play. With this in mind, the trim size of these books usually falls between 8 x 10 or 8.5 x 11, depending on the method of print and available paper sizes.

Icons/Tabs. Pretty much every game manual I have ever seen has had the different sections of the book identified by an icon or a tab on the outer edge of the page, either in the same place at the top of the page or along the outside edge of the page with each section being at a different point on the edge so that players or game masters can easily find the information they need. Kind of the way some dictionaries have cut-outs so you can find the section for each letter easily.

Text Block. Text more often than not flows in two or three columns to a page, with first line indented and justified text. This is, of course, modified if part of the page is taken up by data blocks.

Sidebars. This is related information that is not included in the main text, but is broken out in a side section. For example, if you have a three-column text block on the page but want to reference other information that is relevant without getting confusing you might have the standard text block only run two columns instead of three, and in the space that would have been the third column there is a separate information block with this collateral information. Often it is set off in some way, with a colored or shaded background, or maybe in a box, so that it is clear this is side information and not a continuation of the standard text.

Data blocks. Whether it is text or diagrams, tables or charts, game manuals deal in data. Relevant data should be grouped together in a logical manner in sections and cross-referenced as needed when the data is applied in the manual. If the data element is complicated, with many columns, it is a good idea to differentiate entries by either alternately highlighting every other entry, or dividing entries with a line between each one to make for easier tracking across the columns.

Graphics, Tables, and Charts. These should be well marked and easy to read, with the same style used throughout the book for uniformity and clarity.

The key to game manuals is consistency in how you convey the information. Often there will be a comprehensive table or chart laying out the game mechanics as it applies to different things, such as combat, damage, etc. Then later as elements of those charts apply to specific character types or situations, the relevant data is extracted from the comprehensive chart and replicated in a case-specific version of that chart, using the same formatting but in a smaller scale.

Summing Up

I know. There is someone out there wondering why I didn't cover x, y, or z. There are two camps on the matter. 1) everything else is just variations on what I have covered here; or 2) everything else is so stylistic that there are no "basics" to focus on.

With that in mind, if I missed something you were hoping I would cover, you can contact me and I might have some details I could share. If not, your best bet—as I have mentioned—is to go to where those books are and take a look at some examples in the wild. If one book did it, but the others didn't, it is likely a design choice. If you see elements that many of them used, that make it closer to a standard design element.

As always, in the end, your mantra should be clean, clear, and consistent.

Afterword

I know. I know. It's a lot to take in. Take a moment. Breathe.

If I've done my job right, you now have the blueprint to build better books. A starting place to improve your craft.

Yes. I said starting place. It is an ongoing process.

Book design and layout takes effort and practice. It isn't easy to keep all the fine details straight and to make sure everything is in its place. Often, even when you do everything exactly as you should, things go wrong. It might be because you didn't realize you activated a particular setting or you clicked on something you shouldn't have with the wrong tool selected. It might be because the program glitched and isn't doing what it is supposed to the way it is supposed to. Or it might be because you imported hidden code from your word-processing program without realizing it.

I once typeset a book five times from scratch because of such a hidden code.

To say I wasn't happy about it is a gross understatement, particularly when I discovered why things had glitched. But trust me, each time you work on a book you will learn something new. Every time you venture into the program you are going to use you will discover a new trick or a new tool that will make the next project easier. Don't be afraid to try new things. Don't hesitate to explore the program and see what it can do and how it does it. And don't forget, every program has a help feature. Can't figure out what went wrong or how to do what you want to do? Look it up and see what answers are out there. Or seek out an

online forum where others might have wisdom to share. Heck...
head over to YouTube because you know there's a video for
everything these days.

But most of all, don't give up. Enjoy yourself. Try new things.
Be creative. Make magic!

There can never be too many books.

Appendix
Avoiding Some Mistakes I've Made

I know. I said this book wasn't about how to use the design programs. And I meant it, really. But that doesn't mean I can't share with you some simple tips on avoiding headaches I've encountered on my own path of learning.

Design Problem – My chapters have run all together instead of starting on a new page.

Preemptive Solution – In your word processing program, be sure to use Insert Page Break when a chapter ends to start the next chapter. This is an example of coding that does play well with the design program.

Design Problem – The words are oddly spaced in some of my sentences.

Preemptive Solution – There are two potential causes of this. The first one is that there might be manual line breaks in the manuscript. Before you import your text into your design program make sure to "Find and Replace" all manual line breaks (in Microsoft Word the coding for this is ^ |), replacing them with a (space) or a paragraph mark (^p) as appropriate.

The other cause is when you have words or phrases linked by a / or ... so that the program interprets the whole grouping as one word. The way to fix this is to insert a hair space or thin space before or after the slash or ellipsis. These are small enough they aren't visible, but are enough to break the grouping so the program doesn't see it as one word. Search in your design program for Add Character (In QuarkXpress this is under the Utilities Menu.)

Design Problem – My footnotes/endnotes have integrated with my text.

Preemptive Solution – Do not use the formatting tools in your word processing program to create footnotes in your manuscript before you import it into your design program. Either designate them manually, or create the footnotes/endnotes using the tools in the design program after you import the text.

If you try to do it in the word processing program the note will be linked to the text where it is relevant and it will end up integrated within the text instead of appearing at the bottom of the page or at the back of the book.

Design Problem – The text is leaving large gaps at the bottom of the page.

Preemptive Solution – Before you import your text into your design program make sure to turn off the widow and orphan control and the settings that force lines to remain together. If that doesn't work, you will need to save your source file as a text only document to strip it of existing code and then reformat things like italic or special characters in the new file.

Design Problem - | # | - this code…don't know what it is or what it does, but I used this combination of symbols (with the # representing an actual number) as a decorative section break and when I tried to generate a PDF of the text it failed every time. I discovered the culprit when I tried creating a PDF of the book chapter by chapter and the chapter containing this treatment continued to fail.

Preemptive Solution – Don't do that. And more constructively, see if your design program has a feature that lets you see hidden code.

Design Problem – When I import text it is all in the wrong format.

Preemptive Solution – Before you import text, in the design program click on the *No Style* option in your standard style sheets, then import your text. It should retain all of the original formatting.

Design Problem – When I try to export Text from the design program, parts of it are missing.

Preemptive Solution – Do not import your text elements into your design program piecemeal. Create one manuscript file for your project before importing it. That way all the text blocks are linked together. Otherwise, you will have to identify each separate text block and export the text individually, then combine them into one file in your word processing program.

Design Problem – When I generate the PDF for print my blank pages disappear.

Preemptive Solution – In your design program, before you create your PDF, click on the Options button in the window that pops up when you select Export as PDF. In the window that opens when you click Options click the check box that says 'Include Blank Pages'.

Design Problem – When I upload my production files to the printer I get the error message that my text uses Spot Colors.

Preemptive Solution – With a black-and-white book, it is important that your text be in solid black. Sometimes black text in your word processing program comes across as a spot color when imported into the design program. After you import your text, select all text and then go to the color selector and designate the text to be just 'Black'.

Design Problem – When I upload my production files to the printer I get the error message that my file includes layers.

Preemptive Solution – Before you create your PDF, click on the Options button in the window that pops up when you select Export as PDF. In the window that opens when you click Options, click on the Layers option, once on that tab make sure the box that says 'Create PDF Layers' is not checked.

Design Problem – Have more questions?

Preemptive Solution – Drop me an email at especbooks@aol.com with *Build-A-Book Question* in the subject line.

Glossary

Acknowledgements – This generally goes at the front of the book, though some publishers choose to put it at the back. It is a list or written section where you acknowledge those who helped make the book possible, helped work on it, or supported you while you wrote it.

Appendixes – This is additional or expanded information presented at the end of the book. It is a way for the author to share research, theories, or back story without interrupting the flow of the story or text when the additional information might not be immediately relevant, just of interest.

Back Matter – The extra content located at the back of your book, such as but not limited to the author's biography, Appendixes, Glossary, or Index. Content that is separate from your story or nonfiction, but complements it.

Bar Code – A graphic representation of the ISBN (see below). It is made up of bars of varying widths that represent the individual numbers that make up the ISBN. It is traditionally printed on the back cover.

Bleed – This is extra space that you add to your cover design where the image or background color extends past the boundary of your final trim size. The bleed is there to provide a safety zone when the cover is trimmed down to size by the printer. This ensures that you do not end up with a white border along the edge of your cover if the trim is a little off.

Blurb – The text that appears on the back cover (or jacket flaps, in the case of a hardcover) that describes the book, enticing the reader to want to know more. Also called Cover Copy, Cover Blurb, Book Blurb, or Jacket Copy.

Chapter/Story Title – The identifying text that appears on the first page of your chapter, story, or article, depending on if you are producing a novel, collection/anthology, or nonfiction work.

CMYK – This is a color profile, or mode, that stands for Cyan, Magenta, Yellow, and Black. That means that every color on your cover is made up of different values of some combination of those four colors.

Contents Page – Also called the Table of Contents. The list of sections that appear in your book, including titles and page numbers. If the book involves contributions by multiple individuals, the author's name would appear following the title of their work. This only includes materials that come after the contents page.

Copyright Page – The page following the title page, including the relevant details and disclaimers required in publishing, such as, but not limited to, the publisher's contact information, the copyright notice, the relevant ISBNs, Library of Congress Control Number, and legal disclaimers, also included are the credits for the cover art, any illustrations, the editor, and the designer(s).

Cover Template – A file provided by the printer showing the exact dimension of your book cover, including guidelines indicating where the cover will be folded and trimmed. Templates also include your basic book data, the bar code matching your ISBN, and markings indicating the minimum safe zones for where you can place your text and important elements of your artwork. Templates are provided electronically as PDFs or InDesign files.

DPI – Stands for Dots Per Inch. The clarity of all images is measured in DPI. The more dots per inch, the clearer an image is. The less dots per inch, the more jaggy an image is. The higher the DPI, the bigger the file will be.

Drop Cap – When the first letter of the first word on a page is larger and inset into the first paragraph by two or more lines. Often the font is different and more ornate than that used for the base text. Take care which font you choose as some have florishes that will obsure the surrounding text. The font should be easy to read and complement the feel of the book.

Facing Pages – These are pages that will be visible side by side when you open the book. In other words, you can see them at the same time without turning the page. You can think of it this way, if you close the book they are facing each other. Well…more than facing, but what happens behind closed covers…

Folio – The technical term for the page number.

Front Matter – The extra content located at the front of a book, such as but not limited to the title page, Table of Contents, dedication, maps, list of characters, list of terms, or pronunciation guides. This material is generally numbered with lowercase roman numerals when there is a page number on the page. A running head or page number is generally only used if the element (such as the contents page) is longer than one page.

Full-Bleed – When a background or image extends all the way to the edge of the printed page. To allow for this and make sure there is no white space where there shouldn't be, the designer extends the background or image a quarter inch past the desired trim size of the book.

Glossary – A list of terms that generally appears in the back matter giving greater detail regarding terms or concepts depicted in the book.

Gutter Margin – The extra space you should add to your text design on the inside edge of the page where the book will eventually be bound. Typically, you would add a quarter of an inch or more depending on the thickness of the book. This extra space allows the book to be bound without the text disappearing into the binding of the book.

Half-Title Page – The same as the title page, but with only the title of the book printed on it, not the author and the publisher. When there is a half-title page, it is generally the first page in the book, followed by a blank page, a list of other titles by the author, or a quote or image the author wishes to start off the book with. Half-title pages are a legacy from offset or sheet-fed printing, where a book's pagination must be in increments of four-, eight-, or sixteen-page signatures. If there are too many blank pages at the end of the book (which looks bad) a half-title page is included in the front matter to adjust the signatures and reduce the number of blank pages in the back. In digital printing a half-title page might be included if there is some design element the author or publisher wants to include on the page facing the title page.

Imprint – The brand under which the book is being produced. Sometimes this is the publisher's name, but sometimes a publisher will create a separate sub-brand to group books by genre or type.

Index – These are used for nonfiction, textbooks, and cookbooks. It is a list of the relevant terms in the book and where they are discussed so that readers can go directly to the passages that may contain the information they are looking for.

Introduction – Some books will have an introduction. In most cases, these are collections or nonfiction books. The introduction may be written by the author, or by a notable individual, such as a professional in the industry or a well-known author.

ISBN – International Standard Book Number. A unique identifier assigned by the publisher. Each version of a book requires its own ISBN, which is tied to basic data about the book, such as but not limited to publisher, title, author, format, page count, and price. The ISBN is used by booksellers and librarians to order your book and manage their inventory. All ISBNs are purchased via a service called Bowker. If you purchase from Bowker, the ISBN will show you as the publisher. ISBNs are expensive purchased individually through this service, but the price goes down when you buy in bulk. Standard options are one, ten, and one-hundred ISBNs, with the cost per number going down the more you order at once. If you obtain an ISBN through a publishing service, such as Kindle Direct or Ingram Spark, they are less expensive, or even free, but those numbers indicate that the company you received them from is the publisher of that book, which will also imply to those in the industry that it is self-published, whether it is or not.

Layout – 1. How the elements of your book are arranged on the page. 2. The act of arranging the elements of your book, including placement and style.

Logo – A graphic element representing your brand or imprint. The icon or design should be unique to you. Keep it simple so that it can be scaled up or down as needed and still be legible. It should also be distinct so that it can be readily identified as representing your company. You will want both a black-and-white version, for use in the interior, and a color version, for use on the cover. You will also want to use this logo for advertising purposes.

Margins – The blank space running around the edge of the text block denoting the edge of the page.

POD – Print on Demand. This is a digital printing method that allows you to print as few or as many copies as you need. Rather than a printing press, this method makes use of a more advanced copier-type printer where a book prints on standard paper sheets, which are trimmed down to the desired size.

Price-Specific Bar Code – A graphic representation of the ISBN. It is made up of bars of varying widths that represent the individual numbers that make up the ISBN. It also includes additional bars that represent the retail price you have set. You can find free software online that will generate any type of bar code you need. Your printer should also be provided one by your printer if you request a cover template file. There is no need to purchase a bar code, it is an unnecessary expense.

Review Blurbs – Occasionally, a book will include advance reviews or reviews of a previous edition. When these are particularly favorable and from a reputable source, publishers will often include these at the beginning of the book on the first page following the front cover.

RGB – A color profile, or mode, that stands for Red, Green, and Blue. That means that all the colors on your cover are made up of different values of some combination of these three colors.

Running Foot – When the page numbers appear consecutively at the bottom of the printed page.

Running Head – The text and/or page number that appears at the top of the printed page. For novels, it generally contains the title of the book on one page and the author's name on the facing page, both accompanied by the page number. For collections or anthologies, it generally contains the title of the book on one page with the story or article title and author on the facing page, both accompanied by the page number.

Section Break – A decorative element that appears between two separate sections of text, generally in a work of fiction. It can be a font-generated symbol or an actual art graphic that complements the theme of the book.

Sidebar - In textbooks, manuals, and cookbooks, these are text blocks that are separate from the main content, but convent additional information that is related or that the author feels might be useful, or highlights points they wish to emphasis.

Stock Art – Photographs, illustrations, or works of art that have been posted by an artist on a Stock Art website where individuals can purchase a non-exclusive license to use the art for use as interior illustrations or cover art. The cost of the license depends on which rights you wish to purchase and the cost will differ from site to site. There are subscriptions you can sign up for that reduce the overall cost. It is not unusual for artists to create portfolios on multiple sites and there is no limit to how many individuals may license that image. Once you secure the rights to use an image you are able to modify it or combine it with other art to suit your needs but must credit the original artist or artists on the copyright page of your book.

Style Guides – In many desktop publishing programs—if not all—there are tools where you can define the formatting for different aspects of your book so that when they reoccur all you need to do is select the correct style and the formatting will be implemented. The style guides also allow you to change the style of an element in one place and have it automatically apply to all instances of that style.

Templates – In many desktop publishing programs—if not all—you can create a standard template, or Master, for a type of page in your book that you can drop into place as needed changing the existing layout to the desired layout.

Text Treatment – The words that appear on your cover and any special effects you may employ to embellish them via an art program or internet site.

Title Page – This page includes the basic identifying information of a book. In most cases, the title, series, book number (where applicable), the author or editor's name, the imprint and the publisher's location.

Trim Size – The final dimensions of your printed book. A standard trim size for a Trade Paperback is six inches by nine inches (or 6 x 9). These dimensions are set, though the actual measurements of the book might vary slightly depending on how precisely the book is trimmed on the production line. The spine width of your book is determined by the weight of your paper and the number of pages in the finished book.

The Literary Handyman

Build-a-Book: Anthologies

To all of the unwitting masochists out there who truly believe it might be fun to put together an anthology.

Contents

An Introduction to the Insanity of Anthologies

Some people in the industry will tell you that anthologies are a waste of time, money, and paper, and depending on their business plan they might be right, but for me, I have found great satisfaction and benefit in the anthologies I have been fortunate enough to be involved in, as an author, editor, and publisher.

Let me give you some background, though. I put together my first anthology, *No Longer Dreams*, in 2005. Though I am listed as editor, my involvement in the project was more as a packager. For those not familiar with the distinction, an editor generally reads and selects the stories to be included (or approved by the publisher), coordinates with the publisher and any copy or line editors, determines the order of the stories, and submits an edited manuscript, whereas a packager handles all aspects of the book production and provides the publisher with complete book files ready for print (this may or may not include the cover files). In addition to *No Longer Dreams* I have produced or helped produce thirty-six or more anthologies, including *The Bad-Ass Faeries* series (five collections), *The Defending the Future* series (nine collections), *If We Had Known*, *Footprints in the Stars*, and *The Side of Good/The Side of Evil*, to name a few.

What can I say… I must be at least part masochist.

Each and every one of those projects had its own challenges. The one thing they all had in common? They were a LOT of work. I take the approach that I do because I LOVE creating something from nothing. I love the creative freedom of designing all aspects of a project and then making it happen. Most editors do not have such free rein. I don't even recommend it for the majority of editors for one reason: experience. Not everyone has the knowledge or skills needed to handle *all* the various responsibilities required to create a book from concept to completion. Of course, not everyone needs to, with the number of freelancers available to handle the various tasks involved in producing a book. If you are considering attempting to do so, research what is involved, or better yet, get a mentor. I have the advantage of over thirty years of publishing experience, or I wouldn't even try it myself. Regardless of who is responsible for the work, anthologies take a lot of effort and coordination to produce. But the rewards can be great, if nothing else in satisfaction alone.

The Classification of Anthologies

There are many different approaches to anthologies. Of all of the choices you make as an editor or packager what type of anthology you chose to create will guide your process the most. As with magazines, anthologies come in many varieties. Some are themed, others cater to a particular audience, and yet others feature the best of... well, whatever. Let's look at what all of that means:

Themed – This is pretty self-explanatory: A collection of stories that have an overall theme connecting them. The theme can be broad, or very, very specific, but it serves to unify the content so that it targets a particular market with which that theme is popular. Basically, it means the reader is more likely to pick up the book because they know what to expect, in general, from each story. Examples of themes are Love-At-First-Sight, Vampires, Pirates and Magic. A colleague even published an anthology where the only requirement was that the line "Release the Virgins!" had to appear somewhere in each story. So, yeah, pretty much anything. The benefit of this type of anthology is that readers may be drawn by the topic, even if they are unfamiliar with the authors. These are easier to market as they are focused and hold an appeal to an identifiable fan base.

Unthemed – With this type of collection, writers submit on any topic and there is no unifying factor from story to story, other than that they are in the same collection. One could hope there is some uniformity in genre as well, but not always. This means freedom for the writer, as they are not restricted in what they submit, but not as appealing to the reader because there is the real possibility that they will not be interested in all the stories. These are difficult to sell because the content could vary greatly in genre, theme, and style, leading to an uneven collection. Readers are more likely to be influenced by particular names in the book. In fact, it is possible that if they do buy the collection, they will only read the story by the author they know and follow.

Shared Universe – I know... *what*? This is a kind of very specific themed anthology where the author must write in someone else's established universe. Mostly you see these as media tie-ins (universes based on comic, television, or movie franchises, such as Star Trek, Supernatural, or Marvel), but occasionally you will see them based on gaming systems or popular novels by other authors, or even on a property unrelated to any of those, created specifically as a sandbox for other authors to play in. Examples of this are Eric Flint's *Ring of Fire* or Jeff Sturgeon's *Last Cities of Earth* universes. These collections are most likely—but not always—invitation-only and require the author to either already be conversant with the universe, or adherence to a series bible that familiarizes them with the relevant details before they start writing. Basically, you are in someone else's playground. It can be good for getting your name out there but can also limit you when it comes to writing your own original work, which may not be as well received if the readership has come to expect branded work from you.

Best Of – Mostly, this is here just so I know I'm doing a thorough job. We all hope to be included in one of these someday. Someone else generally decides. Whoever is putting the collection together combs through all the works published during the relevant timeframe that fit the guidelines of the collection. It might be the best of the year, the best of a particular magazine or genre, or the best of a particular author. Consequently, this is a reprint type of anthology usually edited/compiled by a well-respected editor in the industry, such as *The Best Horror Fiction of the Year*, edited by Ellen Datlow, or *The Best Science Fiction of the Year*, edited by Neil Clarke.

In some cases, the editors find the material on their own; in others, you or your publisher might have the opportunity to send in a collection you have worked on for consideration. It is a real honor for all involved to have a selection included in a Best-Of collection. Mostly, you have no control over this, but yes... we can all dream!

Single-Author Collection – Not really an anthology, *per se*, but quite similar in construction and requires some of the same consideration. Will it be themed? Will it be a hodge-podge? Are all the stories the same genre? How do you organize the book? It is very important to go into these with a clear plan or risk some of the same pitfalls as unthemed anthologies where your potential readership is only interested in a portion of the book, or the collection appears uneven because the stories are disjointed in relation to one another.

Organizational – I know that sounds odd, but there isn't really a term for this type of anthology, just the practice of creating them. What I mean here is that different writers' organizations, such as the Horror Writers Association (HWA), Broad Universe, or The Science Fiction and Fantasy Writers Association (SFWA), just for example, have been known to compile anthologies of their members' work. Sometimes it is an annual project, or just a periodic endeavor. The content, either reprint or original, would be dictated by the organization's focus and may or may not be themed.

Charity – Typically — but not always — these are themed in some way to relate to the charity being supported. The key here is that all or most of those involved in the project donate their talents and do not receive payment for their work, beyond, perhaps, copies of the book. The project might be to raise funds and awareness for a particular cause, or just to help out a friend or someone in the industry facing hard times. Examples are *Mine!: A Celebration of Liberty and Freedom for All Benefitting*

Planned Parenthood, published by Comic Mix LLC, or *Dance Like a Monkey*, a collection published by Silence in the Library Press to benefit the late author CJ Henderson.

Nonfiction – While the majority of anthologies are fiction of one type or another, there are those who have made a place for themselves in the market by producing collections of essays on particular topics. Generally, they are related to some type of media or literary fandom, but occasionally they are of a how-to nature, such as writers' guides where those in the industry write on relevant topics, sharing their knowledge and experience with those just getting started. There is a market for these types of collections, but it can be even narrower than those dictated by genre. In addition, Nonfiction can be paired with any combination of the other types of anthologies/collections already discussed in this section. For example, *The Literary Handyman* series that you are currently reading is a single-author nonfiction collection. It is also a themed nonfiction collection in that it is focused on the craft and business of being an author. Another example is *Ardeur: 14 Writers on the Anita Blake, Vampire Hunter Series* produced by Smart Pop, where the essays in the collection focus on and analyze a popular fiction series.

With all these variations, it is important to identify your end goal before you begin as each style has different considerations to take into account if you—and the anthology—are to succeed.

They Must Submit

Now that you have some understanding of the different approaches to anthologies, there is another aspect that we should look at: the terms of submission. After all, you can't produce an anthology or collection without content.

Open Submissions – This is where a call is made public, and anyone can submit as long as they follow the parameters set out by those putting the collection together. There is a lot of competition from hopefuls, and it is not unheard of for an editor to receive hundred, or even thousands of submissions for one call. The editor or publisher either posts this information on their website, or through one of the many websites dedicated to listing calls for submission. Some of those sites even offer tools to both the authors and editors for managing those submissions on that platform. A call for submissions can also be posted in multiple places. I'm not listing examples because the content at some point would become outdated. I recommend doing a web search for "call for submissions" or "open call" for places to post your listing, just be aware that the more broadly you broadcast the signal, the more submissions you are going to receive. That is both a good and a bad thing, depending on your available time, the quality of the submissions, and how well the authors followed the guidelines you posted.

Semi-Open Submissions – Some editors, mindful of the available time and or staff they have to review submissions, make a limited public announcement being very specific where it appears. This can make submissions more manageable, but it could also mean that you don't receive enough quality writing to fill the book.

Invitation Only – Well yeah, it's just what it says. As the editor, you hand-select specific authors you would like to include in the collection—or have authors recommended to you. Generally, the quality of the work you can expect to receive should be more reliable (I mean, seriously, it's not like you're going to invite bad authors to submit, right?), but there is always the chance that an author might not produce what you are looking for, or perhaps they aren't able to deliver their story at all in the end because of outside life events or other issues. You have to decide if you are going to invite more authors than there are planned slots in the anthology, or if you will maintain a list of back-up authors in case your first picks can't deliver or have scheduling conflicts.

In some cases, editors I know will compile a collection in a hybrid manner. Meaning, they will invite a select number of known authors, usually called anchor authors, to contribute but leave a portion of the slots open for submission. Using this method, they have the opportunity to discover new talent, but also have reliable authors to draw in the readership. Another reason for this plan of action is to inspire support for a project if it is being funded through crowdfunding.

Reprint – This is a variation on either Best-of or Invitation Only combined with Themed. Basically, you as the editor, or the publisher decides to compile a particular collection (say, on Lovecraftian Horror or Dog stories... just saying). You can go through a bunch of published fiction that fits the chosen parameters and then attempt to secure the reprint rights, and/or you can post a call for submissions indicating what types of reprint stories you are looking for.

Competition – These collections are usually incidental to a particular writing contest. Meaning, the author enters the contest to win the prize—usually monetary—and the anthology is just a small part of that prize. The most famous (or infamous) of these is the Writers of the Future competition, with four submission periods a year, culminating in a week-long writers' conference for the finalists, ending in a very high-profile awards ceremony and, eventually, a published anthology.

Competitions are generally governed by theme or genre and often have restrictions as to who can submit based on experience level or other criteria. In other words, if an author has too many pro credits or are affiliated with those running the competition, they are excluded from entering. Some editors/publishers use this method to secure submissions in a timely manner and increase visibility. Some also charge a nominal submission fee to fund the award and project. Be cautious of competitions that require a fee. Check them out before submitting to ensure their reputation for completing and delivering what is promised.

The Legalities

Let me start out by saying there are loads of sample contracts out there, so I'm not going to go into exacting detail here, but it is important that when you start an anthology project all parties have a clear understanding — and agreement — of what each both gives and receives in terms of the project. Here are some of the things to consider.

Types of Rights

What do you want to produce, and where do you want to make it available? This is the first thing you need to determine, because your contract needs to detail precisely what you plan, and the author has to agree. What follows are the most common rights you are likely to encounter. And, let me just say, don't be *that* publisher... the one who claims every right possible and more, without any actual intention of pursuing most of them. This is called a rights grab, and it is a good way to get a bad reputation. So, if you don't intent to produce an audiobook, for example, don't claim those rights because you will prevent the author from being able to generate an audiobook themselves, or through an audiobook producer and you will lose out on possible positive exposure for your version of the book.

Grants

Distribution – This is when the contract stipulates where you can sell the end product, either specific to the country where you are publishing, worldwide, or some variation in between. If you are producing an ebook version of your anthology you must secure worldwide distribution rights, because ebooks can be bought from anywhere.

Format – There are many different types of books these days, and your contract must detail what formats you are obtaining the rights for: print, digital, audiobook, etc. Some contracts even make allowances for formats that have not yet been developed but could be.

Media – Beyond publishing the book, if you intend to develop properties based on the content of the book you are producing, those rights have to be secured as well. Examples are merchandise, movies, television shows, or games based on content in the book.

Exclusive – The story is original, and the publisher is obtaining the rights to publish that story exclusively for usually a set amount of time, either in a particular region, or worldwide.

Non-Exclusive – The story has already been published somewhere previously, but the rights have reverted to the author and the new publisher receives the right to print the story over again with the understanding that it has already been published previously.

Work-For-Hire – The author is creating original work based on licensed intellectual property or a literary universe created by someone else, to which the publisher has right of use. In this case, the author does not retain rights to the work produced, and depending on the situation, might not even have their name directly associated with the work produced, depending on the terms agreed upon.

In my contracts, I generally secure first-time publication rights in print and digital, worldwide for one year exclusive, four years non-exclusive; meaning, the author can submit the story elsewhere or publish it in a collection themselves one year after the anthology has been produced.

Reversion of Rights

Every contract should have one of these clauses. It is exactly what it says, the terms and conditions under which the rights will either automatically revert back to the author, or when and how the author can request their rights back.

Warranties

Contracts are there to protect both parties. With this in mind, there is a section of the contract that details the expectations that the work provided is original, that the author has the right to enter into an agreement, and that nothing in the work violates anyone else's copyright. And if, by chance, any of that is not correct, the author is liable if legal action occurs because of said violations.

Payment

There is the assumption that if you are entering a contract with someone, there will be some sort of equitable exchange. You receive rights, they receive payment. Now, that payment in this industry often varies wildly.

Advance – Some publishers offer advances on works being published. Mostly, this is for novels or solo collections, but it bears mentioning. An advance is an agreed-upon amount the author will receive when the contract is signed. This is not a free-and-clear payment, it is (as stated) an advance on projected royalties.

Flat-Fee – Often, particularly with independent presses, anthology contributors are paid a set amount for their work (generally a per-word fee (pro rates currently are considered $.08 a word), but sometimes just an agreed-upon dollar amount, regardless of the length of the story.

Royalties – this is when the contributors receive a percentage of the earnings a book generates, either based on the gross income, the net income, or the profit. The percentage may vary depending on what the royalty is based on. For my titles, the contributors share an equal percentage of 50% of the profits, but if the royalty is calculated based on the gross income, the percentage is generally lower.

For-the-Love – Yeah, you got it. They get bupkis. When this term is in the contract, the authors receive no monetary compensation for the use of their work, either up front or in the future. Some authors will go for this term if they are trying to get their name out there or because it is a project they want to participate in, but unless it is a book raising funds for a charity or a cause, most experienced authors tend to shy away from these.

Comp Copies – Also called author copies, the contract should stipulate how many copies of the book produced the contributors receive. This could be anywhere from three, to one, to none, depending on the publisher. It is also standard for authors to have the option of buying additional copies at a discount. Typically, 50% discount off the retail price, but again, this varies by publisher. Again, most authors aren't interested if they don't at least get a copy for their brag shelf, I know I'm not.

In some cases, an author's payment will be stipulated in books, rather than fund. Contract generally indicate whether an author is or is not free to sell gratis or discounted copies at author events.

These are the basics that all contract should include, but like I said, there is a lot more to a contract than I am really qualified to go into, so check out some of those on-line resources that are out there for more detailed explanation and examples.

Pointers

- Never send out an electronic contract that can be modified, always send a fixed format.
- The contract should have a place for the author's signature/

digital signature, their address, and the date, as well as places at the bottom of each page for both parties to initial to indicate they have reviewed that page. This is to show that no unauthorized changes have been made to the contract by either party.

- If a term or clause is contested or an error is identified in the contract, modifications should be made and initialed by both parties.

- Both parties should sign two copies of the contract, if signing a physical copy, so that both parties will have a fully executed original. If the author returns just one copy, you should sign, then scan the contract. Send the author the copy and you should retain the original.

Putting Together an Anthology: An Overview

Let's assume you have a publisher already (or plan to publish yourself) and you have decided what type of anthology you want to produce. Here are the steps that have to take place pre- and post-production.

Call for Submissions – either post your announcement online, or issue personal invitations to those authors you would like to see submissions from. Your announcement should include the following: Theme (if any), Deadline, Word Count, Rights being secured, Rate, formatting requirements, acceptable submission methods, and where to send submissions. A title (tentative or final) and estimated publication date would be good as well, though optional. There are plenty of places out there to post calls for submissions, but if you go that route, be prepared to receive a LOT of submissions.

Initial reading – everyone has their own procedure for this, and with projects involving more than one staff member, there is often a person designated as first reader. They read through and weed out those submissions that are of low quality or off topic, if there is one.

Second pass – this is the period where those stories being considered are read by the editor or editors and they either reject the story or provide feedback and the author is invited to revise and resubmit the story for further consideration.

Final cut – the editors review the surviving submissions one more time and determine if the feedback has been incorporated to their satisfaction, making final determinations as to what will be accepted and what they will reject.

The Legalities – Acceptances and Rejections sent. Contracts signed and countersigned. Or haggled over...

Editing and Revisions – editors (or copy or line editors) review the final manuscripts and return them to the authors for final edits.

Design and Typeset – depending on the publisher the design aspect of the project can take place independently at any stage in the above process. If a separated designer is responsible for the style of the book they will come up with several concepts for approval, which then will be reviewed with the publisher and/or editor. One is selected or modifications are requested. Once the design is set, the manuscript is approved, and contracts executed the book is typeset. If the book will be illustrated this is the stage where the editor would discuss the project with the artist and provide copies of the stories on which the artwork will be based.

Cover Creation – This is another task that can take place at any stage of the process. Cover art is either created specifically for the project or licensed for a one-time use. The art might be based on a particular story, a combination of elements from multiple stories, or unrelated to specific content in the collection, but representing the theme. Once cover art is approved the cover design is determined and back cover copy is written by either the editor or a copywriter.

Galleys – a pdf or print copy of each typeset story is sent to the authors for review. It is their task at this point to look for errors in formatting or typos that were missed, but no other optional modifications should be made at this stage.

Final Files – the typesetter incorporates any corrections and produces final files that will be sent to the printer to produce the book. If an ebook version is scheduled to be released, this is created at the same time. You can either engage a freelancer for this or there is free software you can download to convert print files to ebook. We use Calibre.

Pre-Release Promotions – the editor or marketer generates press releases, blog entries, and any other advertising materials desired. Announcements are made via social media, internet reporting sites, blogs, websites… any and all venues applicable, many of which are free. Authors are also encouraged to advance promote to spread awareness as widely as possible, making use of the fan base for each person in the book.

Post-Release Promotions – more of the above, with the addition of launch parties, convention appearances, and author signings at bookstores, libraries, and any other applicable venue. And when deeming applicability… be creative! (I've done book and craft fairs, ice cream socials, wine tastings… etc. I have even approached Harley Davidson dealerships to see if they would be willing to host an event centered around my biker faerie books. Hey, you never know! This stage should never end, as long as the book is in print.

Royalties – when applicable – These are paid either directly by the publisher or through the editor, who receives them from the publisher. There are two parts of this, reporting and paying. Generally, but not always, both parts take place simultaneously with a royalty statement outlining sales for a given royalty period being sent by email (PDF format) or conventional mail. Payment may or may not go out at the same time. Some publishers have an amount threshold, generally anywhere between $10 and $25 due, before they issue payment. It may take a while to reach that if sales are low because any royalty is divided between the authors/editors involved in the project. Also, if the anthology is for charity or fundraising, those involved may receive a statement indicating what was raised for the cause, but no payment. Reporting/Payment schedule depends upon the publisher's policy and what was laid out in the contract. Pretty standard is royalties paid on a six-month schedule, though I have seen monthly and quarterly, as well as yearly. Whichever you choose, the actual schedule should be based on when the money from sales for a given period are received. For example, we issue royalty statements/payments twice a year: in March (covering January 1 to June 30), and October (covering July 1 to December 31). The reason for this offset is that most printers or distributors have a built-in agreement that the profits from sales are delivered ninety days after those sales are recorded. By reporting and paying royalties in March and October we ensure we have received all of the funds needed to pay the authors.

The Nuts and Bolts of Building Your Manuscript

There is an art to putting together a collection, be it single-author or anthology. Even if the collection is unified by a theme, you are still taking multiple topics and/or voices (yes… even with a single-author collection. There are many different voices in an author's head) and trying to shape a satisfying or logical arc. That can be very tricky, and your success (or failure) will impact the readers' impression of the collection.

I know… what the heck does that mean?

It isn't enough to pick great stories. Deciding what order to arrange them in is key to a successful collection. Not only do you want to hook potential readers right from the start, but you want to keep them engaged and turning those pages. You also want them to be satisfied when they reach the end. Often, that means putting as much effort into arranging the stories as you did selecting them.

My recommendation is to review all of your stories looking for the inherent patterns that might help you decide the order. This is just a place to start, however. There are many more elements that complicate the process. Here are a few different things to consider:

Quality – One of the rules of thumb for arranging anthologies is to start and end with your best stories. This is because the first story must hook the reader, and the last story will leave them with a better impression of the overall experience. You can take this a step further by putting the third-best story in the middle, then arranging everything else around those three anchor points.

The other consideration is alternating weaker stories with stronger stories. Believe me... every collection has them, in relation to one another. By doing this you avoid frustrating the reader because they have read several stories in a row that stand out as less than the others. If you have weaker stories clumped together and better stories clumped together, the reader will have an uneven reading experience that could impact their enjoyment.

Name Recognition – If you have stories by both established and lesser-known authors, one thing you can do is alternate so that your known names aren't all grouped together.

Progression – Is there a natural order among the stories? For a shared universe or alternate history collection this could mean a historic timeline linked to specific dates or rough periods. For a military collection it could be an arc of stories progressing from planet-based encounters to space based, or likewise Earth, to space, to alien planet. You may or may not find this in your own collection, but it is a place to start.

Avoid Repetition – Make note of the aspects of each story, particularly those elements that appear in multiple stories. It could be a general theme, or a setting, or even a character type. Anything that makes one story echo another in the collection and make sure to spread those out throughout the manuscript. For example, in our collection *Devilish & Divine* several of the stories took place in bars, and half of the stories were about angels, the other half about demons. Several contained both. We had to arrange to stories to alternate angel and devil stories, but also to make sure the bar stories were not in relation to one another. (A side note, one of the ways I avoid repetition in my collections... or try to, anyway... is to have authors submit a synopsis of what they plan to write for approval before they begin. This way if two authors have similar ideas, I can direct one of them in a different direction and have a more balanced book in the end. Of course, that doesn't mean elements of particular stories won't echo others submitted, but you can't control everything, no matter how hard you try.)

Themes – Sometimes there is no easy way to divvy up the stories that is ideal. One way around this is to divide the collection into sections and then apply the above tactics to each section. The first anthology I ever packaged, *No Longer Dreams*, didn't have a theme, so instead we divided the book by genre. Another example is the *Bad-Ass Faeries* anthologies. They had themes, but were more difficult to arrange because of the similar natures of the stories, even with approving a synopsis ahead of time… With those we found the logical sub-themes among the stories and grouped things that way. For example, *Bad-Ass Faeries: It's Elemental* we had five sections: Earth, Air, Fire, Water, and Spirit.

Of course, it is seldom as simple as selecting *one* of the above methods and building your manuscript, but in combination you can structure quite a satisfying experience for the majority of readers, and in the end, isn't that what we are trying to do?

Danielle Ackley-McPhail

An award-winning author, editor, and publisher, Danielle has worked both sides of the publishing industry for longer than she cares to admit. In 2014 she joined forces with husband Mike McPhail and friend Greg Schauer to form her own publishing house, eSpec Books (www.especbooks.com).

Her published works include six novels, *Yesterday's Dreams, Tomorrow's Memories, Today's Promise, The Halfling's Court, The Red-caps' Queen*, and *Baba Ali and the Clockwork Djinn*, written with Day Al-Mohamed. She is also the author of the solo collections *Eternal Wanderings, A Legacy of Stars, Consigned to the Sea, Flash in the Can, Transcendence, Between Darkness and Light, The Fox's Fire, The Kindly One, Dawns a New Day*, and the non-fiction writers' guides *The Literary Handyman, More Tips from the Handyman*, and *Build-A-Book Workshop*. She is the senior editor of the *Bad-Ass Faeries* anthology series, *Gaslight & Grimm, Side of Good/Side of Evil, After Punk*, and *Footprints in the Stars*. Her short stories are included in numerous other anthologies and collections.

In addition to her literary acclaim, she crafts and sells original costume horns under the moniker The Hornie Lady Custom Costume Horns, and homemade flavor-infused candied ginger under the brand of Ginger KICK! at literary conventions, on commission, and wholesale.

Danielle lives in New Jersey with husband and fellow writer, Mike McPhail and two extremely spoiled cats.

The Handyman's Helpers

Anders Håkon Gaut
Anonymous Reader
Aysha Rehm
C.J. Frost
Cato Vandrare
Cheri Kannarr
Christopher J. Burke
Christopher Weuve
Chuck Robinson
Deanna Stanley
eSpec Books
Gary Phillips
Gav
Heather Stephens
Ian Harvey
James Gotaas
Jaq Greenspon
Jen Kappert
Jennifer L. Pierce
Judi Fleming
Judith Waidlich
Kelly Pierce
L.E. Custodio
Lark Cunningham
Lorraine J. Anderson
maileguy
mdtommyd
Mike M.
Peter Engebos
pjk
Scott Schaper
Steph Parker
Stephen Ballentine
The Creative Fund
Tina M Noe Good

www.ingramcontent.com/pod-product-compliance
Lightning Source LLC
Chambersburg PA
CBHW020915140626
46545CB00015B/45